Women, men and language

Second edition

Studies in language and linguistics

General editors: GEOFFREY LEECH & MICK SHORT
Lancaster University

Already published:

A Dictionary of Stylistics
KATIE WALES

The Communicative Competence of Young Children
SUSAN H. FOSTER

Linguistic Purism
GEORGE THOMAS

Women, Men and Language
Second edition
JENNIFER COATES

Lexical Ambiguity in Poetry
SOON PENG SU

WOMEN, MEN AND LANGUAGE

A sociolinguistic account of gender differences in language

Second edition

JENNIFER COATES

Longman
London & New York

Longman Group Limited,
Edinburgh Gate
Harlow
Essex
CM20 2JE, England
and Associated Companies throughout the world.

*Published in the United States of America
by Longman Publishing, New York*

First edition © Longman Group Limited 1986

Second edition © Longman Group UK Limited 1993

First published 1986
Second edition 1993
Fifth impression 1996

ISBN 582 074924 PPR

British Library Cataloguing-in-Publication Data
A catalogue record for this book is
available from the British Library

Library of Congress Cataloging-in-Publication Data
Coates, Jennifer
    Women, men, and language : a sociolinguistic account of gender
differences in language / Jennifer Coates. — 2nd ed.
        p.   cm. — (Studies in language and linguistics)
    Includes bibliographical references and index.
    ISBN 0–582–07492–4
    1. Language and languages—Sex differences. I. Title.
    II. Series: Studies in language and linguistics (London, England)
    P120.S48C62   1993
    306.4′4—dc20   92–30487
                                                                  CIP

Set by 5S in Palatino 9/11
Produced through Longman Malaysia, PA

Contents

Preface to the Second Edition   vi
Acknowledgements   viii & ix

PART ONE: *Introductory*   1
              1 Language and gender   3
              2 The historical background (I) –
                 Folklinguistics and the early grammarians   16
              3 The historical background (II) –
                 Anthropologists and dialectologists   38

PART TWO: *The Sociolinguistic Evidence*   59
              4 Quantitative studies   61
              5 Social networks   87
              6 Gender differences in communicative
                 competence   106

PART THREE: *Causes and Consequences*   141
              7 The acquisition of gender-differentiated
                 language   143
              8 The role of gender differences in linguistic
                 change   168
              9 The social consequences of gender
                 differences in language   187

Bibliography   206

Index   223

Preface to the Second Edition

I was very pleased to have the opportunity of writing a second edition of *Women, Men and Language*. In 1982, when I first considered writing a book about gender differences in language, the topic was perceived as being of interest only to a specialist minority. But things have changed a great deal over the last ten years. The book has been reprinted many times since it was first published in 1986, a phenomenon which reflects the general growth of interest in sociolinguistics – and in women's issues – in recent years. Work in the area of language and gender has increased exponentially; it is certainly no longer a topic of minority interest. Moreover, work on gender-related issues in other fields (history, literary criticism, psychology, sociology, for example) is also flourishing, and there is increasing emphasis on inter-disciplinary research. The establishment of Women's Studies as a subject area in British academic institutions has provided a focus for gender-related research and a support network for those engaged in it.

Rewriting *Women, Men and Language* hasn't always been easy: with a second edition, you can't just say anything you like, but are constrained by the original text. I have tried to preserve the coherence of the first edition at the same time as bringing it up to date. The main changes I've made are of two kinds. First, I've made additions to the text (substantial additions in Chapters 6 and 7) to incorporate new material in the field of language and gender. Second, I've revised the text to ensure a consistent perspective throughout. Work on language and gender can take one of three positions: (1) language reflects gender divisions in society; (2) language creates gender divisions in society; (3) there is an interplay between language and social structure. This book will take the third position.

The main aim of the book has not changed: it is to introduce the reader to the study of gender differences in language. I hope that the book will help to improve our understanding of male–female relationships and of the continuance of male dominance by making clear the key role played by language in sustaining inequality between the sexes.

J.C.
London, 1992

Acknowledgements (first edition)

This book arose from a course I taught for many years at Edge Hill College. I am grateful to Stanley Ellis and Mark Newbrook for providing me with information about their work, and to Chris Baldick, Rhiannon Evans, Sarah Kay and Edward Wilson for their suggestions of folklinguistic material. I have been enormously helped by those who read and commented on earlier drafts of parts of the book: Deborah Cameron, Jenny Cheshire, Margaret Deuchar, Dick Leith, Beryl Madoc-Jones, Lesley Milroy. I would also like to thank my editors, Geoff Leech and Mick Short, for their comments and advice on the manuscript. But my main thanks are reserved for Joy Bowes whose scrupulously careful and detailed comments and criticisms on every chapter of the book have been invaluable. The book is dedicated to the students who took my course – it was their interest in the topic and their frustration with the paucity of texts which stimulated me to write it.

Acknowledgements (second edition)

In revising *Women, Men and Language*, I've had the unstinting help of my colleagues, Vikki Bell, Linda Thomas and especially Shan Wareing, who have suggested material for inclusion, commented on draft chapters, and always been ready to discuss language and gender issues with me. I would like to thank them for their support and encouragement. I would also like to place on record my gratitude to all those who have participated in my ongoing research on talk in single-sex friendship groups. Although I have used only brief extracts from these data in the book, my understanding of gender differences in language has benefited enormously from working on the project, which would have been impossible without their cooperation. Finally, I'd like to thank my son, William, for his fortitude over the last year, when my obsession with revising the book has sometimes taken priority over his needs, and for his invaluable help as a computer expert!

Acknowledgements

We are grateful to the following to reproduce copyright material:

Longman Group UK Ltd for our Table 3.3, from Table 3.2 'Question-naire for *Atlas linguistic et ethnographique due Lyonnais*' trans. W. Nelson Frances in *Dialectology: An Introduction* (1983); Cambridge University Press and the author Dr Peter Trudgill for our Table 4.1 from *The Social Differentiation of English in Norwich* (1974), CUP and the author Susan Philips for our Tables 7.3 and 7.4 from 'Preschool boys' and girls' language used in pretend play' in Philips, Susan, Steele, Susan and Tanz, Christine *Language Gender and Sex in Comparative Perspective* (1987); Edward Arnold Ltd for our Table 4.2 and Figures 4.7 and 4.8 in contribution by R K S Macaulay 'Variation and Consistency in Glaswegian English' also Figure 4.11 in contribution by Suzanne Romaine 'Postvocalic /r/ in Scottish English: sound change in progress?' all in Trudgill, Peter (ed.) *Sociolinguistic Patterns in British English* (1978) also for our Tables 5.1, 5.2 and 5.3 in contribution by Jenny Cheshire 'Linguistic variation and social function' and our Figure 7.1 in contribution by John Local 'Modelling intonational variability in children's speech' all in Romaine, Suzanne (ed) *Sociolinguistic Variation in Speech Communities* (1982) also Figure 4.14 from Edward, John R. *Language and Disadvantage* (1979) and Figure 8.4 from contribution by Jim and Lesley Milroy 'Belfast: Change and variation in an urban vernacular' in Trudgill, Peter (ed) *Sociolingustic Patterns in British English* (1978); Heinle & Heinle for Tables 6.1 and 6.2 and Figure 6.1 in contribution by Don Zimmerman and Candace West 'Sex roles, interruptions and silences in conversation' in Thorne, Barrie and Henley, Nancy (eds) *Language and Sex: difference and dominance* (1975) also our Figure 8.7 in contribution by Patricia Nichols 'Linguistic options and choices for black women in the rural South' in Thorne, Barrie, Kramarae, Cheris and Henley, Nancy (eds) *Language, Gender and Society* (1983); Sage Publications for our Table 6.3 from article

ACKNOWLEDGEMENTS

by Victoria L DeFrancisco 'The sounds of silence: how men silence women in marital relations' in *Discourse and Society* 2 (4) 1991; Australian Professional Publication for our Table 6.4 in article by Janet Holmes 'Hedging, fencing and other conversational gambits: an analysis of gender differences in New Zealand Speech' and our Figure 4.12 in an article by Edna Eisikovits 'Sex differences in inter-group and intra-group interaction among adolescents' both in Pauwels, Anne (ed) *Women and Language in Australian and New Zealand Society* (1987); The Linguistic Society of New Zealand (Inc) and the author Janet Holmes for our Table 6.5 from 'Hedging your bets and sitting on the fence: some evidence for hedges as support structure' in *Te Reo 27* (1984): 54; Longman Group UK Ltd for our Table 6.6 in contribution by Deborah Cameron, Fiona McAlinden and Kathy O'Leary 'Lakoff in context: the social and linguistic functions of tag questions' and our Table 9.1 in contribution by Joan Swann 'Talk control: an illustration from the classroom of problems in analysing male dominance in education' both tables in Coates, Jennifer and Cameron, Deborah (eds) *Women in their Speech Communities* (1989); Praeger Publishers an imprint of Greenwood Publishing Group, Inc., Westport, CT., for our Tables 6.8 and 6.9 in a contribution from Penny Brown 'How and why are women more polite: some evidence from a Mayan community' in McConnell-Ginet, S. et al. (eds) *Women and Language in Literature and Society*; Routledge Publishers for our Table 7.2 in Gordon Wells contribution 'Variation in child language' in Lee, V (ed) *Language Development* (1979); Editions Payot & Rivages for Figure 3.1 from *Les Mots et les Femmes*, page 27, (1978); Basil Blackwell Publishers and Lesley Milroy for our Figures 5.3, 5.4 and 8.5 in *Language and Social Networks* (1980), Basil Blackwell Publishers and Suzanne Romaine for our Figure 7.2 in *The Language of Children and Adolescents* (1984); Cambridge University Press and Jenny Cheshire for our Figures 5.5 and 5.6 from *Variation in an English Dialect* (1982).

We have been unable to trace the copyright holders for Figures 4.4 (8.1) and 8.6 and Tables 3.1 and 8.1 and would appreciate any help that would enable us to do so.

To Simon, Emily and William

Part One
Introductory

CHAPTER 1

Language and gender

1.1 Introduction

Do women and men talk differently? This book is an attempt to answer the question. I shall look at evidence from anthropology, dialectology, sociolinguistics and social psychology, first to establish that the language of women and men *does* differ, and second, to show *how* it differs. I shall also attempt to answer the question that inevitably follows: *Why* do women and men talk differently?

There is now considerable interest in the sociolinguistic variation associated with speaker's gender. Over the last few years, there has been an explosion of research in this field. Many articles have been published, both in learned journals and in edited collections. It is one of the aims of this book to provide a coherent account of such work; to bring together the many accounts of gender differences in language that have been written and to make them accessible to the interested reader. The book is intended both for those with an interest in sociolinguistics who want to study one aspect of variation in depth, and also for those interested in gender differences in general. It will concentrate on sociolinguistic work carried out in Britain and throughout will focus primarily on the English language.

This book, then, is primarily a sociolinguistic account of the co-variation of language and gender. It is not about the relationship between language and sexism, except in a very general sense; that is, it is not about language which denigrates, or is believed to denigrate, women. It will describe language *use*, in particular the differing usage of women and men as speakers.

As far as terminology is concerned, **gender** rather than **sex** will be the key category under discussion. 'Sex' refers to a biological distinction, while 'gender' is the term used to describe socially

3

constructed categories based on sex. Most societies operate in terms of two genders, **masculine** and **feminine,** and it is tempting to treat the category of gender as a simple binary opposition. Much of the work referred to in this book does so. But the reader should be aware that, like class and age, gender may be better described in terms of a continuum or continua. In this book, however, the emphasis will be on **inter-group** variation rather than on **intra-group** variation. In other words, this book will focus on the differences *between* women and men, rather than on differences *within* any one group (such as differences between women as speakers).

In this introductory chapter, I shall begin with a brief outline of sociolinguistics, since subsequent discussion of the language of women and men will be presented in sociolinguistic terms. This outline will be followed by a discussion of women as a social group. There has been a tendency in analysis of social variation (both linguistic and non-linguistic) to fail to differentiate between women and men. If we want to explore the ways in which women's and men's language differs, then it is obviously crucial that we have some idea of how women as a group differ from men as a group. In the final section of the chapter, I shall describe the two main approaches adopted by linguists to the question of gender differences in language, approaches which differ precisely because of disagreement about the status of women as a group.

1.2 Sociolinguistics

Sociolinguistics has been defined as the study of language in its social context. The study of language in its social context means crucially the study of **linguistic variation.** In different social contexts an individual will speak in different ways – this is called **stylistic variation.** Moreover, speakers who differ from each other in terms of age, gender, social class, ethnic group, for example, will also differ from each other in their speech, even in the same context – this is called **social variation.** Sociolinguists are interested in both stylistic and social variation.

Sociolinguists analyse speech in order to show that linguistic variation does not occur randomly but is structured: the aim of sociolinguistics is to expose the orderly heterogeneity of the normal speech community. Unlike theoretically inclined linguists, who concentrate on the imaginary sentences of the ideal speaker-hearer in a homogeneous speech community, sociolinguists choose to grapple with the utterances of real speakers in real (heterogeneous) speech communities.

Sociolinguists are principally interested in the **vernacular**, that is speech used spontaneously among people who know each other well. They have devised all sorts of ways of getting at the vernacular, ranging from the rapid and anonymous survey to long-term participant observation. In a rapid and anonymous survey, the researcher in the guise of, for example, a shopper, asks a question or questions designed to elicit a response of sociolinguistic interest, and then discreetly notes the response in a notebook. In a study involving long-term participant observation, the researcher interacts with a group of informants over a long period of time, becoming so familiar to them that the presence of the tape recorder is ignored. Even when using the standard interview, sociolinguists have structured it to elicit both formal and less formal styles by, for example, asking informants to recount a story about something amusing (or dangerous) that happened to them: the use of personal narrative tends to reduce self-consciousness in speech. This methodological inventiveness has been stimulated by sociolinguists' sensitivity to the Observer's Paradox – which is the problem faced by researchers who want to observe how people behave when they are not being observed.

Quantitative sociolinguists have borrowed the sampling techniques of sciences like botany and zoology, as have other social sciences. Informants have been selected at random from sources such as the electoral roll, and samples have reflected the composition of the community in terms of age, social class, gender, etc. More recent sociolinguistic work – sometimes known as Interactional Socio-linguistics – has used ethnographic methods and has focused on pre-existing groups such as the adolescent peer group; here selection of informants is not random. The best sociolinguistic analyses have shown how linguistic usage varies systematically with aspects of social context such as the social class or ethnic group of the speaker.

Sociolinguists' interest in the vernacular reflects their conviction that the study of language should be the study of the speech of all members of the community, not the study of the dialect spoken by the privileged few. Sociolinguists regard Standard English as just another variety of English, no more and no less interesting than any other variety. Linguists, unlike sociolinguists, start from the premise that Standard English *is* English (it happens, coincidentally, to be the variety spoken by most linguists). Sociolinguists challenge this **majority** view. Not only do they pay equal attention to all varieties, but also they draw attention to the fact that non-standard varieties

5

have their own regular phonology, morphology, syntax and lexis. The sociolinguistic approach, then, is a **minority** approach. The terms 'majority' and 'minority' are used here to refer to differential access to power and control. A majority community is one which has power and control, and majority languages or dialects are those used by majority communities. 'Minority' is a relative term. Minority communities and minority languages are defined as such by their relation to the majority community and language. The term bears no relation to number of speakers – there may be more speakers of minority languages or dialects, but these languages/dialects do not have the same status as majority languages/dialects. By extension, mainstream (Chomskyan) linguistics can be termed the majority approach to language because it concentrates on the language variety of the majority group (the powerful), while sociolinguistics can be termed the minority approach because it focuses attention on the speech of minority communities. (For further discussion of these two approaches, see Deuchar and Martin-Jones 1982.)

1.2.1 Sociolinguistics and Women

Why is it only recently that sociolinguists have begun to pay much attention to the co-variation of language and gender? I should like to suggest two reasons, which stem from sociolinguistics' antecedents in dialectology and linguistics.

First, in traditional dialectology, the informants selected were typically *non mobile, older, rural* and *male* (see Chambers and Trudgill 1980: 33). Sociolinguists rejected this biased selection of informants, but rejection consisted initially of choosing urban rather than rural and younger as well as older informants. While many studies included informants of both sexes, studies confined to male speakers continued to be carried out (e.g. Labov's study of black adolescents in Harlem: Labov 1972b; Reid's study of Edinburgh schoolboys: Reid 1976). Until recently I knew of no sociolinguistic studies which concentrated only on *female* speakers. (Examples of woman-focused research can be found in two edited collections: Bate and Taylor 1988; Coates and Cameron 1989.)[1]

Second, with the reaction against mainstream linguistics came the shift in emphasis from standard to non-standard varieties which has resulted in the minority approach described above. All sorts of minority groups have come under scrutiny, in particular working-class groups, ethnic groups, adolescents. Women, however, were not perceived as a minority group. Linguistic variation co-extensive with social class, ethnicity or age was what appeared salient to early sociolinguists. As we shall see in Chapter 4, most early sociolinguistic work concentrated on the social stratification of speech. Other kinds of variation received less attention. It has taken the development of the social sciences and of women's studies in particular to focus attention on women as a group in their own right.

1.3 Women as a Social Group

Women constitute a very unusual social group. For the sake of comparison, let's look at some 'normal' groups. Let's take working-class people in Belfast, Afro-Caribbeans in London, or adolescents in Reading – social groups which are reasonably easy to identify, and which have been the subject of sociolinguistic analysis (cf. Milroy 1980; Cheshire 1982a; Sebba 1983, in press). While these groups differ from each other in certain crucial ways, they have the following characteristics in common:

1. **Either** they live near each other in a recognised neighbourhood (such discrete homogeneous communities are sometimes called 'ghettoes');
   or they have recognised meeting places (e.g. adolescents hang out on street corners, meet on waste ground, in adventure playgrounds, etc.).
2. They have a recognisable and distinctive sub-culture.
3. Members of the group acknowledge the existence of the group: belonging to the group is part of their identity.

Note that members of the majority group satisfy these conditions as well. Areas like Hampstead in London, or Clifton in Bristol, for example, are sometimes called 'middle-class ghettoes', and it goes without saying that the majority group has a distinctive culture. Since this group is the dominant group, it is unmarked with respect to the other groups (in other words, perceived as normal or neutral, while other groups are 'marked' precisely because they differ from this norm). As a result, the majority culture is often considered to be *the* culture of society at large (just as Standard English is seen as *the* English language).

Women and men are peculiar as far as social groups go because in our society they tend to live in pairs consisting of one woman and one man: they certainly never live in separate areas as in (1)

7

above, except in special circumstances. 'Unlike many minority groups, women are not forced to live closely together in conditions conducive to the development of a collective group consciousness' (Williams and Giles 1978: 436n.). Moreover, where other groups define themselves in relation to out-groups and often come into conflict with these groups (e.g. Afro-Caribbeans in relation to the white community, adolescents in relation to adults), women and men tend to view each other favourably. Perhaps most importantly, it is not clear how far gender is salient as a category to women or men. In the opposition male–female, male is the unmarked term and for men, therefore, social class may be a more salient category than gender.

As far as women are concerned, their awareness of themselves as a group seems to be growing. According to social psychologists, people derive social identity from their membership of various social groups, but it has been pointed out that these groups only have meaning when they are compared with other groups. Henri Tajfel, a social psychologist who developed a theory of inter-group relations and social change (see Tajfel 1974; 1978; 1981), was particularly interested in groups whose members had a poor self-image. This happens when a group has inferior social status and is seen in negative terms by comparison with other groups. Since it can plausibly be argued that women *do* belong to a social group of this kind (in our society they are considered – overtly or covertly – to be inferior to men and thus to have lower status), then it will be enlightening to see what Tajfel's theory predicts about social groups in this position, and what light it throws on women's position in society today, and on women's linguistic usage.[2]

Tajfel argues that members of an inferior social group (a minority group in the sense defined above) can either accept or reject their inferior position in society. If they accept it, they will try to achieve self-esteem and a positive self-image by operating as individuals, not as a group. There are two possible strategies for such people: first, they can measure themselves against members of their own group, not members of the superior group; second, they can try individually to join the superior group. If, on the other hand, they refuse to accept their inferior position in society as just, they will attempt as a group to change things. Tajfel outlines three ways they can do this (these strategies usually occur, historically, in the order given). First, they will try to gain equality with and will adopt the values of the superior (majority) group; this strategy is called **assimilation.** Second, they will try to redefine characteristics which have previously been defined in negative terms by society; they will try to give these characteristics a positive value. Third, they will try to create new dimensions for

Figure 1.1 Tajfel's theory of inter-group relations and social change

comparison with the superior group, so that they are defining for themselves what has positive value, and thereby creating a positive and distinct image for themselves. Figure 1.1 summarises this theory in diagrammatic form.

How far does the theory correspond to the reality of women's position in society today? In the past, women seemed to accept their inferior status; they allowed themselves to be defined by the superior group and they accepted this definition as just. This is still true of many women today. In order to achieve a positive self-image, such women compare themselves *with other women*. The relevant dimensions for comparison are things like cooking, sewing, child-care and personal appearance. The women's magazine industry is kept in business by this need for **intra-group** comparison (comparison with others in the same group). These women avoid comparing themselves with men. Occasionally, a woman who accepts inferior status for women as a group will attempt individually to leave the women's group and become accepted by men. This occurs from time to time in business circles or in politics – a woman operates successfully in the men's world and becomes, to all intents and purposes, a man. However, this is a strategy which can achieve nothing for the group as a whole, but only for the individual. It can be called **tokenism.**

Nowadays women are more aware that they do not have equal status with men, and they are less prepared to accept this state of affairs. Do their attempts to change things fit Tajfel's theory? **Assimilation** is clearly a strategy that is being pursued by women. There has been progress in terms of gaining equality in working conditions and in legal terms: the Equal Pay Act was passed in 1970 and the Sex Discrimination Act in 1975 – the Equal Opportunities

Commission was set up to ensure the effective enforcement of these Acts. Williams and Giles (1978), however, comment that the effort involved in changing *overt* norms may in fact distract attention from the continued existence of *covert* norms which perpetuate women's inferior status. Note that as women become successful in any field – such as teaching or secretarial work – that field tends to lose status.

In terms of *language*, it is clear that certain groups of women (e.g. those in the professions or in politics) have adopted this strategy. They have assimilated into the dominant group in the following ways:

1. they use deeper voices (lower in pitch)
2. they swear and use taboo language
3. they adopt a more assertive style in group interaction
4. they adopt prosodic features more typical of men (e.g. falls rather than rising intonation patterns)
5. they address themselves in public to traditionally male topics: business, politics, economics
6. they are beginning to exploit the use of non-standard accents (BBC employment patterns are a good guide in this area).

The problem with this strategy is that it means that women redefine themselves in terms of *male* values (the values of the dominant group). If women are searching for a satisfactory identity of their own, this is obviously a flawed strategy.

The other two strategies tend to go together: as women succeed in **re-evaluating** characteristics previously described in negative terms, they **create new dimensions** for comparison. Some women have begun to stress the value to society of stereotyped female qualities such as gentleness, caring for others, sensitivity. This has led in turn to a re-evaluation of stereotyped male qualities such as aggression and competitiveness, and an awareness that such qualities are not always socially functional. As far as language use is concerned, the most significant move seems to be a reappraisal by women of the relative merits of cooperative as opposed to competitive strategies in conversation. Research carried out in this field suggests that men typically adopt a competitive style in conversation, treating their turn as a chance to overturn earlier speakers' contributions and to make their own point as forcibly as possible. Women on the other hand, in conversation with other women, typically adopt a cooperative mode: they add to rather than demolish other speakers' contributions, they are supportive of others, they tend not to interrupt each other (this research will be discussed in sections 6.5 and 9.2). Researchers discussing this difference comment that women are beginning to value their style and to resent being forced to adopt the male mode in mixed interaction. (Note that terms like *gossip* are being redefined positively.) It seems that women's less assertive, more cooperative style in group interaction is being revalued positively by women speakers, and conversely, men's style is being criticised.

This area is a good example of the process whereby the redefinition of negative characteristics leads to the creation of new dimensions for comparison. Women's cooperative style in conversation used to be viewed negatively. It was seen as unassertive, tentative, or simply weak. Now, however, there is recognition of the value of cooperative conversational strategies in promoting wide-ranging discussion, in maintaining good social relations, and in negotiating conflict. With re-evaluation has come the notion that the ability to talk cooperatively is a dimension which can be used for comparing speakers – and, for a change, a dimension where comparisons will tend to favour *female* speakers.

There is evidence to suggest that new dimensions of comparison such as this are becoming established in our culture. Two brief examples will illustrate the point. First, research into doctor–patient talk has been extended to compare the styles used by male and female doctors when talking to their patients. Male doctors use a style of talk which is more authoritarian and less sensitive to the patient than that of female doctors. As a result, they are less effective in getting patients to do what they are asked (such as undressing, or agreeing to a course of treatment); patients are more likely to cooperate with female doctors (see West 1990). This new dimension of comparison not only shows women doctors performing better than their male counterparts; it also helps researchers to understand what constitutes effective communication in doctor–patient interaction. (West's research will be discussed in detail in section 6.2.2, p. 125–6.)

The second example comes from the world of education. The new GCSE English examinations (which replaced O level and CSE examinations in September 1986) have a compulsory oral communication component. Students are tested both on individual and group talk, and one aspect of talk which is assessed is **interpersonal skill.** The appearance of this new dimension for comparison in the context of a public examination suggests that a re-evaluation of what constitutes effective talk has taken place. Moreover, this new dimension favours girls, since interpersonal sensitivity is a key component of girls' communicative competence. (Girls' interpersonal skills will be the subject of section 7.3.3; research on the new GCSE oral tests will be discussed in section 9.3.)

As we can see from this brief appraisal of women as a group in the light of Tajfel's theory, women are still in the early stages of the process of change. Not all women feel that their inferior position in society is unjust. Those who *do* feel their subordinate position is unjust are mostly involved in assimilation strategies: that is they are working to change the law and other social structures to give women equality. As I have already pointed out, while such moves are probably an essential prerequisite for social change, the strategy of assimilation is not in the long run healthy for a group in search of a positive social identity, since assimilation essentially means accepting the norms of the dominant group. By refusing to accept men's definitions, and by redefining female characteristics *positively*, some women are moving on to Tajfel's second and third strategies. But the creation of a new positive identity to replace the old subordinate one is an extremely slow process – especially as the dominant group does not accept change passively but will inevitably try by various means to preserve its superior position.

1.4 Women, Men and Language

We have looked at the nature of social groups, at the nature of subordinate (minority) groups in particular, and at the ways in which they seek to change their status. We have looked specifically at women as a social group, at their position in society, and at changes currently taking place in women's position. The reason so much space has been devoted to this assessment of women's and men's relative position in society is that sociolinguistics aims not only to describe linguistic variation and the social context in which such variation occurs, but also to demonstrate the interrelationship of language and society. Sociolinguistic studies reveal that linguistic variation is not random but structured: structured linguistic variation both determines and is determined by the structured social variation found in the speech community.

The structured social variation found in the speech community can be interpreted in more than one way. Women as a social group are clearly *different* from men. As a minority group they can also be seen as *oppressed* and *marginalised* (see Breakwell 1979; Delphy 1984; Moi 1985). The two main approaches to gender differences in language reflect these two views of women's status as a group.

The first – the **dominance** approach – sees women as an oppressed group and interprets linguistic differences in women's and men's speech in terms of men's dominance and women's subordination.

Researchers using this model are concerned to show how male dominance is enacted through linguistic practice. 'Doing power' is often a way of 'doing gender' too (see West and Zimmerman 1983). Moreover, all participants in discourse, women as well as men, collude in sustaining and perpetuating male dominance and female oppression.

The second approach – the **difference** approach – emphasises the idea that women and men belong to different subcultures. This approach is relatively new. As we saw in section 1.3 (p. 7), one of the characteristics of a social group is that it has a distinctive subculture (characteristic no. 2). The 'discovery' of distinct male and female subcultures in recent years seems to be a direct result of women's growing resistance to being treated as a minority group. The invisibility of women in the past arose from the conflation of 'culture' with 'male culture'. But women are now asserting that they 'have a different voice, a different psychology, and a different experience of love, work and the family from men' (Humm 1989: 51). In linguistic terms, the differences in women's and men's speech are interpreted as reflecting and maintaining gender-specific subcultures. A great deal of work is now being done on children's socialisation in single-sex peer groups, and on the consequent development of gender-differentiated linguistic styles[3].

Both approaches seem to yield valuable insights into the nature of gender differences in language. Many sociolinguists have adopted a compromise position, that is, they have tried to combine the two approaches (this should become apparent in discussion of socio-linguistic work in subsequent chapters). The value of these two different approaches will be reviewed in Chapter 9.

This book will restrict itself to linguistic variation related to the gender of the speaker. It will describe differences found in the speech of women and men, and it will relate these linguistic differences to the social roles assigned to women and men in our society. Chapter 2 will expose our society's preconceptions about gender differences in language, while Chapter 3 will assess the contribution of anthropology and dialectology to the study of gender differences. Having dealt with work carried out before the establishment of linguistics as a discipline, we shall move on to look in detail at sociolinguistic analyses of gender differences in language: Chapter 4 will focus on quantitative sociolinguistic studies, Chapter 5 on studies involving the concept of social network. In Chapter 6 we shall look at those studies which examine women's and men's linguistic behaviour in the wider sense of communicative competence: this will include studies on interruptions and silences in conversation, on swearing and on politeness, on different styles in group interaction, among other things. These three central chapters will also try to deal with socio-functional explanations, since the data presented inevitably lead to the question 'Why?' Many explanations for gender differentiation in language have been suggested and these will be reviewed and discussed. The final part, entitled 'Causes and Consequences', will examine three related areas in detail: children's acquisition of gender-differentiated language (Chapter 7), the nature of linguistic change and the role of gender differences in promoting change (Chapter 8), and finally the social consequences of gender differences in language, looking especially at miscommunication between adults and at the use of language in the school setting (Chapter 9).

1.5 Writer's Caveat

Each one of us is either male or female: we have developed an identity which is incontrovertibly gendered. You, reading this book, will bring to your reading a range of experience about what it means to be a female speaker or a male speaker today. You will also have been socialised into a set of preconceptions about the nature of women and men in general and about female and male speakers in particular. You should be alert to these preconceptions and to your own necessarily partial viewpoint when sifting the evidence presented in this book. Also remember that it is not only you, the reader, who have preconceptions and prejudices – I, the writer, have them too, and so have the various scholars whose work on language I shall be referring to. Obviously, the pursuit of any discipline involves an attempt by scholars to rise above their preconceptions. However, it is surely not cynical to say that pure objectivity – especially in an area as sensitive and as controversial as language and gender – is probably a chimera.

As a first step to coming to terms with our preconceptions, and in order to assess which gender differences in language are fiction and which fact, we will look at the cultural mythology associated with gender differences in language. The next chapter will address this subject directly.

Notes

1   If we compare the titles of these two collections – *Women Communicating* and *Women in their Speech Communities* – with those of work

focusing on male speakers, such as Labov's *Language in the Inner City*, we can see that the male-as-norm principle is still alive and well in sociolinguistics.

2 For social psychological aspects of the following discussion I am indebted to Williams and Giles' (1978) article, 'The changing status of women in society'.

3 This approach has been fruitfully applied to the analysis of same-sex talk. However, the reader should be aware that this approach is controversial when applied to *mixed* talk (as in Tannen 1991). See Troemel-Ploetz (1991); Cameron (in press).

CHAPTER 2

The historical background (I) – Folklinguistics and the early grammarians

2.1 Introduction

Differences between women and men have always been a topic of interest to the human species and supposed linguistic differences are often enshrined in proverbs:

A woman's tongue wags like a lamb's tail. (England)
Foxes are all tail and women are all tongue. (England – Cheshire)
Où femme y a, silence n'y a. (France)
The North Sea will sooner be found wanting in water than a woman at a loss for a word. (Jutland)[1]

The comments of contemporary observers, recorded in diaries, letters, poems, novels, and so on, also provide us with evidence of folk-linguistic beliefs about gender differences in language. Beside these more casual observations we can place the work of the early gram-marians. It is not always easy to draw a line between the former and the latter, since much work entitled 'grammar' is no more scientific in its approach to gender differences in language than the observations of 'ordinary' people. In other words, academics and scholars are as much the product of the times they live in as are non-academics, and their work on language can be as subject to prejudice and preconception as are the comments of lay people.

As we shall see, scholarly comments on gender differences in language reflect the ideas of their time. In some cases this tendency has led to startling contradictions. Such contradictions can be accounted for by assuming a general rule, which I shall call **The Androcentric Rule:** 'Men will be seen to behave linguistically in a way that fits the writer's view of what is desirable or admirable; women on the other hand will be blamed for any linguistic state or development which is regarded by the writer as negative or reprehensible.'

2.2   Folklinguistics

In this chapter I shall survey writings from the Middle Ages up to the beginning of this century (that is, work written before the discipline of linguistics was established). Rather than survey the entire field, I shall focus on the following areas of interest: vocabulary, swearing and taboo words, grammar, literacy, pronunciation, and verbosity.

2.2.1   Vocabulary

Interest in the lexical and grammatical structure of the language, that is, in its vocabulary and grammar, was stimulated by the rise of Standard English. Once one variety of a language is selected as the standard, then the process of codification inevitably follows. Codification involves the writing of both dictionaries (dealing with the lexical items of a language) and grammars (dealing with the grammatical structure of a language). In England, the eighteenth century saw the publication of numerous dictionaries and grammars, all written in an attempt to reduce the language to rule, and to legislate on 'correct' usage.

Commentary on gender differences in vocabulary is quite widespread in eighteenth-century writings, as the following extracts will demonstrate. The passage below, written by Richard Cambridge for *The World* of 12 December 1754, implies that the ephemeral nature of women's vocabulary is associated with the unimportance of what they say:

> I must beg leave . . . to doubt the propriety of joining to the fixed and permanent standard of language a vocabulary of words which perish and are forgot within the compass of a year. That we are obliged to the ladies for most of these ornaments to our language, I readily acknowledge.
> (Cambridge 1754, as quoted in Tucker 1961: 93)

Here we see an eighteenth-century gentleman grappling with the problem of linguistic change. The ultimate aim of codification was to 'fix' the language once and for all. However, vocabulary was an area which appeared to elude control. On what grounds Richard Cambridge judged women to be responsible for ephemeral words, we are not told.

Turning to the early twentieth century, we find Otto Jespersen, a Danish professor of English language, writing on the question of changing vocabulary. He asserts that it is *men* rather than women who introduce 'new and fresh expressions' and thus men who are 'the chief renovators of language' (Jespersen 1922: 247). This apparent inconsistency can be accounted for by the Androcentric Rule (see section 2.1). As the rule would predict, in an age which deplored lexical change, women were held to be the culprits for introducing ephemeral words. On the other hand, Jespersen in 1922 accepted that change was inevitable and saw innovation as creative: he therefore credited men with introducing new words to the lexicon.

An anonymous contributor to *The World* (6 May 1756) complains of women's excessive use of certain adverbial forms:

> Such is the pomp of utterance of our present women of fashion; which, though it may tend to spoil many a pretty mouth, can never recommend an indifferent one. And hence it is that there is so great a scarcity of originals, and that the ear is such a daily sufferer from an identity of phrase, whether it be *vastly, horridly, abominably, immensely,* or *excessively,* which, with three or four more calculated for the same swiss-like service, make up the whole scale or gamut of modern female conversation.
> (as quoted in Tucker 1961: 96)

This characteristic women's language is gently mocked by Jane Austen in *Northanger Abbey* (1813), in the speech of Isabella Thorpe:

> 'My attachments are always *excessively* strong.'
> 'I must confess there is something *amazingly* insipid about her.'
> 'I am so vexed with all the men for not admiring her! – I scold them all *amazingly* about it.'
> (*Northanger Abbey*, Ch. 6, my italics)

It is clearly significant that it is Isabella, who is flirtatious, selfish and shallow, who uses these adverbials, and not Catherine, the heroine (who is altogether less sophisticated).

The use of adverbial forms of this kind was a fashion at this time, and was evidently associated in the public mind with women's speech. Lord Chesterfield, writing in *The World* of 5 December 1754, makes very similar observations to those of the anonymous contributor quoted above:

> Not content with enriching our language with words absolutely new [*again the accusation that women destabilise the lexicon*] my fair countrywomen have gone still farther, and improved it by the application and extension of old

ones to various and very different significations. They take a word and change it, like a guinea, into shillings for pocket money, to be employed in the several occasional purposes of the day. For instance, the adjective *vast* and it's [*sic*] adverb *vastly*, mean anything and are the fashionable words of the most fashionable people. A fine woman . . . is *vastly* obliged, or *vastly* offended, *vastly* glad or *vastly* sorry. Large objects are *vastly* great, small ones are *vastly* little; and I had lately the pleasure to hear a fine woman pronounce, by a happy metonymy, a very small gold snuff-box that was produced in company to be *vastly* pretty, because it was *vastly* little.
(as quoted in Tucker 1961: 92)

Lord Chesterfield concludes with a mock-serious appeal to one of the great legislators of the time, Dr Johnson, whose *Dictionary* (1755) was a landmark in the codification process. 'Mr. Johnson', Lord Chesterfield says, 'will do well to consider seriously to what degree he will restrain the various and extensive significants of this great word' [i.e. *vast*].

Johnson's *Dictionary* is well known for its individualistic and biased definitions (*Patron* is defined as 'Commonly a wretch who supports with insolence, and is paid with flattery'). Johnson stigmatises the words *flirtation* and *frightful* as 'female cant'. Such a comment is value-laden. It seems clear that the anonymous contributor to *The World* quoted above is a man: all these passages reveal that their (male) authors believe women to have restricted and vacuous vocabulary, and to exert a malign influence on the language. Note that 'language' is defined by these eighteenth-century writers in terms of male language; the way men talk is seen as the norm, while women's language is deviant.

The androcentric bias is still present in twentieth-century observations on English vocabulary. Jespersen included a chapter entitled 'The Woman' in his book *Language: Its Nature, Development and Origin* (1922). This chapter has the merit of summarising extant research on women's language in many different parts of the world. It has been justifiably criticised, however, for its uncritical acceptance of sexist assumptions about male/female differences in language. Jespersen includes a section on vocabulary in this chapter. He generalises that 'the vocabulary of a woman as a rule is much less extensive than that of a man'. He supports this claim with data from an experiment by an American, Jastrow, in which male college students used a greater variety of words than female college students when asked to write down one hundred (separate) words. This is the only evidence given.

In his section on adverbs, Jespersen says that women differ from men in their extensive use of certain adjectives, such as *pretty* and *nice*. It should be noted that the American linguist, Robin Lakoff, in *Language and Woman's Place*, the work that for many people marks the beginning of twentieth-century linguistic interest in gender differences, specifically singles out ' "empty" adjectives like *divine, charming, cute . . .*' as typical of what she calls 'women's language' (Lakoff 1975: 53).

Women differ from men, according to Jespersen, even more in their use of adverbs. Quoting Lord Chesterfield's remarks on the adverb *vastly* (see pp. 18–19), Jespersen argues that this is 'a distinctive trait: the fondness of women for hyperbole will very often lead the fashion with regard to adverbs of intensity, and these are very often used with disregard of their proper meaning' (Jespersen 1922: 250). (This of course begs the question of 'proper' meaning.) He quotes examples from all the major European languages. This proves that adverbs are widely used in these speech communities, but we are given no evidence to show that it is only, or preponderantly, women who use them.

So is also claimed as having 'something of the eternally feminine about it'. Jespersen quotes *Punch* of 4 January 1896: 'This little adverb is a great favourite with ladies, in conjunction with an adjective'. The extract gives as examples of 'ladies usage': 'It is *so* lovely!'; 'He is *so* charming!'; 'Thank you *so* much!'; 'I'm *so* glad you've come!' Jespersen's 'explanation' for this gender-preferential usage is that 'women much more often than men break off without finishing their sentences, because they start talking without having thought out what they are going to say' (Jespersen 1922: 250).

Lakoff also has a section on the intensifier *so*. She asserts that '*so* is more frequent in women's than men's language, though certainly men can use it' (Lakoff 1975: 54). As we shall see in subsequent sections, there are many parallels between Lakoff's and Jespersen's work, which is surprising in view of the fact that feminists welcomed Lakoff's book, but have been very critical of Jespersen's.

2.2.2 Swearing and Taboo Language

> A whistling sailor, a crowing hen and a swearing woman ought all three to go to hell together.
> (American proverb)

In this section I shall be considering oaths, exclamations, taboo words: anything which could come under the general heading 'vulgar language'. The belief that women's language is more polite, more refined – in a word, more ladylike – is very widespread and has been current for many centuries.

Vulgarity is a cultural construct, and the evidence suggests that it was the new courtly tradition of the Middle Ages which, by creating gentility, also created vulgarity. The issue of vulgar language forms an important theme of French *fabliaux*, comic tales of the Middle Ages, which seem in part to have been written in direct response to the new vogue for 'clean' language. One – *La Dame qui se venja du Chevalier* (Montaiglon et Raynaud, 1872–90: vol VI) – explicitly supports the courtly taboo stigmatising a man's use of obscene language in front of a woman. The man and woman are in bed together when the man commits his faux pas: 'the knight, who was on top, looked right at her face and saw her swooning with pleasure. Whereupon he couldn't suppress his foolishness but said something very vulgar. Right then he asked her "My lady, would you crack some nuts?" ' (as translated in Muscatine 1981: 11). *Croistre noiz* (crack nuts) is a synonym for *foutre* (fuck). The woman is extremely offended and proceeds to take her revenge.

In contrast to this, there is a group of three *fabliaux* (the two versions of *La damoisele qui ne pooit oïr parler de foutre* and *la pucele qui abevra le polain*) which can be read as an attack on linguistic prudery in women, and which defend the use of vernacular ('vulgar') terms. In all three versions of the story, the heroine is a stuck-up (*dédaigneuse*) young woman who can't bear to hear any words to do with sex – they make her feel ill. The father can't keep male servants as they don't speak language suitable for his daughter's ears. The hero is a clever young man who arrives on the pretext of looking for work and feigns disgust at hearing obscene language, thus gaining the confidence of the father and daughter. The girl is so convinced of his purity that she invites him to sleep in her bed. A mutual seduction takes place, with the lovers using elaborate metaphors of ponies, meadows, fountains, etc. to avoid the use of taboo expressions. The writer comments in one version: 'I want to show by this example that women should not be too proud to say *foutre* (fuck) out loud when all the same they're doing it' (as translated in Muscatine 1981: 14). The humour in these tales arises from the ludicrous contrast between the woman's dislike of the *words* and her pleasure in the *act*. A famous passage in the *Roman de la Rose* (*c.* 1277) attacks the use of euphemisms and circumlocutions, and calls for plain language. The writer comments: 'If women don't name them (i.e. *coilles*, bollocks) in France, it's nothing but getting out of the habit' (as quoted in Muscatine 1981: 17). Presumably there have always been taboos on language, but it looks as if the courtly tradition of the Middle Ages, which put women on a pedestal, strengthened linguistic taboos in general, and also condemned the use of vulgar language by women, and its use by men in front of women.

The strength of the folklinguistic belief in male/female differences in swearing is reflected in Elyot's strictures on the upbringing of noblemen's children in *The Governour* (1531). Elyot advises that the child of a Gentleman should be brought up by women who will not permit 'any wanton or unclene worde to be spoken' in the child's presence. To avoid the child's hearing such words, he urges that no men should be allowed into the nursery.

Shakespeare on the other hand makes fun of this cultural stereotype. In *I Henry IV*, Hotspur mocks his wife for her genteel use of oaths:

> *Hotspur*: Come, Kate, I'll have your song too.
> *Lady Percy*: Not mine, in good sooth.
> *Hotspur*: Not yours, in good sooth! Heart! you swear like a comfit-maker's
>   wife! 'Not you, in good sooth'; and
>   'As true as I live'; and
>   'As God shall mend me'; and 'As sure as day';
>   And givst such sarcenet surety for thy oaths,
>   As if thou never walk'st further than Finsbury.
>   Swear me, Kate, like a lady as thou art,
>   A good mouth-filling oath; and leave 'in sooth'
>   And such protest of pepper-gingerbread
>   To velvet-guards and Sunday citizens.
> (*I Henry IV*, III. i. 241ff.)

Shakespeare here reveals an awareness that swearing is related not only to gender but also to social class. Hotspur urges Kate to swear *not* like a comfit-maker's wife and other 'Sunday citizens' (the bourgeoisie), but like 'a lady', that is a female member of the aristocracy.

As section 2.2.1 has shown, eighteenth-century gentlemen were having to come to terms with the fact of linguistic change. Arthur Murphy, in a witty article in *Gray's Inn Journal* of 29 June 1754, suggests that there should be a Register of Births and Deaths for words. He elaborates on this idea with the following conceit:

> A Distinction might be made between a kind of Sex in Words, according as they are appropriated to Men or Women; as for Instance, *D--n my Blood* is of Male extraction, and *Pshaw, Fiddlestick* I take to be female.
> (as quoted in Tucker 1961: 86)

The idea of distinct male and female swear words is still widely held. Lakoff, two hundred years later, makes exactly the same observation as Murphy:

> Consider (a) 'Oh dear, you've put the peanut butter in the refrigerator
>   again.'

(b) 'Shit, you've put the peanut butter in the refrigerator again.'

It is safe to predict that people would classify the first sentence as part of 'women's language', the second as 'men's language'.

(Lakoff 1975: 10)

Lakoff summarises her position later by saying 'women don't use off-color or indelicate expressions; women are the experts at euphemism' (1975: 55).

While noting that she is talking about 'general tendencies' rather than 'hundred-percent correlations', Lakoff seems happy to present such folklinguistic material without the support of any research findings to confirm her statements. It is less surprising that Jespersen, in 1922, held such views:

> There can be no doubt that women exercise a great and universal influence on linguistic development through their instinctive shrinking from coarse and gross expressions and their preference for refined and (in certain spheres) veiled and indirect expressions.

He goes on to the particular case of swearing:

> Among the things women object to in language must be specially mentioned anything that smacks of swearing.

In a footnote to this, he adds:

> There are great differences with regard to swearing between different nations; but I think that in those countries and in those circles in which swearing is common it is found much more extensively among men than among women: this at any rate is true of Denmark.

(Jespersen 1922: 246)

These writers claim to *describe* women's more polite use of language, but we should ask whether what they are actually doing is attempting to *prescribe* how women *ought* to talk. Avoidance of swearing and of 'coarse' words is held up to female speakers as the ideal to be aimed at (as is silence, as we shall see in the section on Verbosity). It is clear that people have thought for a long time that women and men differ in relation to the use of swear words and other taboo expressions. As section 6.2.2 will show, there is still very little evidence to confirm or refute this belief.

2.2.3 Grammar

The rise of Standard English stimulated an awareness of variation in language and with it the growth of the notion of correctness. Once a standard was accepted and codified, then forms which deviated from this standard were frowned on as 'incorrect'. Eighteenth-century notions of grammar were less sophisticated than today's: grammars were prescriptive rather than descriptive, laying down rules of correct usage. They often included sections on spelling and punctuation, which demonstrates how early grammarians took the *written* language as the basis for their work.

The earliest writers on grammar and rhetoric were concerned about the 'correct' ordering of elements in phrases such as *men and women*:

> Some will set the Carte before the horse, as thus, My mother and my father are both at home, even as thoughe the good man of the house ware no breaches, or that the graye Mare were the better Horse. And what thoughe it often so happeneth (God wotte the more pitte) yet in speaking at the least, let us kepe a natural order, and set the man before the woman for maners Sake.
> (Wilson 1560: 189)

This idea of 'a natural order' and of the superiority of the male is unabashedly prescribed for linguistic usage: 'The Masculine gender is more worthy than the Feminine' (Poole 1646: 21). This idea seems to have been a necessary precursor of the sex-indefinite *he* rule, which proscribes the use of *they* or *he or she* where the sex of the antecedent is unknown. Compare the following three sentences:

1. Someone knocked at the door but they had gone when I got downstairs.
2. Someone knocked at the door but he or she had gone when I got downstairs.
3. Someone knocked at the door but he had gone when I got downstairs.

According to prescriptive grammarians, only the last of these three utterances is 'correct' (the first is 'incorrect' and the second 'clumsy'). John Kirkby's statement, from his *New English Grammar* of 1746, is the one most frequently quoted:

> The Masculine Person answers to the general Name, which comprehends both Male and Female; as *Any Person, who knows what he says*.
> (Kirkby 1746: 117)

This is not the place for a full discussion of the rival merits of generic *he* and singular *they* in contexts requiring a sex-indefinite pronoun (for a detailed account, see Bodine 1975b). The important point is that the androcentric (male-as-norm) attitudes so conspicuous in early pronouncements on language were actually used as the basis for some prescriptive rules of grammar. Many people will see feminist opposition to the use of sex-indefinite *he* as misguided and doomed to failure ('I feel . . . that an attempt to change pronominal usage will be futile': Lakoff 1975: 45). What these people are unaware of is the fact that the present rule was itself imposed on language users by male grammarians of the eighteenth century and after. It is naïve to assume that codification was carried out in a disinterested fashion: those who laid down the rules inevitably defined as 'correct' that usage which they preferred, for whatever reason.

Observations on language by men of letters reveal an assumption that women are frequently guilty of incorrect usage, as far as grammar is concerned. The following passage is typical of its time:

> I came yesterday into the Parlour, where I found Mrs. Cornelia, my lady's third Daughter, all alone, reading a Paper, which, as I afterwards found, contained a Copy of Verses, upon Love and Friendship. . . . By the Hand [i.e. *handwriting*], at first sight, I could not guess whether they came from a Lady, but having put on my spectacles, and perused them carefully, I found by some peculiar Modes in Spelling, and a certain Negligence in Grammar, that it was a Female Sonnet.
> (Richard Steele 1713; as quoted in Tucker 1961: 69)

Lord Chesterfield (1741) in a letter to his son remarks: 'most women and all the ordinary people in general speak in open defiance of all grammar'. Henry Tilney tells Catherine Morland that 'the usual style of letter writing among women is faultless, except in three particulars' which are 'a general deficiency of subject, a total inattention to stops, and a very frequent ignorance of grammar' (*Northanger Abbey* 1813). Although he is teasing, we can assume that these were the kinds of taunts about grammatical incorrectness which were commonly made at women's expense at the time.

Jespersen inevitably has much to say on the subject of grammar and male/female differences. As we have seen (in relation to *so*, section 2.2.1), he believed that women often produce half-finished sentences (as a result of not thinking before speaking!). He claims that this happens particularly with exclamatory sentences, and he illustrates his claim with the following examples (both taken from literature):

> 'Mrs. Eversleigh: I must say!' (but words fail her).
> (Hankin, quoted in Jespersen 1922: 251)
> 'The trouble you must have taken,' Hilda exclaimed.
> (Compton-MacKenzie, quoted in Jespersen 1922: 251)

These utterances are precisely the kind of thing that real people, of both sexes, do say. The concept of the half-finished sentence results from treating written language as primary. The sentence is the main unit of written language, but analysis of spoken discourse (a relatively new pursuit) suggests that the sentence may not be a relevant category for speech. In other words, people don't speak in sentences, either finished or half-finished. However, since in the past men received far more education that women, it is likely that their speech was more affected by written norms; in other words, male/female differences may have reflected relative exposure to written language. But we have no quantitative evidence to support this hypothesis.

Jespersen's second claim revolves around the concepts of **parataxis** and **hypotaxis.** Clauses can be joined together in a variety of ways. **Parataxis** is the term used to describe a sequence of clauses where there are no links at all (the clauses are simply juxtaposed): CLAUSE, CLAUSE (e.g. *I got up, I went to work*). Similar to this, but not always included in the term 'parataxis', is **coordination,** where the clauses are linked by **coordinating** conjunctions (*and, but,* etc.): CLAUSE **and** CLAUSE (e.g. *I got up **and** I went to work*). **Hypotaxis** is the term used to describe a sequence of clauses where the links are **subordinating** conjunctions (*after, when, because,* etc.): **after** CLAUSE, CLAUSE/CLAUSE **after** CLAUSE (e.g. **After** *I got up, I went to work/I went to work **after** I got up*).

The crucial difference between these two modes is that parataxis involves a series of main clauses, each clause being of equal value, while hypotaxis consists of a main clause with one or more subordinate clauses dependent on it. The logical connections between the clauses are made *explicit* in a hypotactic style, but left *implicit* in a paratactic style.

There is a long tradition in our culture of scorning parataxis and praising hypotaxis. Paratactic constructions tend to be called 'primitive', presumably because of their surface-structure lack of logical connectives. Hypotactic constructions, on the other hand, are universally admired, especially from the Renaissance onwards. It should be remembered that the classic Latin sentence involves complex subordination, and classical models were revered.

Jespersen's analysis of male/female differences in syntax makes use of this distinction:

> If we compare long periods [i.e. *sentences*] as constructed by men and by women, we shall in the former find many more instances of intricate or involute structures with clause within clause, a relative clause in the middle of a conditional clause or vice versa, with subordination and sub-subordination, while the typical form of long feminine periods is that of co-ordination, one sentence or clause being added to another on the same plane and the gradation between the respective ideas being marked not grammatically, but emotionally, by stress and intonation, and in writing by underlining. In learned terminology we may say that men are

fond of hypotaxis and women of parataxis.
(Jespersen 1922: 251)

The distinction between *grammatically* and *emotionally* is obscure, but *emotionally* is presumably pejorative, and suggests that Jespersen finds the hypotactic style superior. He continues with two famous similes:

a male period is often like a set of Chinese boxes, one within another, while a feminine period is like a set of pearls joined together on a string of *ands* and similar words.
(Jespersen 1922: 252)

At his most sexist, Jespersen is still a gentleman!

More recently, the paratactic/hypotactic distinction has been used to distinguish between Bernstein's restricted and elaborated codes.[2] Without using these terms, Bernstein appeals to our culturally conditioned notion that hypotaxis is a superior mode of construction: he claims that subordination is typical of elaborated code, while restricted code makes use of 'simple' coordinated clauses. Linguists argue that there is nothing intrinsically superior about a construction involving subordinate clauses, but note that hypotactic constructions are typical of written language, while paratactic constructions are typical of speech. We can draw up a simple table (Table 2.1) to show the correspondences.

Table 2.1: The linguistic domains (real and hypothesised) of parataxis and hypotaxis

	Parataxis	Hypotaxis
Typically found in:	Anglo-Saxon prose	Renaissance and post-Renaissance prose
	Speech	Writing
Supposed to be typical of:	Restricted code	Elaborated code
	Women's language	Men's language

As has been said earlier, there has been a tendency for scholars to measure everything against the bench-mark of formal written prose. Both Jespersen's claims about women's syntax seem to relate to differences between the spoken and written language. Written language (in particular, printed material) was produced mostly by men (see section 2.2.4); this means that Jespersen could judge men on their written syntax but he was more likely to have judged women's syntax on the basis of their spoken language.

2.2.4 Literacy

This section is closely linked to the preceding one. There is no doubt that until the coming of state education for all in the twentieth century, women had less access to literacy than men. Before the nineteenth century, only women of the middle class and above were likely to be literate, and even then, when we say literate, we mean literate in the vernacular. The brothers and husbands of these same women were literate in the classical languages as well. Classical Latin and Greek were no longer spoken as mother-tongues by anyone: they survived as languages only in the male world of the school, the university and the church. Latin, in particular, had become 'a sex-linked language, a kind of badge of masculine identity' (Ong 1967: 250). When Milton was asked whether he would teach his daughters other languages, he is alleged to have replied: 'One tongue is sufficient for a woman'.

The following extract shows that, while seventeenth- and eighteenth-century gentlemen agreed that women's language had its defects, especially their written language, they were not all opposed to the idea of changing this state of affairs through education. The extract is taken from the introduction to a work entitled *The Many Advantages of a Good Language to any Nation: with an Examination of the Present State of our own: As also, An Essay towards correcting some Things that are wrong in it*. This work has been ascribed to Thomas Wilson (1663–1755), Bishop of Sodor and Man. After emphasising the Power of Words, the writer warns that an improper use of words reflects badly on the user.

> We could heartily wish that the fair sex would take notice of this last Reason; for many a pretty Lady by the Silliness of her Words, hath lost the Admiration which her Face had gained. And as the Mind hath more lovely and more lasting Charms than the Body, if they would captivate Men of Sense, they must not neglect those best kind of Beauties. As these Perfections do not depend upon the Strength of the Hand, but the Quickness of the Wit, and Niceness of the Eye and Ear; and as in these Talents Nature hath doubtless been as bountiful to that Sex as to our own, those improprieties in Words, Spelling and Writing, for which they are usually laughed at, are not owing to any Defect in their Minds, but the Carelessness, if not injustice to them in their Education. These following Essays are intended for a Help to them as well as others.
> (Wilson? 1724: 37)

He goes on to point out the importance of educating the mothers of the nation's children. We can all admire the liberality of his sentiments, while noting that he addresses his remarks exclusively to men ('Nature has doubtless been as bountiful to that Sex as to our own'). At the time this was written (1724), women's writing was clearly the subject of mockery; moreover, women obviously received very little and very poor education. Swift makes the same point, with typical exaggeration, in his *A Letter to a Young Lady on her Marriage* (1727):

> It is a little hard that not one Gentleman's daughter in a thousand should be brought to read or understand her own natural tongue, or be judge of the easiest Books that are written in it.

Henry Tilney's teasing of Catherine about women's letter writing (quoted in the previous section), shows that little had changed nearly a century later.

Rousseau (1712–78) condemns women's writing, but on different grounds from those we have heard so far. He says:

> that burning eloquence, those sublime raptures which transmit delight to the very foundation of the soul will always be lacking from women's writings. They are all cold and pretty like their authors. They may show great wit but never any soul.
>
> (Rousseau, *La Lettre d'Alembert sur les Spectacles*, as translated by Peggy Kamuf 1980: 290)

In the Romantic Age, then, women are seen as inferior because their writings lack passion. We can contrast this with Jespersen's claim that women prefer paratactic modes of expression (see section 2.2.3), a claim which rests on the assertion that they are 'emotional' where men are 'grammatical'. This contradiction is more easily understood if we take the view that each era redefines what is admirable in language and what is to be avoided (**The Androcentric Rule**). There is consistency in Rousseau's and Jespersen's finding that women are performing less admirably than men.

It is not until the twentieth century that we can take it for granted that women are literate, that women have equal access to education, and that women's voices are heard equally with men's (at least in theory). Women's comments on writing give us an insight into the problems of using a medium which has over the centuries been in the hands of men. Virginia Woolf is particularly concerned with the form of the written sentence:

> But it is still true that before a woman can write exactly as she wishes to write, she has many difficulties to face. To begin with, there is the technical difficulty – so simple, apparently; in reality, so baffling – that the very

form of the sentence does not fit her. It is a sentence made by men; it is too loose, too heavy, too pompous for a woman's use. Yet in a novel, which covers so wide a stretch of ground, an ordinary and usual type of sentence has to be found to carry the reader on easily and naturally from one end of the book to the other. And this a woman must make for herself, altering and adapting the current sentence until she writes one that takes the natural shape of her thought without crushing or distorting it.
(Woolf 1929, as published in Woolf 1979: 48)

Woolf's concern that the written sentence is 'made by men' is part of a wider debate over whether language as a whole is man-made. The inadequacy of 'male' language as a medium for writing about women's experience has been deplored by women writers for centuries.[3] French feminists in particular have pursued this line of argument; Luce Irigaray (1990: 82) claims that even the syntax of the written sentence is irredeemably male, and urges a new 'feminine' syntax. But it is not only the form of the written sentence that has come under attack. The 1980s have seen the publication of several feminist dictionaries and other works on vocabulary,[4] and radical innovations by feminist writers have begun to seep into public consciousness (if only to be ridiculed). Lexical forms like *herstory* (as a substitute for *history*) and *malestream* (as a substitute for *mainstream*) may not, in the long run, be permanent additions to the English lexicon, but they draw attention to the essential **androcentricity** of the written word, and of the culture it represents.

2.2.5 *Pronunciation*

The rise of a standard variety of written English was followed by the rise of a standard variety of *spoken* English. After the development of a standard grammar and lexicon, the need was felt for a standard in pronunciation. The accent normally associated with standard English is RP (Received Pronunciation), an accent which differs from all other English accents in that it no longer has links with any particular geographical region. The growth of a spoken standard is accompanied by the growth of ideas about what constitutes 'good' speech. As the educated speech of the Court in London became prestigious, so other accents began to be stigmatised. Comments by contemporary writers reveal again an androcentric view of linguistic usage with women's speech singled out as deviating from the (male) norms.

Elyot, in *The Governour* (1531), gives the following advice on the subject of nurses and other women who look after noblemen's children when they are infants:

> [they shall] at the lest way . . . speke none English but that which is cleane, polite, perfectly and articulately pronounced, omittinge no lettre or sillable, as folisshe women oftentimes do of a wantonnesse, whereby divers noblemen and gentilmennes chyldren (as I do at this daye knowe) have attained corrupte and foul pronuntiation.
> (Elyot 1531)

Note that the appeal to the idea that no letters or syllables should be omitted is an appeal to the notion of written language as norm. As we have seen (section 2.2.3), spoken English has been compared with written ever since the growth of a written standard. Where writing and speech differ (and we are only now beginning to understand how great these differences are), there has been a tendency to see the spoken form as incorrect, or as deviating from the ideal. The above passage reminds us again that gentlemen, as the educated literate group in society, had a different view of language from women.

The following extract (taken from Gill's *Logonomia Anglica* (1619–21) links the speech of women with that of low-status men:

> in speech the custom of the learned is the first law. Writing therefore is to be adjusted, not to that sound which herdsmen, girls [*mulierculae*] and porters use; but to that which the learned or cultivated scholars [*docti aut culte eruditi viri*] use in speaking and recitation.
> (as translated in Dobson 1969: 435, n.4)

The pronunciation of female speakers (*mulierculae*) is explicitly compared with that of male speakers (*viri*), and readers are urged to imitate educated *men*. The grouping of herdsmen, porters and girls together shows us that prestigious speech was clearly associated with education. It is not clear, however, whether women and men of the same social class in the seventeenth century *did* talk differently – it is only in the twentieth century that quantitative sociolinguistic analysis has been applied to speech.

Jespersen includes an excellent survey of male/female differences in pronunciation in his chapter on 'The Woman', in a section oddly entitled 'Phonetics and Grammar' (where is the grammar?). He interprets the comments of early grammarians as showing that women had a more advanced pronunciation than men. For example, he quotes Mulcaster (1582): '*Ai* is the man's diphthong, and soundeth full: *ei*, the woman's, and soundeth finish (i.e. fineish) in the same both sense, and use, *a woman is deintie, and feinteth soon, the man fainteth not bycause he is nothing daintie*'. Jespersen comments: 'Thus what is now distinctive of refined as opposed to vulgar pronunciation was then characteristic of the fair sex' (Jespersen 1922: 243). He demonstrates that this tendency to innovate was not confined to English women, giving examples from France, Denmark and even Siberia. He devotes a paragraph to 'the weakening of the old fully trilled tongue-point r' (1922: 244). He argues that this change, which has occurred in many languages, has been brought about to a large extent by women. His evidence is slight, and his explanation bizarre: 'The old trilled point sound is natural and justified when life is chiefly carried on out-of-doors, but indoor life prefers, on the whole, less noisy speech habits' (Jespersen 1922: 244). He argues, in effect, that sounds which are appropriate in a rural setting are inappropriate in an urban one. His observation of differences between the speech of 'the great cities' and 'the rustic population' seems plausible, but his correlation of city life with 'refined domestic life' (and therefore under women's influence) seems naïve.

Writing in 1922, Jespersen concludes with the statement: 'In present-day English there are said to be a few differences in pronunciation between the two sexes.' They are listed in Table 2.2 as he gives

Table 2.2: Gender differences in pronunciation in England, 1922 (based on Jespersen 1922: 245)

Men	Women	
[sɔːft]	[sɔft]	*soft*
[gəːl]	[gɛəl]	*girl*
[waɪt]	[hwaɪt]	*white*
[tʃɪldrən]	[tʃʊldrən]	*children*
['weskət]	['weɪs'koʊt]	*waistcoat*

them (the first two are attributed to Daniel Jones, who was Professor of Phonetics at London University). It is interesting to note that, while Jespersen here demonstrates differences in women's and men's pronunciation, his examples, if accurate, do not reveal a consistent pattern: the more 'advanced' forms – [sɔft], [gəːl], [waɪt], [tʃɪldrən] and [weɪskoʊt] – are not correlated with gender.

Jespersen concludes that these are isolated instances: 'on the whole we must say that from a phonetic point of view there is scarcely any difference between the speech of men and that of women: the two sexes speak for all intents and purposes the same language'

(Jespersen 1922: 245). However, his earlier observations on women's more advanced pronunciation have been borne out by much twentieth-century work in sociolinguistics. The relationship between women's speech and linguistic change will be pursued in Chapter 8.

2.2.6 Verbosity

Many women, many words; many geese, many turds.
(English proverb)

There is an age-old belief that women talk too much. The cultural myth of women's verbosity is nicely caught in this fifteenth-century carol which describes the many virtues of women, but undermines the message with a refrain telling us that the opposite is true:

Of all creatures women be best
Cuius contrarium verum est. [of which the opposite is true]
(Davies 1963: 222)

Women are described as 'not liberal in language but ever in secree'. The reader is encouraged to confide in women:

For tell a woman all your counsaile
And she can kepe it wonderly well.

The writer, tongue in cheek, defends women against the charge of being chatterboxes:

Trow ye that women list to smater [chatter]
Or against their husbondes for to clater?
Nay! they had lever [would rather] fast, bred and water,
Then for to dele in suche a matter.

The humour of this poem derives from the reader knowing that the writer intends the opposite meaning throughout. Since the key to understanding this joke is the Latin phrase in the refrain, the joke is clearly a male one, since Latin and Greek were taught only to boys (see section 2.2.4).

English literature is filled with characters who substantiate the stereotype of the talkative women. Rosalind, in *As You Like It* (III.2.264) says: 'Do you not know I am a woman? When I think, I must speak'. Dion, in Beaumont and Fletcher's *Philaster* (II.4.1–3) advises:

Come, ladies, shall we talk a round? As men
Do walk a mile, women should talk an hour
After supper; 'tis their exercise.

Aurora Leigh, the eponymous heroine of Elizabeth Barrett Browning's poem of 1856, says: 'A woman's function plainly is – to talk.'

In a section on 'the volubility of women', Jespersen quotes examples from literature such as those above to prove his point, and refers to research done on reading speed which found that women tended to read a given passage faster than men and to remember more about the passage after reading it. In the face of this evidence, Jespersen asserts: 'But it was found that this rapidity was no proof of intellectual power, and some of the slowest readers were highly distinguished men'! (Jespersen 1922: 252). To support his prejudice, Jespersen refers to Havelock Ellis's work *Man and Woman* (1894), which 'explains' that 'with the quick reader it is as though every statement were admitted immediately and without inspection to fill the vacant chambers of the mind' (Jespersen 1922: 252), and to Swift's assertion that

> the common fluency of speech in many men, and most women, is owing to the scarcity of matter, and scarcity of words; for whoever is a master of language, and hath a mind full of ideas, will be apt in speaking to hesitate upon the choice of both: whereas common speakers have only one set of ideas, and one set of words to clothe them in; and these are always ready at the mouth.
>
> (Swift, quoted in Jespersen 1922: 252)

It must be obvious to any reader today that none of this represents a valid argument. Jespersen obviously accepts the cultural stereotype of the voluble chattering woman; he presents us with some tangential data on reading speed; he then argues that women's facility with words does not correspond to any intellectual power (but rather the contrary), and quotes the dogmatic statements of two famous men, as if this constituted supporting evidence. Since he provides no data on the speed and quantity of women's speech, the passage tells us nothing except that scholars of language in the early part of the twentieth century were subject to the prejudices of their times.

The other side of the coin to women's verbosity is the image of the silent woman which is often held up as an ideal – 'Silence is the best ornament of a woman' (English proverb). This ideal is found very early in literary texts, for example, in the Arthurian romances, in stories such as Erec and Enyd. This exists in versions by Chrétien de Troyes (c. 1170), in *The Mabinogion* (c .1300), and in Tennyson's *Idylls of the King* (1859). The crucial episode involves Erec (Geraint in *The Mabinogion*/Tennyson) and Enyd riding alone on a journey during which Erec tests his wife's loyalty to him. Erec says:

and this
I charge thee, on thy duty as a wife,

Whatever happens, not to speak to me,
No, not a word!
(Tennyson, *Geraint and Enid*)

Silence is made synonymous with obedience.

The tale of Patient Griselda also appears in many different forms, for example, as 'The Clerk's Tale' in Chaucer's *Canterbury Tales*. Again, a wife's loyalty and obedience are tested: this time her children are forcibly taken from her. Even though Griselda believes they may be killed, she does not protest: 'Ne in this tyme word ne spak she noon' ('The Clerk's Tale', l.900). Silence is again portrayed as intrinsic to obedience. (It should be noted that Griselda passes the test of obedience with flying colours, and is thus a character twentieth-century readers have difficulties with; Enyd on the other hand breaks her husband's command in order to warn him of danger – she saves his life by refusing to remain silent.)

During the Renaissance, eloquence was highly acclaimed, but Tasso, in his *Discorso della virtu feminile e donnesca* (1582), makes it clear that while eloquence is a virtue in a man, *silence* is the corresponding virtue in a woman. As one scholar comments: 'The implication is that it is inappropriate for a woman to be eloquent or liberal, or for a man to be economical and silent' (MacLean 1980: 62).

The model of the silent woman is still presented to girls in the second half of the twentieth century: research in English schools suggests that quiet behaviour is very much encouraged by teachers, particularly in girls. This will be discussed at greater length in section 9.3. Such conditioning begins very early in a child's life. It is reported that nursery school children in Bristol are taught a song which goes: 'All the Daddies on the bus go read, read, read . . . All the Mummies on the bus go chatter, chatter, chatter' (quoted in *The Guardian*'s 'Naked Ape' column). Primary school children on Merseyside are taught this song too.

Dale Spender comments on the issue of women and silence:

> The talkativeness of women has been gauged in comparison not with men but with *silence*. . . . When silence is the desired state for women . . . then any talk in which a woman engages can be too much.
> (Spender 1980a: 42)

The idea that silence is 'the desired state for women' is supported by the theory of 'muted groups' proposed by the anthropologists Shirley and Edwin Ardener (Ardener 1975; 1978). Briefly, they argue that in any society there are dominant modes of expression, belonging to dominant groups within that society. If members of a 'muted group' want to be heard, they are required to express themselves in the dominant mode (this ties in with Virginia Woolf's comments: section 2.2.4 above). While muted groups are not necessarily silent, their mutedness means that they have difficulty making themselves heard by the dominant group. However, in many cultures, muted groups are indeed silenced by rules laid down by the dominant group. 'Ritual silence may be imposed on women: in synagogues, for example, and in Greece after weddings' (Ardener 1978: 23). In Britain, the muting of women is more subtle, but there is still overt opposition to women as radio or TV announcers, for example, and the controversy over women's ordination arises in part from the dominant group's resistance to women speaking in authoritative voices.

In relation to the specific topic of women's supposed verbosity, this section has demonstrated that pre-Chomskyan linguistic inquiry provides us with no *evidence* that women talk more than men. Yet there is no doubt that Western European culture is imbued with the belief that women *do* talk a lot, and there is evidence that silence is an ideal that has been held up to (and imposed on) women for many centuries.

2.3 Conclusion

In this chapter we have looked at folklinguistic views of male/female differences in language and those of the early grammarians. We have concentrated on six areas: vocabulary, swearing and taboo language, grammar, literacy, pronunciation, and verbosity. Modern sociolinguistic work on gender differences in grammar and pronunciation will be the subject of Chapters 4 and 5. Chapter 6, which looks at the general topic of communicative competence, will include a discussion of contemporary linguistic research on gender differences in swearing and in verbosity.

Notes

1 The first proverb is taken from *The Oxford Dictionary of English Proverbs*, edited by Smith and Heseltine (1935); the second is from *Cheshire Proverbs*, collected and annotated by Joseph C. Bridge (1917); the last two are taken from Jespersen (1922: 253, n.1).

2 According to Bernstein (a sociologist) restricted code is distinguished from elaborated code in the following ways: it is used
   in relatively informal situations, and speakers assume a great deal
   of shared knowledge; this is reflected linguistically in the high
   proportion of pronouns and tag questions, and in the simple
   syntax. Linguists are not happy with the codes, and Bernstein's
   claim that the ability to use them correlates with social class is
   highly controversial.

3 See Donovan (1980) for a fascinating survey.

4 Examples are: Cheris Kramarae and Paula Treichler (1983) *A
   Feminist Dictionary* (Pandora Press, London); Mary Daly (1988)
   Webster's First New Intergalactic Wickedary of the English Language
   (Women's Press, London); Jane Mills (1989) *Womanwords: A
   Vocabulary of Culture and Patriarchal Society* (Longman, London).

CHAPTER 3

The historical background (II) – anthropologists and dialectologists

3.1 Introduction

There are two major disciplines whose work touches on gender differences in language. These two disciplines – Anthropology and Dialectology – have aims and objectives which are quite distinct from those of sociolinguistics, but there are areas of overlap. Anthropologists have observed language as part of their observation of the whole spectrum of social behaviour in a given community. Dialectologists have analysed the speech of rural communities in order to investigate linguistic change and the decline of rural dialects. Both anthropologists and dialectologists have commented upon gender differences in language; and it is these comments which form the basis of this chapter.

3.2 Anthropologists

Differences between the language of male and female speakers have been noted in anthropological literature since the seventeenth century. Missionaries and explorers came across societies whose linguistic behaviour caused them to speak of 'men's language' and 'women's language'. These terms overstate the case: what we find in these languages are phonological, morphological, syntactic and lexical contrasts where the speaker's gender determines which form is chosen. I shall briefly survey some of this work to illustrate the kind of male/female variation in language that anthropologists commented on.

3.2.1 Phonological Differences

The Chukchi language, spoken in Eastern Siberia, varies phonologically, depending on the gender of the speaker. Women use /ʃ/ where men use /tʃ/ or /r/. For example, the word for *people* is pronounced /ʃamkɪʃʃɪn/ by women and /ramkɪtʃɪn/ by men.

The men and women of the Gros Ventre tribe in Montana also make consistent differences in their pronunciation (Flannery 1946). The velar plosive /k/ is replaced by an affricate in the men's speech, so where the women say /wakinsihiθa/ (newborn child), the men say /waʤinsihiθa/. The word for bread is pronounced /kja'tsa/ by the women, and /ʤa'tsa/ by the men. In this community, pronunciation is a defining marker of sexual identity: if anyone uses the wrong form, they are considered to be bisexual by older members of the tribe. Flannery hypothesises that fear of being laughed at for such errors has helped to erode the use of the language by the younger generation, who tend to speak English.

3.2.2 Morphological Differences

Edward Sapir (1929, quoted in Yaguello 1978) describes a language spoken by the Yana (in California) where the language used between men differs morphologically from that used in other situations (men to women, women to men, women to women). The words used in this men-to-men variety are longer than those used in the communal language. It seems that in a minority of cases the men add a suffix to the primary form, following a rule which can roughly be stated as follows: *When a word in the communal language ends with a long vowel, a diphthong or a consonant, or if the word is a monosyllable, the men's language adds a suffix /-na/, e.g. /ba/ (stag) → /banal/; /au/ (fire) → /aunal/.* In the majority of cases the form in the communal language appears to be a logical *abbreviation* of the male form, following a rule which can roughly be stated as follows: *When a word in the men's language ends in a short vowel – /a, i, u/ – this vowel is lost and the preceding consonant becomes voiceless; thus /b, d, g, ʤ/ + short vowel → /p', t', k', tʃ'/, e.g. /gagi/ (crow) → /gak'/; /p'adza/ (snow) → /p'atʃ'/.*

This second rule can be accounted for by the principle of morpho-phonemic economy (there is a tendency in all languages for words to get simplified – cf *omnibus* → *bus*, *refrigerator* → *fridge*, etc.). In other words, the men's language seems to preserve historically older forms. Sapir suggests that the reduced female forms symbolise women's lower status: the men's fuller forms are associated with ceremony and formality. This is an interesting case of male speech being associated with conservatism and linguistic purity, characteristics now conventionally associated with women's language (this will be discussed at greater length in Chapters 4 and 8).

Among the Koasati, a Muskogean Indian tribe in Louisiana, certain forms of the verb vary according to the speaker's gender (Haas 1944). For example, where the women's form ends in a nasalised vowel, the men's form ends in -s. The following are examples:

Women	Men	
lakawtakkǫ́	lakawtakkós	I am not lifting it
lakawwa	lakawwá.s	he will lift it
ká.	ká.s	he is saying

Where the women's form has the falling pitch-stress on its final syllable and ends in a short vowel followed by /l/, the men's form involves high pitch-stress and replaces /l/ with /s/.

Women	Men	
lakawwîl	lakawwîs	I am lifting it
molhîl	molhís	we are peeling it
lakawhôl	lakawhós	lift it! (to 2nd person plural)

In this community, it is the women's language which is conservative and which represents an earlier stage in the language. In 1944 Haas found that only the older women were maintaining the distinction; the younger women used the men's forms. The women's forms are presumably obsolete now.

3.2.3 Lexical Differences

Gender differences in vocabulary were frequently reported by early anthropologists. I shall look at two examples here; two other examples are given in the next section (section 3.3).

In most languages, the pronoun system marks gender distinctions in the third person (e.g. *he/she*), but the distinction is less commonly made in the first and second persons where speaker's gender is involved. Japanese is a language which marks gender in all three persons of the pronoun (Bodine 1975a, Ide 1991). There is a formal first person form *watakusi* which can be used by either male or female speakers and a formal second person pronoun, *anata*, which can be used to male or female addressees. However, when we look at the full repertoire of personal pronouns available in Japanese, we find that there are significant differences between those used by men and those used by women (see Table 3.1). This table shows us, first, that certain forms are exclusive to men: *boku* as a first person pronoun, and *kimi* as a second person pronoun. The deprecatory pronouns *ore* (first person), *omae* and *kisama* (second person) are also exclusive to men; women have no deprecatory pronouns available to them. Second, Table 3.1 reveals differences in levels of formality: *watasi*, for example, is formal for men, but plain for women. This has the effect of making women's speech sound more polite than men's (see section 6.3 on gender differences in politeness).

Table 3.1: Japanese personal pronouns (Ide 1991: 73)

	Men's speech	Women's speech
First person		
formal	*watakusi*	*watakusi*
	watasi	*atakusi**
plain	*boku*	*watasi*
		*atasi**
deprecatory	*ore*	φ
Second person		
formal	*anata*	*anata*
plain	*kimi*	*anata*
	*anta**	*anta**
deprecatory	*omae*	
	kisama	φ

* marks variants of a social dialect

In his work on the Trobriand islanders, Malinowski (1929, quoted in Yaguello 1978) established that their kinship terminology is organised on the basis of two criteria:

1. same/different gender
2. older/younger.

This means that the word for *sister*, for example, will vary according to whether the speaker is male or female, and whether the speaker is older or younger than the sibling. Figure 3.1 shows how the

Figure 3.1 Trobriand islanders' terms for sister, brother, sister-in-law, brother-in-law (based on Yaguello 1978: 27)

system works for the relationships of brother, sister, brother-in-law and sister-in-law. In the case of the relationship we call *sister*, the Trobrianders have three terms (*luguta, tuwagu, bwadagu*) for our one. Conversely, they make no distinction between a man's sister and a woman's brother (both are *luguta*), nor between a man's brother and a woman's sister if the age difference is the same in both cases (*tuwagu* or *bwadagu*).

We can see why earlier scholars were misled into talking of men's and women's languages. In particular, where English and other European languages distinguish kin on the basis of **gender of the spoken about,** the Trobriand language, like Chiquito, Yana, and many others, distinguishes kinship terms on the basis of **gender of the speaker.** This means that Trobriand islanders give different names to relationships we see as 'the same', but only one name to relationships we perceive as 'different'.

3.3 Anthropological Explanations

It is clear that none of these examples constitutes a case of separate languages for women and men. Observers mistakenly described the phenomena they came across in terms of separate male/female languages as a result of both linguistic naïvety and a tendency to exaggerate. Their hypotheses about the origins of gender differences in language were inevitably skewed by their belief in polarised gender varieties. The two main explanatory factors put forward by anthropologists were **taboo** and **contact with speakers of other languages.**

Taboo operates in all societies, proscribing certain forms of behaviour, including linguistic behaviour. In British society today, topics of conversation such as excretion or sexual activity are taboo in many contexts. In so-called 'primitive' societies, what is or is not permitted is stringently controlled socially. Taboos are part of the structure which maintains social order.

A good example of taboo and its effects on language is reported by Caroline Humphrey in an article on women and taboo (Humphrey 1978). She investigated what constituted incorrect or improper behaviour for women in Mongolia. Most linguistic taboos in Mongolia are concerned with *names*. Mongols avoid using the names of dead people, predatory animals and certain mountains and rivers thought to be inhabited by spirits. More particularly, women are absolutely forbidden to use the names of their husband's older brothers, father, father's brothers or grandfather. This taboo extends beyond the names of the husband's male relatives: women are not allowed to use *any word or syllable* which is the same as, or sounds like, any of the forbidden names. For example, where the name *Shar* is taboo, the woman must not use either the name or the word *shar* (= yellow), but has to substitute *angir*, a word which refers to a yellow-coloured duck. Or if the tabooed name is *Xarzuu* (derived from *xarax* = to look at), the woman must also avoid the word *xar* (= black) and has to use instead *bargaan*, which means 'darkish or obscure'. It is not surprising that earlier reports talked of 'women's language' among the Mongols. However, such taboos affect only vocabulary; other aspects of language are unaffected. Moreover, each woman affected by such a taboo will have different linguistic problems, depending on the names of her male relatives-by-marriage. So while it can result in distinct female vocabularies, taboo as a social force is hardly sufficient explanation of the other gender differences which occur in language.

Contact with speakers of other languages occurs when there is an invasion, or when men marry women from outside their village or tribe (as is the custom in some societies). The most well-known case of gender differences in language said to result from the marrying of people speaking different languages is that of the Carib Indians. In his account of the people of Lesser Antilles, written in 1665, Rochefort claimed that the men and women spoke different languages:

> The savage natives of Dominica say that the reason for this is that when the Caribs came to occupy the islands, these were inhabited by an Arawak tribe which they exterminated completely, with the exception of the women, whom they married in order to populate the country. Now, these

> women kept their own language and taught it to their daughters. . . . It is
> asserted that there is some similarity between the speech of the continental
> Arawaks and that of the Carib women.
> (as quoted in Jespersen 1922: 237)

It is clear from other evidence that this is another case of separate
lexical items for women and men in certain areas; it is not a case of
two separate languages. Moreover, the invasion theory is not totally
convincing, especially as the linguistic variation found among Carib
Indians is similar to that found in other American Indian groups
(Trudgill 1974b: 86). Contact with speakers of other languages will
not do as an explanation for gender differences in language in general,
since such differences occur in all known languages.

3.4 Some Problems with Anthropological Work on Gender Differences

The major defect of anthropological work is that anthropologists failed
to see that gender differences in language were not exclusively a feature
of 'primitive' people and of distant exotic cultures. It is reasonable
to ask the question: Why did they ignore gender differences in the
European languages they were familiar with? The answer seems to be
that they defined the problem in terms of **gender-exclusive** differences.
That is, they commented on differences between women's and men's
usage where certain linguistic forms were reserved exclusively for the
use of one gender or the other. All the examples quoted so far in
this chapter are of this kind. The variation in male/female language
found in European languages, however, involves **gender-preferential**
differences, that is, while women's and men's language differs, there
are no forms associated exclusively with one gender; rather there
is a tendency for women or men to prefer a certain form. For
example, as we shall see in the following chapters, women in
Britain tend to use forms closer to Standard English, while men
tend to use a higher proportion of non-standard forms. The difference
between gender-exclusive and gender-preferential usage seems to be
a reflection of the difference between pre-literate, non-industrialised
societies and literate, highly industrialised societies; the former tend to
have clearly segregated gender roles, unlike modern European societies
where gender roles are much less rigidly structured.

Despite their failure to generalise their discoveries to more familiar
societies, anthropologists at least drew attention to the way in which

human societies use gender as a salient social category, and to the linguistic differences which arise directly from this social structure and which re-create and perpetuate this structure. More recently, anthropology has had an important influence on the developing discipline of sociolinguistics. In general terms, the anthropologists' insistence on the significance of cultural context has underpinned the sociolinguist's conviction that the study of the ideal speaker/hearer in a homogeneous speech community is too narrow a field. More particularly, sociolinguistic methodology has borrowed directly from anthropological field techniques; the study of groups as working wholes and the concept of the social network as a tool of analysis are leading to exciting new developments in sociolinguistic research. Such research will be described in detail in Chapter 5.

3.5 Dialectologists

Dialectologists, unlike anthropologists, have always been sensitive to gender differences in their own (that is, European) languages. Ironically, this has resulted in our having virtually no data on such differences, for reasons which will become apparent during the following discussion. I shall discuss the work of dialectologists as it relates to gender differences under three headings: women as informants, the questionnaire, and the fieldworker.

3.5.1 Women as Informants

The choice of informants is of crucial importance in any linguistic survey. Since the Holy Grail of traditional dialectology was 'pure' dialect, which had to be recorded before it died out, dialectologists chose as informants those who, in their view, spoke 'pure' dialect. The circularity of this procedure was uncritically accepted. Their methodology contrasts markedly with that of modern sociolinguistic surveys using a quantitative approach: these have adopted the methods of the social sciences, and take a representative sample of informants chosen randomly from the electoral roll, or some equivalent list. Because dialectologists' choice of informants was so unrepresentative, we have little idea what sort of linguistic variation existed in the rural communities studied. Certain members ·

of the community were included; others were excluded. We have no comparative data to confirm or refute the dialectologists' claim that some members of the speech community spoke a more 'pure' form of the dialect than others.

Who did dialectologists choose as informants? The answer to this question reveals that their choice depended largely on folklinguistic beliefs. Dialectologists favoured older members of the community as informants (for obvious, if not scientific reasons), but they disagreed about the merits of female as opposed to male informants. One view was that women were the best informants because of their innate conservatism. This view was expressed by a great variety of dialectologists, from the end of the nineteenth century up to the 1940s, in areas as different as Slovenia, Switzerland, Flanders and Romania. The general view is that stated by Wartburg in his review of Griera's Linguistic Atlas of Catalonia (which is criticised for its lack of women informants):

> Everyone knows that as far as language is concerned women are more conservative than men; they conserve the speech of our forebears more faithfully.[1]
> (Wartburg 1925: 113 as quoted in Pop 1950: 373)

This view is supported by the following 'reasons':

1. Women hardly ever leave their village, unlike men.
2. Women stay at home and talk ('chat') to each other, and don't mix with strangers.
3. Women don't do military service.

The opposite view – that women are *not* conservative – was held by many other dialectologists, including the hugely influential Gilliéron, director of the linguistic survey of France (the first major survey to use a trained fieldworker). These dialectologists preferred *men* as informants, since they considered men's speech to be closer to the 'pure' dialect. The general view is clearly stated by Harold Orton in his *Introduction to the Survey of English Dialects*:

> In this country men speak vernacular more frequently, more consistently, and more genuinely than women.
> (Orton 1962: 15)

The innovative nature of women's speech is stressed:

> Women's speech is not conservative. Women, who are usually said to be more conservative than men, accept new words quite readily.[2]
> (from Pop's account of Gilliéron 1880)

Unlike those who believe in women's conservatism, these dialect-ologists offer us no explanations. Gauchat, for example, tells us that women are more innovative and then describes their lives as follows:

> They spend much more time in the home, with other people, cooking and washing, and talking more than men, who are busy with their agricultural work; you see the men at their work, silent and often on their own for the whole day.[3]

We are presumably meant to infer from the different life styles of the two sexes a reason for their differing linguistic usage. But this description does not explain why women should be more innovative than men. In fact, the female way of life described here is virtually identical to that described by dialectologists in the 'women are conservative' camp. As far as we can see any difference, it is in the way the *men*'s lives are described: the dialectologists in the first group stress the men's interaction with strangers, their involvement in travel and military service; while those in the second group either don't describe the men's lives, or portray them as isolated.

The explanation which seems to underlie the second group of studies is women's supposed sensitivity to linguistic norms. It is assumed that standard norms will have more influence on women's speech than on men's; women, who have little status in society, seek to acquire status through their use of language. Stanley Ellis, chief fieldworker for the Survey of English Dialects, comments:

> Women were always seen as a refining and 'improving' influence. It was suggested that this often came about because young country girls used to have a spell as indoor servants in better class homes and came under the influence of better speech.
>
> (Ellis, personal communication)

The concepts of both conservatism and status-consciousness on the part of women are introduced into dialect studies in a somewhat ad hoc manner, depending on how women's speech is perceived. Neither seems a very satisfactory explanation of gender differences in language. (For a fuller critique of conservatism and status-consciousness as explanatory factors, see Cameron and Coates 1989.)

The evidence suggests, then, that attitudes to informants were preconceived and highly subjective. Not surprisingly, we find contra-dictions: Gilliéron, whose survey covered the whole of France, argued that women were not conservative linguistically, while Meunier, in his much smaller study of the Nivernais region of France, favoured women as informants because of their conservatism. Jaberg and Jud, in their major dialect survey of Italy and southern Switzerland, also assume the linguistic conservatism of women, but one of their fieldworkers (Rohlfs) is quoted as saying 'the pronunciation of vowels by women doesn't differ only from that of men – who possess vowels which are purer and clearer – but from area to area' (Jaberg 1936: 21, n.3 as quoted in Pop 1950: 579).[4] Rohlfs definitely seems to be claiming that men's pronunciation of vowels was 'purer' than women's. Pop, in his comprehensive account of dialect study (Pop 1950), can hardly fail to notice such discrepancies. He is basically an adherent of the 'women are conservative' camp, but he advocates a detailed comparative study of the pronunciation of men and women, since, he says, 'it certainly seems, although people often assert the contrary, that women's language displays more innovations than men's in certain cases' (Pop 1950: 195).[5]

Only one dialectologist, out of all those I have surveyed, states specifically that he is *not* aware of gender differences in the speech community he is studying. This is Angus McIntosh, director of the Survey of Scottish Dialects. He writes: 'As to sex, there is no evidence which shows conclusively whether men or women make better informants in Scotland' (McIntosh 1952: 90).

So who did the dialectologists choose as informants? On the basis of their published views, we would expect the first group to select women (since they describe women as linguistically conservative) and the second to select men (since they describe men as linguistically conservative). In fact, with the exception of the German–Swiss survey and McIntosh's Scottish survey (in both of which the fieldworkers interviewed one man and one woman in each locality), *all* the dialect surveys for which I have figures favoured men. Table 3.2 gives details.

As Table 3.2 shows, women were very poorly represented in dialect surveys. Moreover, a detailed examination of dialect survey findings shows that the few female informants are not spread evenly. The Survey of English Dialects, for example, investigated the thirty-nine counties of England, but this does not mean that 12 per cent of informants in each county were women, as we would expect (see Table 3.2); in fact, in seven counties, *no* women were interviewed (Worcestershire, Gloucestershire, Northamptonshire, Huntingdonshire, Cambridgeshire, Wiltshire and Devon).

When we look for explanations for this uneven pattern of sampling, we find that dialectologists express reservations about women as informants. Even dialectologists who see women as better informants on *linguistic* grounds (because of their supposed conservatism) reject them for non-linguistic reasons. For example, women are said to be too busy or too timid, or embarrassed at being asked to speak patois in front of a researcher. A typical 'explanation' for failing to interview

Table 3.2: Table to show proportion of women informants in dialect surveys (source: Pop 1950)

Dialect survey	Date of publication	Male informants	Female informants	Total informants	% women
France (Gilliéron)	1902–10	640	60*	700*	8.57
Catalonia (Griera)	1923–39	107	1	108	0.93
S. Austria (Tesniere)	1925	70	18	88	20.45
Italy/Switz. (Jaberg and Jud)	1928–40	380	40*	420*	9.52
Sardinia (Pellis)	1933–35	55	5	60	8.33
Corsica (Bottiglioni)	1933–42	61	6	67	8.96
Italy (Bartoli)	1933	316	48	364	13.19
Belg. Congo (De Boeck)	1942	?	0	?	0.00
North China (Giet)	1946	495	29	524	5.53
England (Orton)	1962–78	867	122	989	12.34

* = approximate figure

more women is that of Sever Pop, who was director of the dialect survey of Romania:

> The investigator comes up against problems in persuading women to give up two or three days to the project, since household chores prevent them from doing so, and they feel embarrassed at sitting down at the table with a 'city gentleman'.[6]
> (Pop 1950: 725)

Pop at least adduces reasons which seem relevant to the fieldworker's task. Other dialectologists, however, explain their omission of women on blatantly sexist grounds. The following is taken from an article by Griera, a Catholic priest who was responsible for the Linguistic Atlas of Catalonia:

> The reasons for my doing so [*excluding women*] are: the impossibility of their maintaining attention during a long questionnaire lasting several days; the fact that their knowledge of objects is, in general, more limited than men's, and, above all, their lack of firm concepts which is reflected in imprecise naming of objects.
> (Griera 1928)[7]

Even though dialectologists are aware that they tend to favour men as informants, it seems probable, to judge from the following comment of an expert fieldworker, that they had no idea *how few* women were actually involved as informants: 'The informants I used during my spell as fieldworker for the Survey of English Dialects in the 1950s were far more men than women. I would estimate about one informant in four or five were [*sic*] female' (Ellis, personal communication). As we can see from Table 3.1, fewer than one informant in eight was female.

There are two aspects of dialect study which may help us to explain the predominance of men as informants. These are the questionnaire, which was traditionally used to structure the interview, to guarantee comparability, and to ensure that the desired responses were obtained from every informant; and the fieldworker, usually a trained scholar who was sent out into a given area by the director of the survey, to conduct interviews with informants.

3.5.2 The Questionnaire

The questionnaire, 'the central instrument used in the systematic collection of dialect' (Francis 1983: 52), may seem an innocent tool of research, but besides determining in advance what linguistic items are to be scrutinised, it predetermines in other ways what is to be included and what not.

Most questionnaires, both those in postal surveys and those employing fieldworkers, were divided into sections, and some of these sections would be aimed specifically at women, and some at men. The German–Swiss Linguistic Atlas based its choice of informants on this division: 'The responses for the dialect of each locality were given by a man and a woman of the district: the man replied to the questions concerning men's work; the women to those concerning feminine occupations'[8] (Pop 1950: 770). The German–Swiss survey was unusual in interviewing as many women as men, but we should note the rigid segregation of questions into those for women and those for men. This presumably reflects the dialectologist's concern with **lexicon**. Traditional dialectology aimed to establish 'what a three-legged milking stool is called in several hundred different places' (McIntosh 1952: 70). Many dialectologists assumed that men's and women's vocabularies differed as a reflection of their social roles. As McIntosh comments:

> Experience has shown that a conventional portmanteau questionnaire cannot be filled in completely with the help of only one person; the housewife lets one down on agricultural terms, the farmer on kitchen terms, and often some local expert has to be hunted out specially to deal with such items as flowers or birds.
>
> (McIntosh 1952: 89)

I shall look at two examples of dialect study to show how the structure of the questionnaire affected the choice of informant.

1. Navarro, who was responsible for the Linguistic Atlas of Puerto Rico, is reported as justifying his virtual exclusion of women informants on the grounds that they wouldn't know the replies to his questions:

   'Since the questionnaire was designed to find out in particular about agricultural terminology, women could not give good replies. For this reason there are only two women among the informants.'[9]

   (Pop 1950: 452)

2. Wirth, director of the Linguistic Atlas of Sorabe (a Western Slav dialect), was particularly interested in domestic vocabulary. As Pop says:

   'Since his questionnaire was principally concerned with the terminology of the dwelling place and housework, he was obliged to appeal to women to collaborate.'[10]

   (Pop 1950: 981)

Table 3.3 gives details of the thirty-one sections included in the questionnaire for the *Atlas linguistique et ethnographique du Lyonnais* (Gardette 1968). This is one of the more recent regional atlases produced by French dialectologists, yet the built-in assumption of male-as-norm is still there: of the thirty-one sections, two (nos 20 and 21) are specifically marked as 'Women's Life'. Women's life has to be marked because it is taken for granted that the majority of sections will relate to men.

We can see from the preceding discussion that one of the reasons women were not used as informants was that (male) dialectologists defined which areas of life and therefore which lexical sets were worthy of study from an essentially androcentric viewpoint.

Table 3.3: Questionnaire for *Atlas linguistique et ethnographique du Lyonnais* (Francis 1983: 60)

Section	Number of questions
1 Meadow, hay, rake, fork	57
2 Grain, sowing, harvest	58
3 Threshing, the flail	57
4 Yoke, goad	39
5 Plows and working the land	55
6 Carts and wagons	66
7 The vineyard	89
8 The wood	54
9 The garden, potatoes, root vegetables	36
10 Cattle, horses, donkeys	63
11 Sheet, goats, swine	62
12 The barnyard	50
13 The barnyard (concluded), bees, dog, cat	43
14 Milk, butter, cheese	64
15 Bread	43
16 Trees (other than fruit-trees)	59
17 Fruit-trees	59
18 Birds, flies, parasites	58
19 Harmful animals, snakes, water creatures, insects	48
20 Women's life: 1. The bed, housekeeping, meals	59
21 Women's life: 2. Washing, sewing	52
22 The house: 1. Generalities, doors and windows, kitchen	61
23 The house: 2. Lamps, fireplace, bedroom, outbuildings	56
24 Weather: winds, rain, snow, sun	70
25 The stars, landscape	45
26 The calendar	44
27 The day, kinship	48
28 From cradle to grave	107
29 The body	85
30 Clothing; manure; occupations	50
31 Hemp	31
Total lexical items	1,875
Morphological items	68

> It is especially common for the interviewer to shift to a woman – often the wife of a principal male informant – for those parts of the questionnaire which deal with the house, the kitchen, the children, and other areas commonly considered to be women's province.
>
> (Francis 1983: 86)

Since men's work was regarded as of prime interest, women's work, and therefore women's vocabulary, was normally regarded as peripheral. Since dialectologists were also interested in phonology and grammar, this concentration on male language does not seem defensible. There are indications, however, that women may have been involved more than at first appears. The description of the principal informant at point number 2 for the Dialect Atlas of SubCarpathian Poland (published in 1934) tells us that he was called Jean Klamerus, that he was 75 years old, that he was rather deaf and slow. He was interviewed in the presence of his daughter-in-law, who is described as an energetic, intelligent woman, a good informant from a grammatical point of view, and very good from a phonetic and lexicological point of view. Pop comments that it was the daughter-in-law who replied to most of the questions[11] (Pop 1952). How often a female relative gave the responses which are credited to a man, we cannot tell.

3.5.3 The Fieldworker

Another reason why men were chosen as informants rather than women was probably that the vast majority of fieldworkers were themselves men. This is so much the normal pattern that McIntosh defines the fieldworker as 'a man [sic] specially trained to listen to peculiarities of speech' (McIntosh 1952: 66). The first women fieldworkers were those involved in the Linguistic Atlas of New England (two women out of ten fieldworkers) and the Survey of English Dialects (two women out of eleven fieldworkers).

If we imagine Edmont Edmont, fieldworker for the French Linguistic Atlas, arriving on his bicycle at one of the 639 localities he surveyed between 1896 and 1900, it seems plausible to argue that he was far more likely to get into conversation with, and subsequently to interview, other men. Edmont did in fact interview only about 60 women out of his 700 informants. Kurath, director of the New England survey, writes the following in his section on choosing informants:

> After some experience in the field, he [the fieldworker] may discover that

> informal contacts in the general store, barber shop or local tavern can
> provide him with useful leads.
> (Kurath 1972: 13)

(Note the use of *he/him* in this extract.) This is the advice of an eminent
dialectologist to others in the field after a century of dialect study:
presumably it reflects traditional practice. If the norm was male
fieldworkers making contact with potential informants in the male
setting of the barber shop or the tavern, then it is hardly surprising
that women were rarely interviewed.

If we look at what happened when the fieldworker was *female*, we
can test the hypothesis that the gender of the fieldworker influenced
the selection of informants. An examination of those sections of the
Survey of English Dialects where a woman was the fieldworker shows
a significant increase in the number of women interviewed. As Table
3.2 shows, for the survey as a whole, 12 per cent of informants were
women. For Leicestershire and Rutland, the two counties wholly
investigated by a woman fieldworker, the figures are 33 per cent and
40 per cent respectively.

The fieldworker's gender should be taken into account for other
reasons too. Only recently have linguists become fully aware of the
effect an interviewer can have on an informant's language. Labov
(1969) has demonstrated convincingly that by replacing a white
middle-class interviewer with a younger, Black interviewer (and also
by reducing the formality of the situation by sitting on the floor,
eating crisps, etc.), the Black child who was previously thought to
have virtually no language can be shown to be a fluent speaker. It
seems highly probable that women feel constrained in the presence
of a male interviewer (see Pop's comment quoted above, p. 49), and
will therefore produce more formal language. This may help to explain
the experience of Orton and others that women's speech was closer
to standard norms. (However, modern sociolinguistic surveys, carried
out by both women and men, are still finding that in Britain women's
speech tends to be closer to standard, as we shall see in Chapter 4.)

In more recent dialect surveys, despite the growth of sociolinguistic
research and methodology, the presence of women as fieldworkers is
still a matter for comment. The following is an extract from Gardette's
discussion of methodology in his *Atlas linguistique et ethnographique du
Lyonnais*:

> The four female fieldworkers of our team had in general as good results
> as those of Monsieur Girodet and myself. Those who interviewed in areas
> where they were known, among informants who claimed common friends,
> often received a particularly sympathetic welcome.
> (Gardette 1968: 44)

This shows an understanding that the relationship between fieldworker and informant is one which can vary. But it is also patronising, since it is surely gratuitous to comment on the women's results being as good as those of the two male fieldworkers. In a discussion of women as fieldworkers, Francis (1983) argues that women may not be ideal, since male informants may not want to respond frankly in their presence. I shall quote this passage in full as it is very revealing of attitudes in dialectology:

> It has been pointed out that women [*as fieldworkers*] do have one disadvantage: the kind of old-fashioned rustic who constituted the usual informant in traditional surveys is likely to be squeamish about discussing some topics and using some lexical items considered to be improper in the presence of a woman. This is true, but such items constitute a very small part of most questionnaires. On the other side it may be said that a woman fieldworker may have much better success than a man in eliciting some of the special vocabulary of women from female informants.
> (Francis 1983: 84)

Note how the writer doesn't feel any need to make explicit the fact that the 'old-fashioned rustic who constituted the usual informant' is obviously male. Just as women are often included as informants only for the sake of special 'women's vocabulary', so women fieldworkers become accepted since they may be better at eliciting this 'women's' language. Female informants and female fieldworkers are viewed as essentially tangential to the central concerns of traditional dialectology.

3.6 Conclusion

It is now seen as a major weakness of traditional dialectology that it selected informants on such an unscientific basis. Because of assumptions made by fieldworkers and their directors about male/female differences in language, women have been largely ignored in dialect studies. Where they have been included, it has been to supplement the fieldworker's information, rather than as full members of the speech community. Dialectology, in other words, has marginalised women speakers. Traditional dialectologists defined the true vernacular in terms of male informants, and organised their questionnaires around what was seen as the man's world.

A desire to improve on the methodology of dialect surveys, combined with a growing interest in *urban* dialects, gave impetus to the growth of sociolinguistics. Sociolinguists, like dialectologists, are interested in variation in language and in the phonology, grammar and lexicon of non-standard varieties. But where dialectologists focused on the *spatial* dimension, studying regional variation, sociolinguists have shifted attention to the *social* dimension and study variation due to factors such as age, gender, social class, education, ethnic group. Dialectologists tended to ignore the speech of women, for all sorts of conscious and unconscious reasons: some dialectologists claimed that women's speech was more standard than men's and therefore less interesting for their research; others, as we have seen, saw women as more conservative linguistically. We have no hard evidence that women's speech was more or less standard, more or less vernacular than men's. If dialectologists had sampled populations in the way quantitative sociolinguists do, by interviewing a representative cross-sample, then we might have had some very interesting data on linguistic sex differences. As it is, we have, as the end-product of most dialect surveys, a record of the language of non-mobile, older, rural *men*, and we don't know whether women's language differed significantly from theirs or not.

It is only with the advent of quantitative sociolinguistic studies that we have reliable data on gender differences in language. Quantitative sociolinguistic studies which explore gender differences in language will be described in the two following chapters (Chapters 4 and 5).

Notes

1 'Tout le monde sait qu'en matière de langage les femmes sont plus conservatrices que les hommes, qu'elles conservent plus fidèlement le parler des aieux' (Wartburg 1925: 113, as quoted in Pop 1950: 373).

2 'Le parler des femmes n'est pas conservateur. Les femmes, que d'ordinaire on affirme être plus conservatrices que les hommes, acceptent assez facilement les mots nouveaux' (Pop's account of Gilliéron, *Patois de la commune de Vionnaz (Bas Valais)* (1880), Pop 1950: 180).

3 '[les femmes] passent beaucoup plus de temps à la maison, en société, à cuisiner, à laver et qui parlent plus que les hommes, pris par les travaux de la campagne, au milieu desquels on les voit taciturnes, et souvent isolés toute la journée' (Pop's account of Gauchat, *L'Unité phonétique dans le patois d'une commune* (1905), Pop 1950: 194).

4 'La prononciation des voyelles chez la population féminine ne diffère pas seulement de celle des hommes – qui possèdent des voyelles plus pures et plus claires – mais de quartier à quartier et quelquefois même d'individu à individu' (K. Jaberg, *Aspects géographiques du langage*, 1936, as quoted in Pop 1950: 579).

5 'il semble bien, quoique l'on affirme souvent le contraire, que le langage des femmes présente dans certains cas plus d'innovations que celui des hommes' (Pop 1950: 195).

6 'L'enquêteur recontre des difficultés à persuader les femmes de sacrifier deux ou trois jours pour l'enquête, car les soins du ménage les en empêchent, et elles se trouvent gênées de s'attabler avec "un monsieur de la ville"' (Pop 1950: 725).

7 'Les raons que m'hi obligaren son: l'impossibilitat de guardar atencio durant un llarg interrogatori d'alguns dies; el tenir els coneixements de les coses, generalment, mes limitats que els homes i, sobretot, la falta de fixesa s'idees que es tradeix en una denominacio imprecisa de les coses' (A. Griera, *Entom de l'Atlas linguistique de l'Italie et de la Suisse Meridionale*, 1928, as quoted in Pop 1950: 373). I am grateful to Max Wheeler for translating this extract.

8 'Les réponses pour le parler de chaque localité ont été données par *un homme et par une femme du pays*: le premier répondait aux demandes concernant les travaux faits par les hommes; la seconde à celles touchant les occupations féminines' (Pop 1950: 770).

9 'Le questionnaire ayant été rédigé en vue de connaître surtout la terminologie agricole, les femmes ne pouvaient pas donner de bonnes réponses. Pour cette raison, il n'y a que deux femmes parmi les informateurs' (Pop's account of Navarro's fieldwork for the *Linguistic Atlas of Puerto Rico*, 1948, in Pop 1950: 432).

10 'Son questionnaire regardant en premier lieu la terminologie de l'habitation et du ménage l'obligeait d'ailleurs à faire appel à la collaboration des femmes' (Pop 1950: 981).

11 'c'est plutôt elle [i.e. the daughter-in-law] qui a donné les réponses' (Pop 1950: 977).

Part Two
The Sociolinguistic Evidence

CHAPTER 4

Quantitative studies

4.1 Introduction

In this chapter I shall look at gender differences in language revealed by quantitative sociolinguistic studies. The chapter begins with a brief description of classic sociolinguistic work, with its analysis of linguistic variation in relation to social class of speaker and speech style (formal or informal). The central section will examine in some detail five examples of sociolinguistic work which reveal significant gender differences. The chapter ends with a discussion of the reasons underlying this kind of sociolinguistic variation.

4.2 The Standard Paradigm

Classic sociolinguistic research, such as William Labov's in New York and Peter Trudgill's in Norwich, aimed to examine the correlation between linguistic variation and other variables, in particular social class. These quantitative studies revealed clear social stratification, and gave rise to the related concepts of **prestige** and **stigma**. **Prestige** is said to be attached to those linguistic forms normally used by the social group with the highest social status. The process of standardisation almost always leads to the development of notions of correctness; members of a given speech community will come to acknowledge that one particular variety – the standard dialect – is more 'correct' than other varieties. Correct usage will be seen as being enshrined in this variety, which will accordingly have high prestige. The use of the standard variety in the major institutions of society – the law, education, broadcasting – perpetuates this prestige. Conversely, **stigma** is attached to non-standard forms. This stigma may be overt, as in the case of forms which are the subject of heated condemnation on newspaper correspondence pages, or which are frowned on in school[1] (e.g. 'dropping' initial /h/, *ain't, disinterested* for *uninterested*); or it may be beneath the level of public consciousness, as in the case of many of the forms investigated by sociolinguists. As interest in the use and persistence of non-standard forms has grown, non-standard varieties have come to be known as the **vernacular.**[2]

Another important concept employed in quantitative sociolinguistic studies is that of the **linguistic variable.** A variable, to put it simply, is something which varies in a socially significant way. A linguistic variable, then, is a linguistic unit with various realisations: these are called **variants.** An example of a linguistic variable in contemporary British English is (t) (note that round brackets are used to indicate that we are talking about a variable, not a sound – [t] – or a letter – ⟨t⟩). When (t) occurs intervocalically (between vowels) in words like *butter* or phrases like *bit of,* it has two variants, the voiceless alveolar plosive [t] and the glottal stop [ʔ]. In other words, depending on circumstances, *bit of* may be realised as [bɪtəv] or [bɪʔəv]. Linguistic variables can be phonological (like (t) in the example) or grammatical or lexical. Not all linguistic units are variables, of course.

Sociolinguists are interested in linguistic variables because they don't vary randomly – they vary systematically in relation to other variables, such as social class, age and gender. In other words, linguistic variables are involved in **co-variation** with other variables. Londoners who say [bæʔə] for *butter* will still be referring to a substance made from cream which we spread on bread, but they will be revealing something of their social/regional origins in choosing that particular variant. Speakers' use of linguistic variables is one of the ways in which they locate themselves in social space. Linguistic variables, in other words, are linguistically equivalent but socially different ways of saying something.

4.2.1 Social Stratification

The classic pattern of social stratification revealed by quantitative studies is shown in diagrammatic form in Figure 4.1. The vertical axis represents group score (measured as the average of the scores of all the individuals in that group and converted to a percentage figure); a score of 100 per cent represents consistent use of the prestige form.

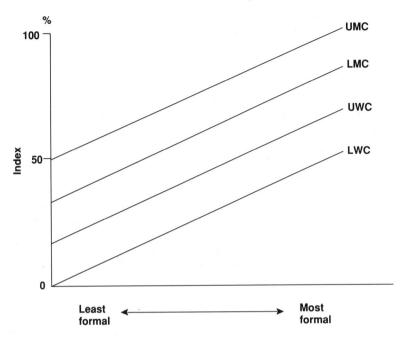

Figure 4.1 A diagrammatic representation of social stratification

The horizontal axis represents the degree of formality in the speech situation. Notice the following three points:

1. Each social class group uses a higher proportion of prestige forms (has a higher score) in formal speech, and a lower proportion of prestige forms (a lower score) in informal speech: this produces the sloping lines.

2. In any given speech style (i.e. at any point on the horizontal axis from least formal to most formal) social class stratification is maintained; each group maintains its position relative to other groups: this produces the parallel, non-overlapping lines in the diagram.

3. Use of the imaginary linguistic variable plotted here varies from 100 to 0 per cent: the prestige variant is used consistently by the upper middle class in the most formal contexts, but it is not used at all by the lower working class in the least formal contexts (such consistent use of non-standard forms in non-formal contexts is what many sociolinguists are now trying to observe, in order to arrive at accurate descriptions of the vernacular).[3]

As you might expect, representations of social stratification as it is actually found in modern urban communities are not as tidy as Figure 4.1. Figure 4.2 is adapted from Peter Trudgill's Norwich survey (Trudgill 1974a), and shows the relative scores for the variable (ng), as found at the ends of words like *hopping, skipping*. Trudgill's informants are divided into five social class groups: the middle middle and the lower middle class, the upper, middle and lower working class. Four different speech styles are represented: Casual Speech (CS), Formal Speech (FS), Reading Passage Style (RPS) and Words List Style (WLS). These names are roughly self-explanatory: informants were interviewed by the investigator (who was not known to them) – this produced Formal Speech. Informants were asked to read a passage aloud, and to read a list of words – data obtained from these tasks were labelled Reading Passage Style and Word List Style respectively. Casual Speech occurred spontaneously when, for example, a third person interrupted the interview or during breaks for coffee; it also occurred in planned contexts, for example, in response to the interview question 'Have you ever been in a situation when you had a

Figure 4.2 Social stratification in Norwich – the variable (ng) (based on Trudgill 1974a: 92)

good laugh?' The variable (ng) is scored for two variants only. A score of 100 per cent represents consistent RP pronunciation: [ŋ] (*hopping*), while a score of 0 represents consistent non-standard pronunciation: [n] (*hoppin'*).

Here you can see that, although the five lines do not slope evenly (as in the idealised diagram), they all rise from left to right; in other words, all five social class groups in Norwich use the prestige variant [ŋ] more in more formal speech styles. And while the lines are not equidistant from each other, they do not cross over each other; in other words, social stratification is maintained in all the four speech styles investigated. Note the difference between the three working-class groups and the two middle-class groups in the two less formal speech styles: there is a noticeable gap between the two sets of lines at the left hand side of the diagram. Scores range from 0 per cent (the lower working class in Casual Speech) to 100 per cent (the two middle-class groups in Word List Style). Figure 4.2 demonstrates the range of social class and stylistic variation which (ng) is involved in in Norwich.

The complex but regular pattern exhibited here by (ng), and represented in idealised form in Figure 4.1, is thought to be typical of a linguistic variable with stable social significance, that is, a linguistic variable not involved in change.

4.2.2 *Linguistic Variables Undergoing Change*

The other classic pattern revealed by quantitative sociolinguistic research is typical of a linguistic variable undergoing change. An idealised diagram is given in Figure 4.3. Note that both social stratification and the slope up from left to right are maintained. The main difference between Figure 4.3 and the diagram for a stable linguistic variable (Figure 4.1) is the **crossover** pattern which Figure 4.3 shows. The lower middle class (the second highest status group) shows a much greater shift towards the prestige form in formal styles than any other social group – note the steepness of the slope – so great in fact that it has a higher score than the upper middle class in these more formal styles. In less formal styles, however, (where Labov argues less attention is paid to speech and pronunciation is therefore less under the speaker's control) the lower middle class, like the two working-class groups, uses proportionately few of the prestige variant. This results in the line which joins lower-middle-class scores **crossing over** the line joining upper-middle-class scores.

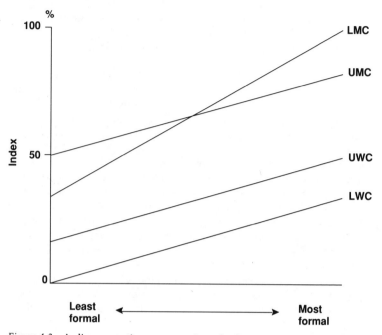

Figure 4.3 A diagrammatic representation of a linguistic variable undergoing change

The behaviour of the lower middle class here, reflected in their scores, is known as **hypercorrection.** The most famous example of hypercorrection is that of post-vocalic (r) in New York City, as analysed by Labov (1972a). The variable post-vocalic (r) involves pronunciation or non-pronunciation of (r) in words such as *car* or *guard*, where (r) occurs after a vowel. Figure 4.4 reproduces Labov's diagram. Only two variants are involved: presence or absence of post-vocalic (r) (e.g. /kar/ or /ka:/). A score of 100 represents consistent usage of (r) after a vowel; a score of 0 represents consistent absence of (r). Labov's informants were divided into six groups, and their speech measured in five different styles. (The fifth style, MP – Minimal Pairs – involves pairs of words where (r) is the only differentiating element, e.g. *sauce: source.*)

Figure 4.4 reveals clearly that, while in less formal styles only the UMC uses the prestige variant with any degree of consistency, in the more formal styles LMC usage surpasses that of the UMC. The reason for hypercorrection seems to be the sensitivity of the LMC as a group to social pressures: their insecurity (because of

Figure 4.4 Social stratification of a linguistic variable in process of change: post-vocalic (r) in New York City (Labov 1972a: 114)

their position on the borderline between the middle and working classes) is reflected in their concern with correctness and speaking 'properly'. When a linguistic variable is in the process of change, Labov argues, the LMC becomes sensitive to the use of the new prestige variant (in this case, use of r-full pronunciation). In more formal styles (i.e. when paying more attention to speech) they make a conscious effort to speak 'correctly', and style-shift sharply from a virtually r-less casual (informal) style to a keeping-up-with-the-Jones', more r-full formal style.

4.3 Gender Differences

Most early sociolinguistic work was concerned primarily with social class differences. However, it was soon apparent that other non-linguistic variables, such as ethnic group, age and gender, were involved in structured linguistic variation. In the case of gender, it was established that in many speech communities female speakers will use a higher proportion of prestige forms than male speakers. In

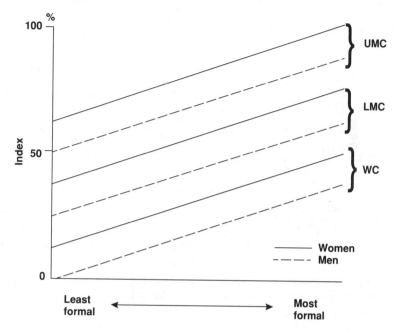

Figure 4.5 A diagrammatic representation of stratification according to social class and gender

other words, the prestige norms seem to exert a stronger influence on women than on men. In the case of stable linguistic variables, we can expect a pattern like the one shown in Figure 4.5. In the case of linguistic variables in the process of change, it appears that LMC *women* are particularly sensitive to the new prestige variant and are therefore prone to hypercorrection. Let's look at five examples of sociolinguistic research where gender differences have emerged as significant, to examine in detail the form such differences take. (The relationship between gender differences in speech and linguistic change will be taken up in Chapter 8.)

4.3.1 *Norwich*

Trudgill's demonstration of social stratification in the case of the variable (ng) in Norwich has been given in Figure 4.2. A closer analysis of the data, including speaker's gender as well as social

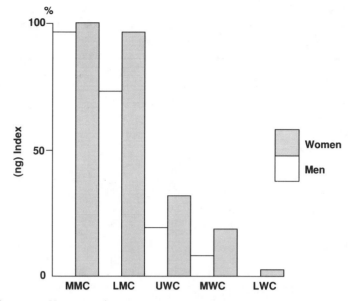

Figure 4.6 Histogram for (ng) in Norwich, showing social class and gender differences (based on Trudgill 1974a: 94)

class and contextual style, reveals that scores for male and female speakers are quite different. The general pattern revealed here is that shown in Figure 4.5: women speakers in Norwich tend to use the prestige variant [ŋ] more (and the stigmatised variant [n] less) than men, and this holds true for all social classes.[4] Such a diagram is highly complex and difficult to read; Figure 4.6 gives the results for formal style only, in histogram form. The contrast between the scores of women and men of the same social class is very striking.

Table 4.1 gives the actual scores of women and men in five social class groups and in four styles. As in Figure 4.2, a score of 100 represents consistent [ŋ] pronunciation (the prestige form), and a score of 0 represents consistent use of [n] (the stigmatised variant). The most interesting point to notice is that in fourteen out of twenty cases (i.e. 70 per cent) women's scores are higher than men's scores. Among other things these figures tell us the following:

1. In all styles, women tend to use fewer stigmatised forms than men.
2. In formal contexts (where Trudgill got informants to read lists of words) women seem to be more sensitive to the prestige pattern

Table 4.1: The variable (ng) in Norwich – index scores broken down by social class, sex and contextual style* (based on Trudgill 1974a: 94)

		CS	FS	RPS	WLS
MMC	M	69	96	100	100
	F	100	100	100	100
LMC	M	83	73	80	100
	F	33	97	100	100
UWC	M	5	19	82	100
	F	23	32	87	89
MWC	M	3	9	57	76
	F	12	19	54	80
LWC	M	0	0	0	34
	F	0	3	46	83

* I have reversed Trudgill's scores for consistency's sake (i.e. to keep 100 as the score representing the most prestigious pronunciation)

than men (look at the last column – the lowest score for women is 80).

3. Lower-middle-class *women* style-shift very sharply: in the least formal style, they use quite a high proportion of the stigmatised variant, but in the three more formal styles, they correct their speech to correspond to that of the class above them (the middle middle-class) – Labov argues (1972a: 243) that extreme style-shifting of this kind, often resulting in hypercorrection, is particularly marked in LMC women.

4. Use of non-standard forms (that is, of the vernacular) seems to be associated not only with working-class speakers, but also with *male* speakers.

4.3.2 Glasgow

Ronald Macaulay's (1977; 1978) study of Glasgow English revealed a similar pattern (though Macaulay's results are based on one style only, that of the formal interview). The diagram for the variable (i), as in *hit, kill, risk*, is given in histogram form in Figure 4.7. A score of 100

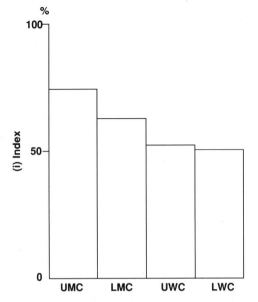

Figure 4.7 Social stratification of (i) in Glasgow (based on Macaulay 1978: 135)

represents consistent pronunciation of (i) as [ɪ] (the prestige form); a score of 0 represents consistent pronunciation of (i) as [ʌˆ] (Glasgow vernacular form).

The diagram showing social class stratification presents the usual tidy picture: each social class group uses proportionately more of the prestige form than the next group down in the social class hierarchy. When the figures are broken down into male and female scores, however, as in Figure 4.8, this superficial tidiness disappears. Women in each social class are revealed as using more of the prestige form [ɪ] than men of the same social class. Note that the women in each social class pattern like the men in the group *above* them. Conversely, the men in each social class pattern like the women in the group *below* them (see Table 4.2). Macaulay pointed out that the major break in the women's scores comes between the lower middle class and the upper working class, while for men it comes between the upper middle class and the lower middle class. So LMC women speak more like UMC women, while LMC men speak more like UWC men. This shows yet again the pivotal nature of the lower middle class.

Macaulay's data, like Trudgill's, suggests that social class scores conceal more than they reveal. In the case of the variable (i) in

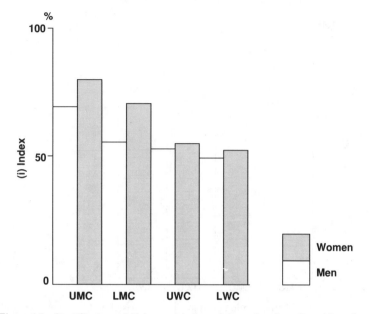

Figure 4.8 Stratification of (i) by social class and gender (based on Macaulay 1978: 135)

Glasgow, social class scores give us only an average of male and female scores, and fail to differentiate male and female usage.

Table 4.2: Male and female scores for (i) in Glasgow (based on Macaulay 1978: 135)

	Men	Women
UMC	69.00	80.00
LMC	55.25	71.25
UWC	53.25	55.00
LWC	50.00	53.00

4.3.3 West Wirral

Mark Newbrook's (1982) study of West Wirral aims to establish how far the urban vernacular of Liverpool ('Scouse') has spread into the surrounding area and, in particular, how far Scouse features have

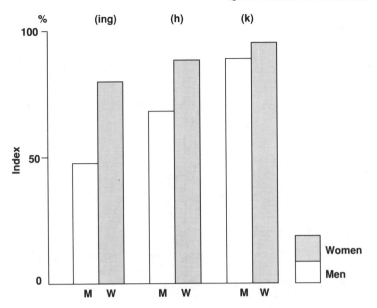

Figure 4.9 Gender differences in West Wirral for three phonological variables: (ing), (h) and (k)

replaced local Cheshire forms as the usual non-standard forms occurring in this locality. He investigated a number of phonological variables, and found that there were significant gender differences for most of them. Figure 4.9 shows male and female group scores for the three variables (ing) as in *jumping*, (h) as in *house*, and (k) as in *kick*. The variants for (ing) are [ɪŋ] and [ɪn]; the variants for (h) are [h] and ø; the variants for (k) are the standard form [k] and the non-standard affricated form [kˣ] (or sometimes [x]). In all cases, a score of 100 indicates consistent use of the prestige variant.

With all three variables, we find the expected pattern: women's pronunciation is closer to the prestige standard than men's. Moreover, these group scores conceal the fact that the range of individual scores involved differs greatly between men and women. The typical score for a working-class man was much lower than that for a middle-class man, whereas women's scores covered a much narrower range. This suggests that social class is a more important factor in determining men's speech than women's, at least in West Wirral.

Figure 4.10 is the histogram for the variable (a) as in *bath, grass*. In this case, informants are analysed in terms of age as well as gender.

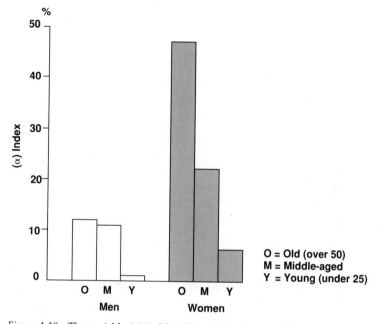

Figure 4.10 The variable (ɑ) in West Wirral showing stratification by age and gender

A score of 100 represents consistent RP pronunciation: [ɑ:]; a score of 0 represents consistent non-standard pronunciation: [æ]. Note that women's scores are higher than men's in each age group. Note also the age-grading that occurs with this variable: scores are higher for older speakers than for younger ones. Older *women* are much closer to the standard norms than other speakers, while young men are virtually consistent [æ] users. It looks as if young women are participating in the increasing dominance of [æ]. This non-standard variant seems to be a marker not only of male speech, but also of the speech of the young.

4.3.4 *Edinburgh*

Our fourth example is taken from Suzanne Romaine's (1978) work in Edinburgh. Her study was confined to primary-school children with working-class fathers; each child was interviewed alone, and the 10 year olds also read a passage. Note that this study is more selective than the others we have looked at: informants belong to a narrow age range (6–10 years), to the working class (as far as father's occupation can be said to define this), and the data are obtained in one context only (with the exception of the 10 year olds).

One of the variables included in Romaine's investigation was post vocalic (r) as in *car*, *door*, etc. South of the Scottish border, this variable is found only in rural mid-north Lancashire and in the Welsh Marches and the West Country; Scots speakers, however, are generally believed to pronounce their r's. Romaine wanted to see if this were true. She identified three variants of (r): an alveolar tap: [r], a frictionless continuant: [ɹ], and ø (no r at all). Informants were given a separate score for each variant, with usage of each variant being expressed as a percentage of total (r) use.

Romaine's analysis of the data revealed that speaker's gender was the single most important factor correlating with (r). Figure 4.11 gives the results for each variant with informants grouped according to gender. This histogram conflates the scores of children in the three age groups investigated, since clear-cut differences in the use of (r) emerged between male and female speakers in each age group. Note that male speakers consistently use more of the [r] variant than female speakers, and are also more likely to use ø. Girls on the

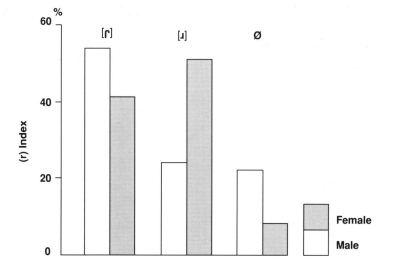

Figure 4.11 Gender differences in the use of the variable (r) in Edinburgh (based on Romaine 1978: 150)

other hand consistently prefer the frictionless continuant [ɹ]; girls, moreover, seem to avoid r-less pronunciation.

This variable, then, again reveals sharp gender differentiation. In terms of frequency, the most striking feature is the girls' use of [ɹ]. Clearly [ɹ] is a marker of female speech in Edinburgh.

4.3.5 Sydney, Australia

The studies we have looked at so far were all carried out in Britain, and all investigated phonological variation. But gender-differentiated language seems to be a world-wide phenomenon, and is not confined to pronunciation. Our final example comes from Australia and involves grammatical variation. Edina Eisikovits (1987; 1988) investigated the speech of adolescents living in working-class areas of Sydney. Three of the grammatical features she studied were the

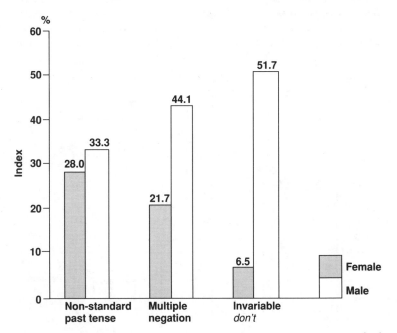

Figure 4.12 Gender differences in Sydney, Australia, for three non-standard grammatical features (based on Eisikovits 1988)

following:

1. non-standard past tense forms such as *seen* and *done*
   e.g. *he woke up an' seen something*
2. multiple negation
   e.g. *they don't say nothing*
3. invariable *don't*
   e.g. *Mum don't have to do nothing*

Figure 4.12 gives the results for these three forms in the speech of her 16-year-old informants. (Note that, because of her focus on non-standard forms, Eisikovits's results are scored with 100 representing consistent *non-standard* usage.)

Here we see the expected pattern once again, with female speech closer to the standard, and male speakers consistently using a higher proportion of non-standard forms. However, this pattern was *not* apparent in the speech of younger adolescent speakers interviewed by Eisikovits. The development of gender-appropriate speech will be discussed in Chapter 7; I shall look at Eisikovits' results in more detail as part of that discussion (section 7.3.1).

4.3.6 Summary

These five studies show us the regularity of gender differentiation in speech. Where variation exists, it often seems to be the case that male and female speakers prefer different variants. Further, where it is possible to label one of the variants as prestigious, then it is typically *female* speakers who are found to use this variant. This was the case with Norwich (ng), Glasgow (i) and West Wirral (ing), (h) and (k). Use of non-standard, non-prestige forms, in other words, seems to be associated not only with working-class speakers, but also with *male* speakers. Where we find a given variant consistently used by one set of speakers rather than by another, we call that variant a **marker.** Our examples show us that [n] is a marker of male speech in Norwich, that [æ] is a marker of male speech (and of younger speakers) in the Wirral, that [ɹ] is a marker of female speech in Edinburgh and that invariable *don't* is a marker of male speech in Sydney, Australia.

4.4 Explanations

The examples given above show us the form that linguistic variation between the sexes takes. This brings us to the question, Why? The main goal of quantitative studies such as those used as examples in this chapter is the collection and analysis of data on linguistic variation. Many sociolinguists are not primarily concerned with *why* such variation exists, and their methodology is not usually designed to probe such questions.

4.4.1 Women's Sensitivity to Linguistic Norms

Women's sensitivity to linguistic norms is often asserted, and this is attributed to their insecure social position. Such insecurity on the part of women offers a clear parallel with the lower middle class, who, as we saw in section 4.2.2, provide the classic example of hypercorrect linguistic behaviour. Are sociolinguists really saying that women's linguistic behaviour is hypercorrect?[5] Let us look at some examples.

1. *(ng) in Norwich*
   Besides showing a regular pattern of sex differentiation, Table 4.1 (index scores for (ng) in Norwich) also exemplifies the extreme style-shifting of LMC women. In formal styles, LMC women pattern like the UMC as a whole, but in more informal speech they use a high proportion of stigmatised forms.
2. *The glottal stop in Glasgow*
   The glottal stop is the most overtly stigmatised feature of Glasgow speech. Macaulay found that it was widely used, but with clear social stratification (working-class groups using it considerably more than middle-class groups). The biggest contrast was between LMC men and women: LMC female informants used 40 per cent fewer glottal stops than LMC male informants. One LMC woman used fewer glottal stops than *any* UMC informant, a finding which conforms to the classic definition of hypercorrect behaviour.
3. *(o) on Merseyside*
   This linguistic variable – which occurs in words like *coat, go* – has many variants. One of these, [ɛʊ], is generally considered to be hypercorrect.[6] In his work in West Wirral, Newbrook established that, when they used Scouse variants, a minority of male informants but *all* the females preferred this variant.

The first two examples show that the hypercorrect pattern of the second highest status group, the lower middle class, is crucially connected with the usage of LMC *women*. The third example shows a more general pattern, with women of all classes showing sensitivity to [ɛʊ]. But these examples, and the material examined earlier in this chapter, do not justify labelling women's speech as a whole as hypercorrect. As Figure 4.5 shows, gender differences lead to regular stratification, with women using fewer stigmatised forms and more prestige forms than men in each social class. It is no more justifiable to call this pattern of female usage hypercorrect than it would be to call the usage of the middle class hypercorrect in relation to that of the working class.

4.4.2 Self-Evaluation Tests

In order to test sensitivity to linguistic norms, Trudgill (1972; 1974a) carried out self-evaluation tests on his informants. He presented them with a recording of certain words, with two or more different pronunciations, varying from prestigious pronunciation (RP) to non-standard Norwich pronunciation. Informants were asked to indicate which of the forms most closely resembled the one they habitually used. The variables (er), as in *ear, here, idea*, and (a) as in *gate, face, name*, were both involved in this test. In the case of (er), only 28 per cent of male informants and 18 per cent of female informants responded accurately (that is, claimed to use the form which corresponded to their actual usage in Casual Speech, as recorded in the interview). A staggering 68 per cent of the women (and 22 per cent of the men) **over-reported,** that is, claimed to use the prestige form when their index scores revealed they actually didn't. On the other hand, half the men (50 per cent) and 14 per cent of the women **under-reported,** that is, they claimed to use non-standard forms when their index scores revealed that they habitually used forms closer to standard pronunciation.

The results for the variable (a) repeat this pattern: 50 per cent of the men and 57 per cent of the women evaluate their pronunciation accurately; 43 per cent of the women (and 22 per cent of the men)

Table 4.3: Percentage scores for self-evaluation for (er) and (a) in Norwich (based on Trudgill 1972)

	(er)		(a)	
	M	F	M	F
Over-report	22	68	22	43
Under-report	50	14	28	0
Accurate	28	18	50	57

over-report, while 28 per cent of the men (and none of the women) *under*-report. Table 4.3 summarises these figures.

The first thing to notice is that Trudgill's test reveals significant *over*-reporting by *women*. This suggests that women *are* sensitive to prestige norms. Many women in Norwich believe that they are producing forms close to standard pronunciation when they are not. This suggests that they are *aiming at* standard pronunciation, and that they are trying to avoid stigmatised forms.

The second thing to notice is that Trudgill's test reveals significant *under*-reporting by *men*. They claim to use non-standard forms when in fact they do not. Such behaviour can be explained by hypothesising that non-standard speech must have **covert prestige.**

4.4.3   Covert Prestige

The concept of covert prestige arose when linguists attempted to explain the persistence of vernacular (non-standard) forms in the speech of working-class speakers. In view of the resistance of working-class speakers to the overt prestige of Standard English, we have to postulate the existence of another set of norms – vernacular norms – which have covert prestige and which therefore exert a powerful influence on linguistic behaviour. In the light of Trudgill's self-evaluation tests and the examples of male/female differences given earlier in the chapter, it seems reasonable to infer that vernacular forms have covert prestige not just for the working class but also for *men*. Under-reporting is equally common among middle-class men as among working-class men in Norwich. It looks as if many Norwich men are actually aiming at non-standard working-class speech.

This also seems to be the case for the male adolescents in Sydney, Australia, studied by Eisikovits (see section 4.3.5). While female speakers self-correct towards the standard, for example:

(1)   'me an' Kerry – or should I say, Kerry and I – are the only ones who've done the project'

the self-corrections of male speakers are *from* standard *to* non-standard forms:

(2)   'I didn't know what I did – what I done'
(3)   'we were skating around – we was skating along an' someone walked bang in front of me.'

A study of language attitudes in Kentucky (Luhman 1990) also provides evidence that male speakers place high value on non-standard varieties (in this case, Appalachian English).

We see here the development of a stronger explanatory model. Early work on gender differences in language emphasised women's apparent sensitivity to prestige forms. The concept of prestige as a force which attracts different speakers more or less powerfully depending on their gender is supported by the sociolinguistic evidence: men do indeed use fewer prestige forms than women. But the introduction of the concept of covert prestige strengthens the model, by postulating the existence of two opposing sets of norms competing for speakers' loyalty: Standard English with its overt prestige, and vernacular norms with covert prestige. It is claimed that women are attracted by the norms of Standard English while men respond to the covert prestige of the vernacular. This model is also used to explain social class differences – in other words, it is argued that social class differences in language exist because middle-class speakers give allegiance to the institutionalised norms of Standard English while working-class speakers reject these norms and instead give allegiance to the vernacular. This reveals an interesting parallelism between women and the middle class, on the one hand, and men and the working class, on the other (Figure 4.13).

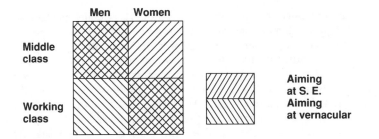

Figure 4.13 The intersection of social class, gender and language

Middle-class *women* and working-class *men* have no conflict of interests. Both their gender and their social class point to the same affiliation. For middle-class men and working-class women, however, there is a conflict of interests: the behaviour predictable on the basis of their social class will be incompatible with the behaviour predictable on the basis of their gender.

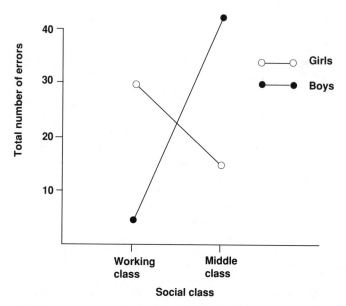

Figure 4.14 Interaction between gender and social class of children in terms of errors of gender identification (Edwards 1979b: 93)

The ambiguity of the position of middle-class male speakers and working-class female speakers is nicely pinpointed by the results of the following experiment (Edwards 1979a). Adult judges were presented with tape recordings of twenty middle-class and twenty working-class children and asked to identify whether children were male or female from their speech. In a minority of cases, the judges were not able to do this accurately. As Figure 4.14 shows, the judges did not make random mistakes; they made mistakes about two sets of children: middle-class boys and working-class girls. Middle-class boys sounded like girls to the judges, while working-class girls sounded like boys.

4.4.4 Status and Solidarity

These explanations themselves require explanations. If we accept that, in speech communities such as those described in this chapter, speakers choose between opposing sets of linguistic norms, we still have to explain why it is that women are more likely to be influenced by the publicly legitimised standard norms, and that men are more likely to be influenced by vernacular norms which are not publicly recognised. In this section, I shall look at the explanatory framework provided by social psychology; while the following section (4.4.5) will describe an explanation which draws on the notions of face and power.

Social psychologists have studied attitudes to speech in some detail. Their research confirms that RP has far more prestige than regional accents in Britain. One of the 'rewards' (to use the social psychologists' term) for speakers who use speech closer to standard norms is that they acquire greater **status.** Another reward seems to be that RP speakers are perceived as being more ambitious, more intelligent and more self-confident. However, while RP speakers are rated highly in terms of competence, regionally accented speakers are rated highly in terms of personal attractiveness: they are perceived to be serious, talkative, good-natured, and as having a sense of humour. This suggests that there are also rewards, though of a different kind, for those speakers who choose non-standard forms.

Most social psychological studies are designed to explore attitudes to different varieties of English without considering gender as a variable. A rare study (Elyan et al. 1978) designed to test reactions to women speaking with standard and non-standard accents (RP and Lancashire) revealed that women using an RP accent were rated by judges as being more fluent, intelligent, self-confident, adventurous, independent and *feminine* than women with a regional accent. In addition, RP-accented women were also rated as being more *masculine* (judges had to rate each speaker for both masculinity and femininity on a nine-point scale). This may seem contradictory, but if masculinity and femininity are seen as two independent dimensions, then individuals have the choice of both characteristics. American research shows that between 30 per cent and 45 per cent of American women college students score high on both feminine and masculine dimensions: this is called **psychological androgyny** (Bem 1974; 1975). It is suggested that androgynous behaviour offers many rewards for women in contemporary society, allowing them a wide repertoire of behaviour to cope with the wide variety of social roles they have to take on. We can argue that, in Britain, RP is part of androgynous behaviour for speakers who are both female and middle class, because of these rewards.

Speakers, however, are not isolated individuals; they are members of social groups, and it is one of language's functions to act as a symbol of group identity. For all sorts of reasons, working-class speakers diverge linguistically from middle-class speakers, in order to mark the social distance between the two groups. At the same time, working-class speakers will converge linguistically with each other, in order to show **solidarity,** to mark their membership of the same social group. The conscious effort by members of the working class *not* to speak Standard English is well documented, as the following quotations demonstrate:

1. 'you'd get battered off a' the pals'
   (George W., Edinburgh, in response to a suggestion that he should 'talk nice', quoted in Reid 1978).
2. A Cockney grandmother claimed her grandson would be labelled 'a queer' if he talked with a 'la-di-da' accent
   (quoted in Bragg and Ellis 1976).
3. 'I don't think I would change the way I speak. I wouldn't like to have an English accent. I think it's a very daft one. They pronounce words correctly but they don't sound very nice. In your own environment you'd feel out of place. If you live in Glasgow you must talk like a Glaswegian'
   (15-year-old Glasgow boy, quoted by Macaulay 1977).

Notice that all these examples come from *male* speakers. There are clearly very strong pressures on speakers who are both working class and male to diverge from Standard English. By using non-standard forms, male speakers signal their solidarity with each other.

Social groups need to assert their distinctiveness, and language is one way of doing this. It looks as though there are strong cultural pressures on men and women to distinguish themselves from each other, even though other groupings (such as social class, ethnic group, age) notionally place them together. It is important for groups to maintain their identity, and language variation contributes to this in two ways:

1. Linguistic differences strengthen in-group unity (that is members of a group recognise each other as being linguistically *similar* to each other and *different* from people outside the group).
2. Linguistic differences increase the distance between groups (which helps to maintain distinctive group identities).

So linguistic differences between women and men can be seen as functioning to maintain their separate identities.

4.4.5 Face and Power

A different explanation of women's greater use of standard forms is proposed by Margaret Deuchar (1989). Deuchar uses the notions of **face** and **power,** drawing on Brown and Levinson's (1978; 1987) model of politeness. The term *face* is used as in everyday phrases such as *to lose face*. Respecting face is defined as showing consideration for people's feelings. We show consideration by respecting two basic human needs: (1) the need not to be imposed on (this is called **negative face**); and (2) the need to be liked and admired (this is called **positive face**). *Power* is defined as 'an asymmetric dimension of relative power'; in any interaction, the speaker can be described as relatively more or less powerful than the addressee.

Deuchar makes the following four assumptions:

1. participants in an interaction wish to protect their own face
2. attention to other's face is affected by relative power in relation to other
3. attention to other's face may involve damage to one's own
4. women have less relative power than men.

(The first three of these are derived from Brown and Levinson; the last is Deuchar's.) Deuchar argues that the use of prestigious standard speech can be a strategy for protecting the face of relatively powerless speakers without attacking that of their addressees. Given women's relative lack of power, use of more standard forms allows them to pay attention to other's face (to avoid threatening it) at the same time as protecting their own face. Deuchar's explanation enables us to see women's linguistic behaviour as a positively chosen strategy; it also reminds us that any account of gender differences must take into account the issue of power. The subject of women and politeness will be taken up in Chapter 6 (section 6.3).

4.5 Conclusion

In this chapter we have looked at some examples of sociolinguistic research which demonstrate gender differentiation, and we have discussed some of the reasons put forward to explain this phenomenon. In all known communities, male and female are important categories; that is, members of a community are distinguished from each other in terms of *gender*, as well as in other (more culture-specific) ways. Not surprisingly, in sociolinguistic research, gender has emerged as an important variable, and sociolinguists have found that gender differences in language often cut across social class variation. Women – like middle-class speakers – are shown to use proportionately more standard forms (those accorded overt prestige by society), while men – like working-class speakers – are shown to use proportionately more non-standard forms. Why women should regularly select forms closer to Standard English, while men select forms closer to the vernacular, is a phenomenon which is still little understood. The next chapter (Chapter 5) will look at work which explores the hypothesis that the level of integration of speakers in a community will be directly reflected in their language, and will show in what ways such work refines our understanding of male/female differences in language.

Notes

1 Note that, in order to pass public examinations, pupils need to internalise these concepts, and to acquire a facility in written Standard English.
2 The perceptive reader will have spotted that the term *vernacular* is used in this book – and in sociolinguistics generally – to mean both (1) non-standard varieties of a language; and (2) spontaneous speech between equals in private. Clearly these two senses are not coterminous: in particular, sense (1) excludes the informal talk of speakers of the standard variety, while sense (2) loses the contrast *vernacular-standard*. In practice, most sociolinguists slide without comment between the two senses, but readers need to be alert to the ambiguous nature of the term. (See Milroy 1987: 57–60 for further discussion of this point.)
3 See note 2.
4 This rests on the assumption that men's and women's social class has been accurately assessed. However, since Trudgill, like most other researchers, assessed women's social class partly on the occupation of their husband or father, it is not clear that this assumption is justified. (See Delphy 1981 for an incisive critique of stratification studies in relation to women.)
5 See, for example, Labov 1972a: 243.
6 Note that the term *hypercorrection* is being used here in a different sense, since the variant is never used by UMC informants: it is a qualitative rather than a quantitative overshoot. Knowles (1974) and De Lyon (1981) both consider [ɛʊ] to be hypercorrect on Merseyside, but Newbrook (who refers to it as [↑ʊ] feels it is not synchronically hypercorrect in West Wirral.

CHAPTER 5

Social networks

5.1 The Concept of Social Network

One of the most fruitful explanations of linguistic variation in recent years has been the concept of social network. This concept has been current in the social sciences for some years, but was not mentioned in sociolinguistic analysis until Blom and Gumperz (1972), and not well known before publication of the Milroys' Belfast study (Milroy and Milroy 1978; Milroy 1980).

Members of a given speech community – such as Belfast – can be seen as being connected to each other in social networks which may be relatively 'closed' or 'open'. An individual whose personal contacts all know each other belongs to a closed network. This is shown diagrammatically in Figure 5.1. The arrows represent mutual knowing.

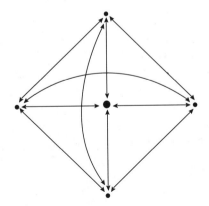

Figure 5.1 A closed network

An individual whose personal contacts tend not to know each other belongs to an open network (see Figure 5.2).

Figure 5.2 An open network

Closed networks are said to be of **high density;** open networks are said to be of **low density.** Moreover, the links between people may be of different kinds: people can relate to each other as relatives, as neighbours, as workmates, as friends. Where individuals are linked in several ways, e.g. they live in the same street, work in the same factory, and share leisure activities, then the network ties are said to be **multiplex.**

It seems that the networks typically found in socially mobile, highly industrialised societies are of low density and **uniplex** (that is individuals are not linked in more than one way). In rural village communities and in traditional working-class communities, on the other hand, the networks typically found are of high density and multiplex.

Relatively dense networks, it is claimed, function as norm-enforcement mechanisms. In the case of language, this means that a closely knit group will have the capacity to enforce *linguistic* norms. Lesley Milroy, working in Belfast, showed that in the working-class communities there (both Catholic and Protestant) there is polarisation of gender roles, with men's and women's activities being sharply distinguished. Such polarisation is typical of communities with dense networks. What Milroy established was that the men's networks are denser and more multiplex than the women's, and that this difference in network strength is matched by linguistic differences.

Let's now look at two pieces of sociolinguistic research where network strength is shown to be a significant factor in predicting male/female differences, starting with Lesley Milroy's work on Belfast, and then considering Jenny Cheshire's study of adolescents in Reading.[1]

5.1.1 Belfast

Milroy investigated three working-class communities in Belfast: Ballymacarrett (a Protestant area in East Belfast), the Hammer (a Protestant area in West Belfast) and the Clonard (a Catholic area in West Belfast). All three areas are poor working-class districts with a high incidence of unemployment.

Milroy's analysis of these communities was based not on interviews but on **participant observation.** Through informal contacts with core members of these communities, she was able to approach them in the capacity of 'a friend of a friend'. This role meant that she was accepted with friendliness and trust; it also enabled her to observe and participate in prolonged and informal interaction. Her tape recorder was soon accepted in the various households she visited, and she could be reasonably confident that the conversations she recorded were representative of the vernacular.

She observed not only the language of the people she contacted, but also their social networks. Because all three communities revealed dense and multiplex networks, she decided to give each individual a Network Strength Score, depending on five factors. Scores for each individual were calculated by assigning one point for each condition fulfilled. The five factors were as follows:

1. Belonging to a high-density, territorially based group.
2. Having substantial ties of kinship in the neighbourhood (more than one household in addition to the nuclear family).
3. Working at the same place as at least two others from the same area.
4. Working at the same place as at least two others of the same sex from the area.
5. Associating voluntarily with workmates in leisure hours.

The total score was designed to reflect the individual's level of integration into localised networks.

Individual scores, then, ranged from 0 to 5. As will be apparent, factors 3, 4 and 5 will give high scores to men in traditional employment. In Ballymacarrett, where traditional employment patterns still prevail to some extent (the men working in the shipyards), the men typically had high scores. In the Hammer and Clonard, on the other hand, which are both areas of high *male* unemployment, individual women often scored as high as or higher than men.

The value of the social network as a concept, and of the Network Strength Score as an analytical tool, lies in their ability to demonstrate a correlation between the integration of an individual in the community, and the way that individual speaks. Individuals who participate in close-knit networks are also those who most consistently use vernacular forms in speech. It would be a common-sense assumption that the speech of members of a close-knit group would tend to be more homogeneous than that of members of a loosely knit group; the Network Strength Scale allied with linguistic analysis allows the assumption to be examined more closely.

THE VARIABLE (th)

One of the variables examined by Milroy was the interdental voiced fricative (th) occurring intervocalically in words such as *mother, bother, together*. Vernacular speakers in Belfast delete (th) in such words; they pronounce *mother*, for example, as [mɔ.ər]. In Figure 5.3, a score of 0 represents consistent pronunciation of (th) intervocalically, while 100 represents consistent deletion of (th). (Note that a score of 100 now represents consistent *vernacular* pronunciation.) Both studies described in this chapter focus on working-class communities and their speech. Their scoring is therefore the inverse of that used in Chapter 4: speakers are measured against the set of norms which constitute the vernacular, not against the set of norms known as Standard English. Figure 5.3 shows the distribution of (th) by age, gender and area.

This variable shows the pattern typical of stable sociolinguistic markers. All three communities are revealed as sharing the same attitude to (th). The gender differences are very marked, particularly in Ballymacarrett, the most traditional of the three areas. The two generations are shown to pattern similarly, though men's and women's pronunciation is more polarised in the younger generation, with higher scores for 18–25-year-old men and low scores for 18–25-year-old women (particularly Ballymacarrett women).

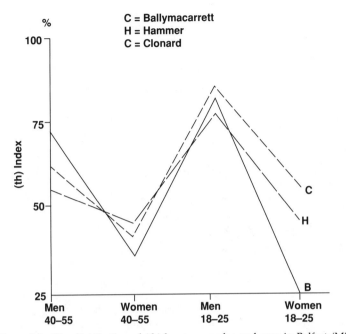

Figure 5.3 The distribution of (th) by age, gender and area in Belfast (Milroy 1980: 128)

It's important to consider individual scores as well as group scores. In the three communities, individual scores confirm the striking gender differentiation of intervocalic (th) – the men's and women's scores do not overlap at all. Even the men with the lowest scores (the men who delete (th) least) score more than the women with the highest scores. In other words, even the men whose pronunciation is furthest from the vernacular norms delete (th) intervocalically more than any woman.

THE VARIABLE (a)

This pattern is not found with all variables, however. Consider Figure 5.4, for the variable (a).

This is a much more complex variable, since it cannot be scored in the simple binary fashion that (th) was. A five-point scale was used to measure the degree of retraction and back-raising of (a) in words like

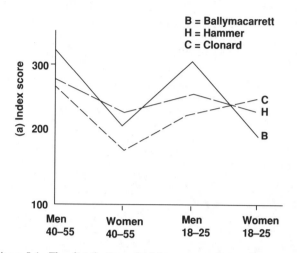

Figure 5.4 The distribution of (a) by age, gender and area in Belfast (Milroy 1980: 124)

hat, man, back, with a score of 1 for [æ] ranging through [a], [ä], [ɑ] to a score of 5 for [ɔə]. (The higher the score, the greater the backing of (a).) First, consider the pattern for Ballymacarrett. As we saw with (th), there is clear gender differentiation in this community, with the same zig-zag line as before. The Hammer and the Clonard, however, do not show this pattern. In the Hammer, the difference between men and women for (a) is insignificant, while in the Clonard, the *young women* use *more* backed variants of (a) than the young men (quite unlike the older women, whose scores are significantly lower than those of the men of their generation, following the usual pattern).

So what do the data on these two variables in Belfast tell us? First, for certain stable variables such as (th), there is clear differentiation between the sexes. As earlier sociolinguistic studies had established, this difference is the result of the men using variants consistently closer to the vernacular norms, and of the women using variants consistently less close. Milroy suggests as an explanation of this difference that men in working-class inner city areas belong to denser, more multiplex networks than women. By using her Network Strength Scale, she was able to show that a high Network Strength Score was clearly correlated with use of the vernacular. In most cases, this meant that men whose speech revealed high usage of vernacular forms were also found to belong to tight-knit social networks. If it is accepted that social networks operate as important norm-enforcing mechanisms, then it would seem to be the case that, in inner city Belfast, with stable linguistic variables such as (th), the tight-knit social networks in which most of the men participate serve to enforce the vernacular speech norms. Conversely, vernacular forms are less evident in women's speech in these communities because the women belong to less dense, less multiplex social networks, which therefore have less power to enforce norms.

The second variable above, however, does not follow this pattern. While the women and men in Ballymacarrett differ in their use of (a) in the expected way, this pattern is not found in the Hammer or in the Clonard. It is the Clonard findings which are particularly interesting: while the older generation conform to the expected pattern, the younger generation reverses it. How can we explain the high scores of the young Clonard women for this variable? It seems that Ballymacarrett as a community differs from the other two: it suffers little from male unemployment, largely because of its location by the shipyards. The Hammer and the Clonard both had unemployment rates of around 35 per cent at the time of Milroy's research, which clearly affected social relationships. Men from these areas were forced to look for work outside the community, and also shared more in domestic tasks (with consequent blurring of gender roles). The women in these areas went out to work and, in the case of the young Clonard women, all worked together. This meant that the young Clonard women, by contrast with all the other female groups, belonged to a dense and multiplex network; they lived, worked and amused themselves together. The young Clonard women have the highest network score of any sub-group (mean = 4.75); the mean for the young Clonard men is 3.0. This is in complete contrast with the scores for Ballymacarrett, where the mean network score for men is 3.96, compared with 1.33 for the women. The contrast is between a traditional working-class community (Ballymacarrett) and a working-class community undergoing social change because of severe male unemployment (Clonard). The tight-knit network to which the young Clonard women belong clearly exerts pressure on its members, who are linguistically homogeneous. Because of their social circumstances, the young Clonard women are linguistically more like the young Ballymacarrett men than like the other women in the three communities. Social networks in this case help to explain not only linguistic differences between the sexes, but also the seemingly divergent behaviour of the younger Clonard women.

5.1.2 Reading

It seems to be the case that social networks are most close-knit around the age of 16. This means that adolescents will be more consistent vernacular speakers than adults. Labov's famous study of Black English Vernacular focused on adolescent peer groups in New York (Labov 1972b), and Cheshire's more recent work in Reading was based on three groups of adolescents. While Labov studied only male peer groups, Cheshire studied both boys and girls, which enabled her to examine gender differentiation in vernacular usage.

Cheshire, like Labov and Milroy, gained her data through long-term participant observation. That is, having decided to analyse the speech of working-class adolescent peer groups, she located three groups (two of boys, one of girls) in two adventure playgrounds in Reading, and was gradually accepted by them. (She told the first group that she had a vacation job, finding out what people in Reading thought of the town. They sympathised with her need to earn some money and accepted the tape recorder as an aid to her supposedly poor memory.) She visited the playgrounds two or three times a week for nine months, and was soon on very friendly terms with the adolescents. She took care, through details like informal dress and riding a motor-bike, to reduce the social distance between the adolescents and herself as far as possible.

Cheshire examined non-standard morphological and syntactic features in the speech of the adolescents. Examples of eleven of these variables are given below.

1. non-standard -s
   'They calls me all the names under the sun, don't they?' (Derek)
2. non-standard has
   'You just has to do what the teachers tell you.' (Mandy)
3. non-standard was
   'You was with me, wasn't you?' (Ann)
4. negative concord
   'It ain't got no pedigree or nothing.' (Nobby)
5. non-standard never
   'I never went to school today.' (Lynne)
6. non-standard what
   'Are you the little bastards what hit my son over the head?' (Nobby)
7. non-standard do
   'She cadges, she do.' (Julie)

8. non-standard *come*
   'I come down here yesterday.'
9. *ain't* = auxiliary *have*
   'I ain't seen my Nan for nearly seven years.' (Tracey)
10. *ain't* = auxiliary *be*
    'Course I ain't going to the Avenue.' (Mandy)
11. *ain't* = copula
    'You ain't no boss.' (Rob)

Table 5.1 gives percentage scores for male and female speakers for these eleven variables. A score of 100 represents consistent use of the non-standard forms. The non-standard forms are all used less often by the girls than by the boys, apart from non-standard *do*, a feature which seems to be involved in linguistic change. These findings, then, conform to the expected pattern, with female speakers adhering more closely to standard norms, while male speakers use non-standard forms more consistently.

Table 5.1: Gender differences in non-standard features of Reading speech (Cheshire 1982b: 163)

	Frequency indices	
	Boys	**Girls**
non-standard **-s**	53.16	52.04
non-standard **has**	54.76	51.61
non-standard **was**	88.15	73.58
negative concord	88.33	51.85
non-standard **never**	46.84	40.00
non-standard **what**	36.36	14.58
non-standard **do**	57.69	78.95
non-standard **come**	100.00	75.33
ain't = aux **have**	92.00	64.58
ain't = aux **be**	74.19	42.11
ain't = copula	85.83	61.18

In terms of the social networks they belong to, it seems that the boys belong to structured peer groups of the kind described by Labov in his work with Black adolescents in New York, while the girls belong to a much less tightly knit group. The sociometric diagram (Figure 5.5) shows the friendship patterns obtaining between the boys in the Orts Road group. Each boy was asked which friends he spent most of his

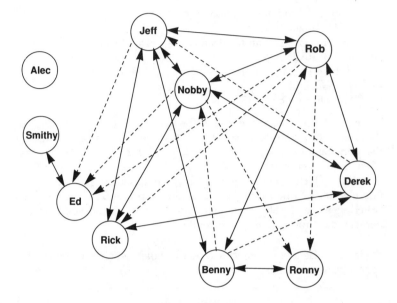

Figure 5.5 Friendship patterns in the Orts Road group (Cheshire 1982a: 89)

time with; solid lines represent reciprocal naming and thus the main social links within the group.

On the basis of the boys' responses, Cheshire divided them into three groups: core members, secondary members and non-members. Cheshire investigated the relationship between use of non-standard linguistic features and peer group status. She found some positive correlations: of the nine most frequently occurring non-standard features in the boys' speech, six were used more by core members than by others, and four of the features (non-standard present tense forms, *has*, *was*, and *never*) were used most by core members and least by non-members. But this correlation is not as regular and systematic as that found by Labov in his work on black adolescent peer groups. It seems that adolescent peer groups in Britain have a more flexible structure. The hierarchically structured and tight-knit adolescent groups in New York show a corresponding high correlation between peer group status and use of non-standard language. Cheshire also suggests that not *all* the non-standard features of Reading English necessarily serve as markers of peer group status. In order to investigate *which* variables function as markers of vernacular loyalty, she constructed a vernacular culture index, based on the following six factors:

1. skill at fighting
2. carrying of weapons
3. participation in minor criminal activities
4. sort of job preferred
5. style (i.e. dress, hairstyle)
6. swearing.

Each boy was given a score for each of these factors, and on the basis of their total scores the boys were divided into four groups: group 1 boys are those who adhere most closely to the norms of vernacular culture, and group 4 boys are those who do not adhere to these norms. Cheshire was able to show that six of the non-standard features of Reading English seem to be closely linked to the speaker's involvement in the vernacular culture. Table 5.2 gives the scores for these six variables. As the Table shows, the four variables in group A are very sensitively linked to vernacular loyalty, while those in group B are less sensitive markers.

Table 5.2: Adherence to vernacular culture – scores for frequency of occurrence of six non-standard forms (based on Cheshire 1982b: 156)

		Group 1	Group 2	Group 3	Group 4
	non-standard -s	77.36	54.03	36.57	21.21
Class A	non-standard has	66.67	50.00	41.65	(33.33)*
	non-standard was	90.32	89.74	83.33	71.43
	negative concord	100.00	85.71	83.33	71.43
Class B	non-standard never	64.71	41.67	45.45	37.50
	non-standard what	92.31	7.69	33.33	0.00

* Number of occurrences of this variable was low, so the index score may be unreliable.

Cheshire found that the girls did not form structured peer groups like the boys. All the girls in the group studied by Cheshire knew each other, but they tended to break up into pairs of 'best friends', and these pairings would be intense but short-lived. In terms of their

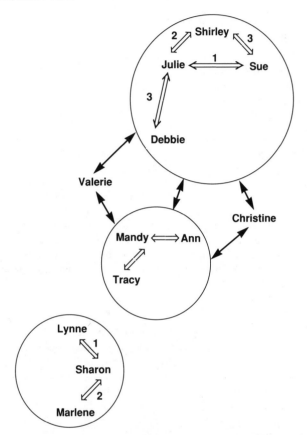

Figure 5.6 Friendship patterns in the Shinfield girls' group (Cheshire 1982a: 93)

main friendship patterns, the girls can be divided into three separate sub-groups, as shown in Figure 5.6. When asked who they spent most of their time with, each girl named her 'best friend' (double lines in Figure 5.6). When asked who else they spent time with, they named all the other girls in the group, except for the three 'outsiders', Lynne, Marlene and Sharon, who form a separate sub-group. Valerie and Christine are also peripheral and spend less time at the playground: Valerie is older and gave her boyfriend's name in answer to the first question; Christine is younger and named a schoolfriend.

Cheshire found no systematic pattern of variation in language correlating with this rather unstructured pattern of relationships. Moreover, she decided that the vernacular culture index which she had used to measure the boys' adherence to vernacular values could not be used for the girls. Although the girls took part in activities which could be called delinquent, such as stealing and setting fire to the playground, their attitude to such activities differed from the boys'. They did not boast about what they had done, and although they had fights from time to time, they did not value certain girls as 'good fighters'. In other words, they did not seem to value the vernacular norms of toughness and violence in the same way the boys did. In some ways – in terms of their interest in pop music, films, television and boyfriends – they were closer to mainstream culture. But they also clearly rejected many of the values of mainstream society; most of them, for example, did not attend school regularly.

Cheshire finally made a simple binary distinction between those girls who seemed in part to adhere to the vernacular norms defined earlier, and those who did not. The three 'good' girls in the latter group did not swear, steal, set fire to the playground or play truant from school. Table 5.3 shows a comparison between the scores for the two groups.

Table 5.3: Frequency indices for eight variables for two groups of girls (Cheshire 1982b: 163)

	'Good' girls	'Bad' girls
non-standard **-s**	25.84	57.27
non-standard **has**	36.36	35.85
non-standard **was**	63.64	80.95
negative concord	12.50	58.70
non-standard **never**	45.45	41.07
non-standard **what**	33.33	5.56
non-standard **come**	30.77	90.63
ain't = copula	14.29	67.12

As this table shows, there are five features which are used more by the 'bad' girls than by the 'good' ones: non-standard *-s, was, come*, negative concord, and *ain't* as copula. Three of these, as we saw earlier, function as markers of vernacular loyalty for boys too:

non-standard -s suffix, *was* and negative concord. Non-standard *come* is, however, invariant for the boys (they all use it 100 per cent of the time) whereas it clearly functions as a marker of vernacular loyalty for the girls, being almost categorical for 'bad' girls, but occurring much less frequently in the speech of the three 'good' girls (30.77 per cent). *Ain't* too seems to function as a marker of vernacular loyalty for girls, but not for boys, who all use it with relatively similar frequency. Non-standard *never* and *what* function only loosely as markers of vernacular loyalty for the boys; for the girls they seem not to be markers at all, since the 'good' girls use them more.

Cheshire concludes that different speakers exploit the system in different ways. While some non-standard linguistic features act as markers of vernacular loyalty for both male and female adolescents in Reading (non-standard present tense verb forms, non-standard *was*, and negative concord), there are other non-standard features which act primarily as gender markers: that is they function as markers of vernacular loyalty only for girls (non-standard *come* and *ain't* as a copula) or only for boys (non-standard *never* and *what*). These results implicitly challenge the notion that members of a speech community can be defined in terms of shared norms.

5.2 Explanation in the Light of Social Network Theory

The concept of the social network, which enables us to see the individual in relation to the group, clearly refines our understanding of gender differences in language. The evidence is that a tight-knit network structure is an important mechanism of language maintenance. Men's speech in many speech communities is closer to the vernacular than women's, and we can see that it is the close-knit social networks to which men have traditionally belonged which serve to maintain vernacular speech norms. Women's speech, then, is closer to the standard not because women are deliberately aiming at Standard English but because the less tight-knit networks to which women belong are less efficient at enforcing vernacular norms. In other words, women may use forms closer to Standard English for the negative reason that they are relatively less exposed to vernacular speech and more exposed to Standard English.

Cheshire's examination of style-shifting in the speech of her informants gives us additional information on the nature of peer group pressure. She made a set of recordings in the schools attended by the adolescents in her groups, and she used this material to see whether the speech of the adolescents was affected by the more formal school context. She found that all three groups in her study used fewer non-standard verb forms in school (i.e. non-standard -s). Interestingly, it emerged that the girls' use of non-standard verb forms decreased more sharply than the boys'. We can infer from the fact that the girls were not part of a cohesive peer group, and that their friendships fluctuated frequently, that they are less under pressure from the group to use vernacular forms, and consequently more exposed to the prestige norms of Standard English valued by institutions such as schools. In other words, the girls are more likely to see non-standard forms as being inappropriate in the school context, and to style-shift accordingly.

Not all the boys used fewer non-standard verb forms in school (as would be predicted by the Labovian model, with non-standard features reducing as the situation becomes more formal). The boys' speech in school is shown to be linked to their relationship with their teacher. Where they have a good relationship with the teacher, they use fewer non-standard present tense verb forms; that is, they adapt their speech in the direction of school norms. Where they have a poor relationship with their teacher, on the other hand, they either maintain their vernacular usage or actually increase the proportion of non-standard forms in their speech. One of the boys studied by Cheshire used non-standard speech in this way to mark his hostility to the school: he diverged from Standard English more in school than in the adventure playground, presumably to mark his loyalty to the vernacular culture. (*All* of the boys in Eisikovits' study (see section 4.3.5) used *more* non-standard forms when interacting with an adult in the school context than when interacting with each other.)

Milroy suggests that a status-based model of the kind initially developed by Labov in New York City (and described in section 4.2.1) is inadequate to deal with the language patterns of urban populations such as Belfast. She asserts the importance of **solidarity** as a factor in influencing patterns of language use. The status-based model would predict that speakers who belong to relatively loose-knit networks will change their speech in the direction of publicly legitimised norms (Standard English). However, in Belfast, speakers from the Hammer, with more loose-knit networks resulting from re-housing and unemployment, are *not* more standardised than Ballymacarrett or Clonard speakers. The change in their speech patterns shows a drift away from the focused vernacular norms of more tight-knit groups, but not a drift towards the prestige norms of Standard English. In these working class communities, then, it is more accurate to say that men's speech differs from women's because men's tight-knit networks exercise control over their members and maintain vernacular norms. It seems that working-class women are not aiming at prestige norms; they belong to relatively loose-knit networks which have less capacity to enforce focused linguistic norms, and they therefore use vernacular forms less consistently than men. This is quite different from claiming that women and men are aiming at different norms.

5.3 Woman as Lames

In his work on the speech of Black adolescent peer groups in New York, Labov introduces the term *lame* to refer to isolated individuals on the fringes of vernacular culture: 'To be lame means to be outside of the central group and its culture' (Labov 1972b: 258). Labov demonstrated that lames differ systematically in their use of language from full members of the peer group: while their speech is still very non-standard, it is much less close to the vernacular than is the speech of members of the street culture. For example, if we look at one grammatical feature of the Black English Vernacular – negative concord – we find that the adolescent peer group known as the Thunderbirds uses negative concord 98 per cent of the time, while the lames use it only 76 per cent of the time. For the Thunderbirds it is a semi-categorical rule; for the lames it is a variable rule. (Note, however, that 76 per cent as a score for the use of negative concord is still very high: the lames are certainly not approximating to (white) prestige norms.)

Can we describe women as lames? The work of both Milroy and Cheshire demonstrates that female speakers are less closely integrated into vernacular culture, that female speakers use vernacular norms less consistently than male speakers, and that these two findings are interrelated. In this respect, women are like Labov's lames. But Labov used the term to refer to isolated individuals. Most women are not isolated: among the women in Belfast studied by Milroy only three had a Network Strength Score of 0; among the Reading adolescents, only two of the girls are clearly peripheral (see Figure 5.6). Women do belong to social networks, but these seem to be less dense and multiplex than those of men.

There are other reasons for pausing before labelling women as lames, that is, describing women as deviant. The Androcentric Rule (see p. 16) predicts that commentators will describe the linguistic behaviour of men as 'normal' and the linguistic behaviour of women as deviating from that norm. Is it possible that sociolinguistic research has an androcentric bias?

Certainly, conventional criteria for network strength may be less applicable to the particular circumstances of women's lives. Out of the five criteria used by Milroy, for example (see p. 89), the third, fourth and fifth are male-oriented, because they relate specifically to waged work. While it is true that women do participate in waged work (especially in working-class communities like those studied by Milroy), they also have domestic responsibilities which these criteria do not recognise.

Second, we need to beware of defining the vernacular in such a way that it excludes female speakers. Sociolinguists frequently write of working-class vernacular culture and male culture as if they were one and the same thing. It is important to stress the fact that vernacular norms are features which mark a speaker's loyalty to a particular network. Women's loyalty to vernacular norms is not always marked with the same linguistic features that mark men's identification with vernacular culture. Cheshire's work in Reading (see p. 100) showed this clearly: some non-standard features functioned as markers of vernacular loyalty only for the girls, while others functioned as markers of vernacular loyalty only for the boys.

Finally, the claim that women in general belong to less dense and multiplex networks than men is controversial. Work in other cultures suggests that this is not always the case. In her study of Tenejapa (a Mayan community in Mexico), Penelope Brown observes that 'where men dominate the public sphere of life and women stick largely to the domestic sphere, it seems likely that female relationships will be relatively multi-stranded, male ones relatively single-stranded' (Brown 1980: 134).

In the final section of this chapter, I shall examine two counter-examples, both involving communities in Britain. In both examples, it is women, not men, who use a higher proportion of non-standard forms, and women who belong to dense, multiplex networks.

5.4 Women and Vernacular Speech

The sociolinguistic studies described in Chapters 4 and 5 found that, in Norwich, Glasgow, West Wirral, and Ballymacarrett in Belfast, men consistently used more non-standard speech. Using the social network approach, Milroy and Cheshire concluded that dense multiplex social networks have the capacity to sustain vernacular norms and that it is working-class *male* speakers who typically belong to such networks. However, such patterns are not immutable, nor are they found in all communities. The two examples to be described in this section demonstrate that, while the more common pattern seems to be that men use more non-standard speech than women, in some communities it is women who are closer to the vernacular.

As we saw in section 5.1.1, recession and growing male unemployment in parts of Belfast are coinciding with new patterns of interaction and employment for women. The Clonard community in Belfast shows that, where men lose their interaction patterns and women live as neighbours and work and amuse themselves together, then it is *women* who display consistent usage of vernacular forms.[2] The young Clonard women have the highest Network Strength Score of any sub-group studied by Milroy. The strength of their network ties is reflected in the homogeneity of their linguistic forms. In other words, the tight-knit network to which they belong acts as a powerful norm-enforcing mechanism.

Our second example comes from Wales. Beth Thomas (1989) studied the East Glamorgan dialect of Welsh in the small community of Pont-rhyd-y-fen, and discovered that only older *women* retained the local vernacular variant [ɛ:]. The social networks of both men and women of the older generation in Pont-rhyd-y-fen are dense, multiplex and localised, but those of the women are even more community-based than those of the men. Their lives revolve around the home, the immediate neighbourhood and the chapel. Use of the [ɛ:] variant is confined to those women who have networks based on the two chapels at the eastern end of the village.

Thomas's study shows that the fact that women have a traditional domestic role does not necessarily correlate with weaker networks and more standard pronunciation. Her findings indicate how important it is to examine the conditions of people's lives at a very local level. While employment opportunities were crucial factors in the formation of social networks in Belfast, involvement in the chapel was crucial in shaping interaction patterns in Pont-rhyd-y-fen.

It is one of the strengths of the social network approach that it is sensitive to both individual and small group differences. Sociolinguistic work using the social network approach provides us with valuable insights into why individual speakers use vernacular forms with greater or less consistency. At the same time, the approach helps us to understand linguistic differences between male and female speakers.

Notes

1   The Belfast material is based on Milroy and Milroy 1978; Milroy 1980; Milroy 1982. The Reading material comes from Cheshire 1978; Cheshire 1982a; Cheshire 1982b.
2   It should be noted that the Clonard young women's use of other variables was in line with 'normal' female usage, but Lesley Milroy points out that (a) is a particularly important variable in Belfast and is currently undergoing change (see section 8.3.4).

CHAPTER 6

Gender differences in communicative competence

6.1 The Concept of Communicative Competence

So far I have used the term *language* in the narrow sense of grammar and phonology, the formal structure of language. The gender differences in language described in Chapters 4 and 5 were differences in women's and men's syntax, morphology and pronunciation. This focus on linguistic form, with the sentence as the highest unit of structure, was established in linguistics and has been carried over into sociolinguistics: there are many sociolinguists who consider studies of social variation in grammar and phonology to be 'sociolinguistics proper'. It is becoming more and more apparent, however, that this view of language is far too narrow. The sociolinguist has to deal with real language data from a wide variety of situations; anyone who has ever studied conversational interaction will know that they cannot deal adequately with it if they restrict themselves to sentence grammar.

In response to the growing awareness that the study of language should be more than the study of grammar and phonology, new disciplines have emerged such as discourse analysis and pragmatics; while others, such as ethnomethodology and speech act theory, have experienced a revival of interest. The concept which marks the beginning of this revival of interest in language in its broadest sense is **communicative competence**. The term was first used by Dell Hymes (1972). He argued that it was essential to incorporate social and cultural factors into linguistic description. In his view, the Chomskyan notion of the child internalising a set of rules which enable her/him to produce grammatical sentences doesn't go far enough: the child learns not just grammar but also a sense of **appropriateness**. It is not sufficient for the child to be linguistically competent; in order to function in the real world, s/he must also have learned when to speak, when to remain silent, what to talk about – and how to talk about it – in different circumstances. Imagine someone who speaks at the same time as others, who doesn't respond to questions, who looks away when addressed, who stands embarrassingly close to another speaker, who doesn't laugh when someone tells a joke. . . . Such a person might use well-formed sentences, but we would all recognise that they were *incompetent* in an important sense. It is this knowledge of how language is used in a given society which constitutes communicative competence.

6.2 The Communicative Competence of Women and Men

In this chapter I shall look at ways in which women and men seem to differ in terms of their communicative competence. They differ, in other words, in their sense of what is *appropriate* for them as speakers. Much work – some of it contradictory – has been done in this area, though in some cases the evidence is suggestive rather than conclusive.

Gender differences in communicative competence are part of folk knowledge (as we saw in Chapter 2). In Britain, for example, we all grow up to believe that women talk more than men, that women 'gossip', that men swear more than women, that women are more polite, and so on. Research in this area often directly challenges cultural stereotypes, since much of the folklore associated with male/female differences turns out to be false.

In this chapter I shall look first at turn-taking and conversational dominance, then at certain aspects of conversational style where male and female usage seems to differ, then at politeness and its linguistic correlates. I shall examine the question, 'How far is women's language really powerless language?' and the chapter will end with a brief appraisal of linguistic interaction in all-female groups.

6.2.1 Turn-Taking and Conversational Dominance

Any analysis of conversational interaction needs a model of normal conversation structure. Figure 6.1 is a flow chart which represents the way turns are taken in conversation. It is based on Sacks et al's (1974) model of turn-taking in naturally occurring conversation. (The

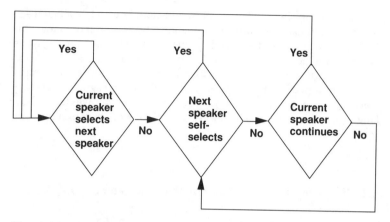

Figure 6.1 Flow chart showing turn-taking in conversation (based on Zimmerman and West 1975: 110)

diamonds represent decision points.) The current speaker in conversation may select the next speaker (by asking them a question, for example, or addressing them by name), in which case the person selected must speak next. If the current speaker does not select the next speaker, then one of the other participants in the conversation can opt to speak next. If none of them does so, then the current speaker has the option of continuing to speak.

Zimmerman and West (1975; West and Zimmerman 1977) taped thirty-one conversations involving two participants 'in coffee shops, drug stores and other public places' on the campus of the University of California; ten conversations took place between two women, ten between two men, and eleven between one woman and one man. They analysed these conversations in terms of the model shown in Figure 6.1, because they were particularly interested in the mechanisms of turn-taking. How do speakers know when it is their turn to speak? It seems that participants in conversation anticipate the end of the current turn by using syntactic and semantic clues. Evidence for the close syntactic and semantic monitoring we do of others' speech is provided by cases where one speaker contributes to or completes another's turn (so you get either speaker A and B speaking together, or B finishing A's utterance). The following examples, both from spontaneously occurring conversation, illustrate this.

(1) ⎰A:　but we've got　　four still alive now
　　⎱B:　　　　　　　　four　　　　　　　mhm
　　(Coates 1984a)

(2) {A: the continentals I suppose they came in late and
    {B:

    {A: they build them
    {B: properly
    (Crystal and Davy 1975: 21)

This ability to anticipate the end of a speaker's turn means that one turn follows another very smoothly, often with no pause intervening. (Minimal responses such as *yeah* or *mhm* as in example (1) don't constitute a turn: they are a way of indicating the listener's positive attention to the speaker, and thus a way of supporting the speaker in their choice of topic.)

Zimmerman and West examined irregularities in the transcribed conversations, that is, points in the conversations where turn-taking did not follow the smooth pattern described above. They found profound differences between the conversations involving two speakers of the same sex and those involving one speaker of each sex. The two sorts of irregularity they identified are called **overlap** and **interruption**.

Overlaps are instances of slight over-anticipation by the next speaker: instead of beginning to speak immediately following current speaker's turn, next speaker begins to speak at the very end of current speaker's turn, overlapping the last word (or part of it). **Interruptions**, on the other hand, are violations of the turn-taking rules of conversation. Next speaker begins to speak while current speaker is still speaking, at a point in current speaker's turn which could not be defined as the last word. Interruptions break the symmetry of the conversational model: the interruptor prevents the speaker from finishing their turn, at the same time gaining a turn for themselves. The following is an example of an interruption from Zimmerman and West's data:

(3) *Female*: it just strikes me as too 1984ish y'know to sow your
              seed or whatever (#) an' then have it develop miles
              away not caring i ⌈f
    Male: ⌊now:: it may be something uh quite
              different

Tables 6.1 and 6.2 show the number of overlaps and interruptions occurring in the conversations analysed by Zimmerman and West. Table 6.1 deals with the conversations which took place between speakers of the same sex (two women or two men). Here, in twenty conversations, there were twenty-two overlaps, divided twelve and ten between the participants, and there were seven interruptions, of which three involved the first speaker and four the second. (For the

Table 6.1: Turn-taking irregularities in twenty same-sex pairs (based on Zimmerman and West 1975: 115)

	1st speaker	2nd speaker	Total
Overlaps	12	10	22
Interruptions	3	4	7

Table 6.2: Turn-taking irregularities in eleven mixed-sex pairs (based on Zimmerman and West 1975: 116)

	Male speakers	Female speakers	Total
Overlaps	9	0	9
Interruptions	46	2	48

purposes of the analysis, the person speaking first in a given stretch of conversation was labelled 'first speaker'; this does not mean that this speaker initiated the conversation.)

These results are in complete contrast with those given in Table 6.2, where the conversations involved one woman and one man. In these eleven conversations there were nine overlaps and forty-eight interruptions. All of the overlaps were caused by the male speaker, and forty-six of the forty-eight interruptions were cases of the man interrupting the woman. These results were checked to see that they weren't caused by one abnormal conversation: the interruptions occurred in every conversation except one.

Note that the number of interruptions is very high when we consider that there were only seven in the twenty same-sex conversations. The ratio of interruptions to conversation is 0.35:1 (seven out of twenty) for same-sex conversations, and 4.36:1 (forty-eight out of eleven) for mixed-sex conversations. Second, note that Table 6.1 shows us that men rarely interrupt one another; it is when they are talking to women that they use interruptions. These results indicate that in mixed-sex conversations men infringe women's right to speak, specifically women's right to finish a turn. Conversely, the fact that women used no overlaps in conversation with men (while they did use some in same-sex conversations) suggests that women are concerned *not* to violate the man's turn but to wait until he's finished.

What effects do such violations of normal turn-taking in conversation have? It seems that after overlaps and especially after interruptions, speakers tend to fall silent. Since most interruptions (according to Zimmerman and West's data) are produced by men in mixed-sex conversations, the speaker who falls silent is usually a woman. Silence is often a sign of malfunction in conversation: under ideal conditions, participants in conversation alternate their turns smoothly, with little or no gap between turns. Zimmerman and West found that the average silence in single sex conversations lasted for 1.35 seconds, while the average silence in mixed-sex conversations lasted for 3.21 seconds. The following, more extended, example from their data shows clearly the effect of interruption on a speaker, and demonstrates why interruptions can be viewed as displays of dominance. (Figures in brackets indicate seconds and tenths of seconds between turns; (#) indicates a silence of one second or less.)

(4) *Female*: how's your paper coming? =
     Male: =alright I guess (#) I

     Male: haven't done much in the past two weeks
     (1.8)
     Female: yeah, know how that ⌜can
     Male: ⌞hey ya' got an extra

     Male: cigarette?
     (#)
     Female: oh uh sure ((hands him the pack)) like *my*

     Female:⌜pa-
     Male: ⌞how 'bout a match?
     (1.2)
     Female: ere ya go uh like *my* ⌜pa-
     Male: ⌞thanks
     (1.8)
     Female: sure (#) I was gonna tell you ⌜my –
     Male: ⌞hey I'd really

     Male: like to talk but I gotta run (#) see ya
     (3.2)
     Female: yeah

Silences in Zimmerman and West's data resulted not just from interruptions and overlaps, but also from delayed minimal responses. Minimal responses, such as *mhm* or *yeah*, as was pointed out above (p. 109), are a way of indicating the listener's positive attention to the speaker. The listener has an active, not a passive, role in conversation,

111

and minimal responses (as well as paralinguistic features such as smiling, nodding, grimacing) signal active attention. The following extract illustrates this (listener's responses in brackets):

(5) and this put her into a bit of a flap (*mhm*) so before she could do anything about this she had to pull forwards (*mhm*) in order to er to open the gates so she took the car out of reverse, put it into first gear (*yeah*) and pulled forward very gently (*yeah*).
(Crystal and Davy 1975: 44)

Zimmerman and West found that in mixed-sex conversations male speakers often delayed their minimal responses. In other words, they said *mhm* or *yeah* at an appropriate point but only after a pause. It seems that a delayed minimal response may function to signal a lack of understanding or a lack of interest in what the current speaker is saying. Just as a well-placed minimal response demonstrates active attention on the part of the listener and support for the speaker's topic, so a delayed minimal response signals a lack of interest in and lack of support for the speaker's topic.

The following is an extract from a malfunctioning conversation, where the woman is struggling to keep the conversation going, but is receiving no support from the male participant. Note the frequent silences (figures in brackets indicate length of pause in seconds):

(6) in other words black women are white (2) *y'know* it's really a simplistic article (0.5) *you know* he starts off saying – this – (1) *y'know* (0.8) sort of this gross indiscriminate black versus white (1) vision and . . .
(Fishman 1980a: 130)

This example comes from data collected by Pamela Fishman (1980a), who taped the daily conversations of three young American couples (a total of fifty-two hours of speech). She found that the women used *you know* five times more than the men in the twelve-and-a-half hours of conversation which she transcribed (women 87: men 17). In example (6), note how the *you knows* occur immediately before or after pauses, at points where the woman might expect (but doesn't get) some response from the man. *You know* reveals malfunction in turn-taking: change of speaker is not occurring because the man is not participating in the conversation (he rejects the topic under discussion). This use of *you know* by women in mixed-sex conversation is evidence of the work they have to do to try to keep conversation going. Women use *you know* more than men because it is men rather than women who fail to respond minimally or with a full turn at appropriate points. (In the cases where Fishman *did* find men using *you know*, it was doing the same work.) *You know* will be discussed further in the section on 'hedges' (section 6.2.2, p. 116).

Control of topics is normally shared equally between participants in a conversation. In conversations between speakers of the same gender, this seems to be the pattern, but when one speaker is male and one female, male speakers tend to **dominate**. **Conversational dominance** is the focus of research by Leet-Pellegrini (1980) which looks at the interaction of the independent variables speaker's gender and expertise. Expertise refers to the speaker's level of knowledge of the topic under discussion. By examining linguistic features such as talkativeness, interruptions, overlaps and minimal responses, Leet-Pellegrini was able to establish that *in conjunction* the variables of gender and expertise were a good predictor of dominance. In other words, speakers who were both male *and* well-informed tended to dominate conversation. They talked more and infringed the other speaker's turns more. On the other hand, speakers who were both female and uninformed talked less and used more minimal responses and other supportive linguistic behaviour. Male speakers who were well-informed dominated conversation because they used a style of interaction based on power (asserting an unequal right to talk and to control topics) while well-informed female speakers preferred an interactional style based on solidarity and support. These findings will be taken up in Sections 6.4 and 6.5.

Conversational dominance seems to be realised more through silence than through grabbing the floor when the subjects are married couples. In a study which extends Fishman's work, Victoria DeFrancisco (1991) got seven married couples to tape themselves at home for a week or more. She subsequently interviewed each of the participants on their own and asked them to comment on extracts from their recorded conversations. Her overall finding was that the women worked harder than the men to keep conversation going, but were less successful at achieving this. In contrast to Leet-Pellegrini's findings, DeFrancisco found that, although the women in her study talked *more* than the men, and introduced more topics, this was not associated with dominance. In fact, the women were less successful than the men in getting their topics accepted. The following is an extract from DeFrancisco's data (figures in brackets represent pauses in seconds).

(7) *Mary*: I've got this all figured out (3) I talked to Doyle today? (4) and (4) you know explained to him the fact that you know, come April I'll probably have to (1) ahm (#)

    Bud: Excuse me, open the back door, I'm gonna give this to ((the dogs)) (8)

    Mary: I'll probably have to terminate my appointment

Note how the man fails to give any responses, not even *mhm* or *yeah*, at appropriate moments during his wife's story, and how he interrupts her story by leaving the room. When he was interviewed by DeFrancisco, he said he didn't feel like talking at the time the conversation was recorded, and anyway he'd 'heard it all before'. His behaviour was typical of the men in this study. The men were responsible for more turn-taking violations across all categories studied; Table 6.3 gives the detailed results.

Table 6.3: Turn-taking violations in the daily interaction of seven couples (based on Defrancisco 1991: 416)

	Women (%)	Men (%)
No response	32	68
Delayed response	30	70
Inadequate response	40	60
Interruption	46	54

Overall, DeFrancisco concluded that the men's strategies allowed them control over domestic interaction. They defined the day-to-day reality of each couple's communication patterns, while the women had to adapt to the patterns imposed. This finding is supported by Sattel (1983), who argues that silence is used by men as part of male dominance. He claims that male inexpressiveness is a method for achieving control in both mixed and all-male conversation.

In this section, we have seen how male speakers infringe the normal turn-taking rules of conversation in order to establish their dominance. They interrupt other speakers, delay or omit minimal responses, and sometimes withdraw from interaction altogether. Work on adult–child conversations shows a similar pattern, with adults abusing the system in order to dominate (see West and Zimmerman 1977). We shall look at adult–child conversation in Chapter 7.

6.2.2 Gender and conversational style

The claim that women and men typically employ different linguistic 'styles' is followed up in a wide range of studies. We shall summarise some of these in this section, under the headings Verbosity, Minimal responses, Hedges, Tag questions, Questions, Commands and directives, Swearing and taboo language, and Compliments.

GENDER DIFFERENCES IN COMMUNICATIVE COMPETENCE

There is a widespread belief in our society that women talk more than men, yet research findings consistently contradict this. Men have been shown to talk more than women in settings as diverse as staff meetings (Eakins and Eakins 1978), television panel discussions (Bernard 1972), experimental pairs (Argyle et al. 1968), e-mail discussion via computer (Herring 1992; Herring et al. in press), and also husband-and-wife pairs in spontaneous conversation (Soskin and John 1963). When asked to describe three pictures, male subjects took on average 13.00 minutes per picture compared with 3.17 minutes for female subjects – more than four times as long (Swacker 1975).

Research on conversational dominance (see section 6.2.1) establishes unambiguously that it is men who dominate the floor in mixed interaction. Spender (1980a) explains the persistence of the myth of the talkative women by suggesting that we have different expectations of male and female speakers: while men have the right to talk, women are expected to remain silent – talking at any length, then, will be perceived as talkativeness in women (see section 2.2.6).

Spender's hypothesis is borne out by a study of electronic discourse (discussion via computer) among academics in the United States (Herring, Johnson and DiBenedetto in press). During a discussion of 'men's literature' which lasted five weeks, there were two days when women's contributions exceeded men's (note that men contributed 70% of the total words in this discussion). The resulting disruption, with men claiming they were being 'silenced' and threatening to 'unsubscribe' from the network, suggests that women and men do not have equal rights to speak. '[B]y contributing more even temporarily . . . . . women in the group violated the unspoken convention that control of public discourse belongs rightfully to men' (Herring, Johnson and DiBenedetto: in press).

The word *chatter*, which is nearly always used of women rather than men, has two main semantic components: verbosity and triviality. The idea that women discuss topics which are essentially trivial has probably contributed to the myth of women's verbosity, since talk on trivial topics can more easily be labelled 'too much'. The evidence is that women and men *do* tend to discuss different topics (see Aries 1976; Haas 1979; Aries and Johnson 1983; Coates 1987; Seidler 1989), as do girls and boys (this will be discussed in Chapter 7). However, the fact that topics such as sport, politics and cars are seen as 'serious' while topics such as child-rearing and personal relationships are labelled 'trivial' is simply a reflection of social values which define what men do as important, and conversely what women do as less important.

MINIMAL RESPONSES

Research on the use of minimal responses is unanimous in showing that women use them more and at appropriate moments, that is, at points in conversation which indicate the listener's support for the current speaker (Strodtbeck and Mann 1956; Hirschmann 1974; Zimmerman and West 1975; Fishman 1980a; Coates 1989a; 1991). Fishman (1980b) describes women's skilful use of minimal responses in mixed interaction as 'interactional shitwork'. She concludes that there is a division of labour in conversation which supports men and women in positions of power and powerlessness. As we saw in section 6.2.1, when men *do* use minimal responses, these are often delayed, a tactic which undermines the current speaker and reinforces male dominance.

HEDGES

Women's speech is often described as 'tentative', and this assertion is linked to the claim that women use more **hedges**. Hedges are linguistic forms such as *I think, I'm sure, you know, sort of* and *perhaps* which express the speaker's certainty or uncertainty about the proposition under discussion. Robin Lakoff explicitly linked women's use of hedges with unassertiveness. She claimed that women's speech contains more hedges (a claim based on no empirical evidence), and argued that this is because women 'are socialised to believe that asserting themselves strongly isn't nice or ladylike, or even feminine' (Lakoff 1975: 54).

Surprisingly few researchers have carried out empirical work designed to investigate Lakoff's claims. The few studies there have been show that in some situations women *do* use more hedges, but suggest we need to be sensitive to the different *functions* of hedges, and also need to query the (androcentric) assumption that more frequent use of hedges is a weakness.

One relatively straightforward piece of research focusing on the expression of tentativeness was carried out by Bent Preisler (1986). He recorded groups of four people (both single-sex and mixed) discussing controversial subjects such as violence on television or corporal punishment for children. His sample consisted of women and men from two different age groups (20–25 and 45–50) and from three occupational groups. All the informants lived and worked in Lancaster (northern England). His analysis showed that the women in his sample used significantly more hedges than the men.

Janet Holmes's analysis (based on a corpus consisting of equal amounts of male and female speech) is more delicate than Preisler's, because she distinguishes between the different functions served by hedges (Holmes 1984; 1987). Instances of *you know* in her data, for example, are categorised into two broad groups: one where *you know* expresses the speaker's confidence or certainty, as in the following example (examples from Holmes 1987):

(8) and that way we'd get rid of exploitation of man by man all that stuff/ *you know*/ you've heard it before
[*radio interviewee describing past experience*]

and one where *you know* expresses uncertainty of various kinds (note the rising intonation here):

(9) and it was quite// well it was it was all very embarrassing *you knów*
[*young women to close friend*]

Table 6.4 summarises the distribution of these two different functions in women's and men's speech.

Table 6.4: Distribution of *you know* by function and speaker's gender (Holmes 1987: 64)

Function of *you know*	Female	Male
Expressing confidence	56	37 (p=0.05)
Expressing uncertainty	33	50
Totals	89	87

This table shows that the women recorded by Holmes use *you know* more frequently than men when it expresses confidence, but less frequently when it expresses uncertainty. Holmes's sensitive analysis demonstrates that hedges are multi-functional, and that any analysis of gender differences needs to allow for this. Moreover, her findings challenge Lakoff's blanket assertion that women use more hedges than men, as well as Lakoff's claim that women's use of hedges is related to lack of confidence, since female speakers used *you know* more in its confident sense.

Both these studies included *mixed* discourse in their analysis, that is talk involving both women and men. My own research on hedges (Coates 1987b; 1989a; forthcoming b) focuses on *single-sex* discourse. When When women friends talk to each other, it is clear that they exploit the multi-functional capacity of hedges. In particular, women's use of addressee-oriented hedges to mitigate the force of an utterance can be seen as a strength rather than as a weakness. Women in my corpus often discuss highly sensitive topics; the use of hedges prevents such talk from being too **face-threatening** (see section 4.4.5 and 6.3). The two examples below illustrate this. In the first, speaker A's description of an old friend enters the taboo area of (malicious) criticism (note how the hedges become more frequent as the speaker becomes more embarrassed) from which she is rescued by C's jokey comment:

(10) A: but I did see what amounted to *sort of* chest hair black, she's a very dark *sort of* dark skinned and sallow complexion and a [1D] *I mean* I – *I mean* I hope I'm *just* reporting this without any edge to it . *you know*, so *I mean* I *probably*

   C: you mean you really feel that she's turning into a gorilla? (laughter)

The second example comes from a discussion of the Yorkshire Ripper case. After someone has raised the point that the police appealed to the public to consider men in their households, B reveals that she forced herself to consider her husband.

(11) oh god yes *well I mean* we were living in Yorkshire at the time and I — *I mean* I . *I mean* I did+ I *sort of* thought *well could* it be John?

The number of hedges present in this example is unsurprising, given the sensitivity of the topic. Self-disclosure of this kind can be extremely face-threatening and speakers need to hedge their statements.

A possible reason for men's apparently lower usage of hedges is their choice of topics: unlike women, men on the whole avoid self-disclosure and prefer to talk about impersonal subjects. In other words, a comparison between all-male and all-female conversation will often be a comparison between discussion of impersonal issues (current affairs, travel, sport) and discussion of highly personal issues involving mutual self-disclosure. For example, using an all-male sample designed as far as possible to match my all-female sample, Janis Pringle (1991) identifies the main topic in one of the all-male conversations she recorded as 'The Sixties', with sub-topics such as Bob Dylan; revolution has never happened in Britain; Marxism; and students today. Compare this with the main topic sequence in one of the all-female conversations in my data (see Coates 1989a: 105): mother's funeral; child abuse; wives' loyalty to husbands; the Yorkshire Ripper case; fear of men. When topics such as the latter are under discussion, then hedges become a valuable resource for speakers.

TAG QUESTIONS

Lakoff (1975) nominated the tag question as one of the linguistic forms associated with tentativeness, but provided no empirical evidence to show that women use more tag questions than men. According to Lakoff, tag questions decrease the strength of assertions. Compare the two sentences below:

(12a) The crisis in the Middle East is terrible.

(12b) The crisis in the Middle East is terrible, isn't it?

Lakoff claims that women use sentences like (12b), which contains the tag question *isn't it*, more often than men, who are supposed to favour (12a).

Siegler and Siegler (1976) presented students with sixteen sentences, four of which were assertions with tag questions like (12b) above. The students were told that the sentences came from conversations between college students, and were asked to guess whether a woman or a man produced the sentence originally. The results of this test supported Lakoff's hypothesis: sentences with tag questions were most often attributed to women, while strong assertions, like (12a), were most often attributed to men (the difference in attributions was statistically significant). This however only confirms what speakers' *attitudes* are; it doesn't prove that women actually use more tag questions.

While several studies have confirmed that English speakers *assume* a connection between tag questions and female linguistic usage (see O'Barr and Atkins 1980; Jones 1980, to be discussed in section 6.4 and 6.5 respectively), one of the rare studies which set out to test this assumption empirically found it unproven. Dubois and Crouch (1975) used as their data the discussion sessions following various formal papers given at a day conference. They listed all examples of formal tag questions (such as 'Probably industrial too, isn't it?') as well as 'informal' tags (such as 'Right?', 'OK?' as in 'That's not too easy, right?'). A total of thirty-three tag questions was recorded (seventeen By contrast, Preisler's (1986) research reveals that tag questions, *in combination with* other linguistic forms (e.g. certain modals and other stressed auxiliaries) are used significantly more by women than by men. auxiliaries) are used significantly more by women than by men.

All this work is based on the questionable assumption that there is a one-to-one relationship between linguistic form (tag question) and extra-linguistic factor (tentativeness) (see Cameron 1985: 55 for a discussion of this point). Refreshingly, Holmes (1984) analyses tags according to whether they express primarily **modal** or **affective** meaning. Tags with primarily **modal** meaning signal the speaker's degree of certainty about the proposition expressed:

(13) She's coming around noon isn't she
     (*Husband to wife concerning expected guest*)

Such tags can be described as **speaker-oriented** since they ask the addressee to confirm the speaker's proposition. Tags whose primary function is **affective** express the speaker's attitude to the addressee (and are therefore **addressee-oriented**). They do this either by supporting the addressee (facilitative tags):

(14) The hen's brown isn't she
     (*Teacher to pupil*)

or by softening the force of negatively affective speech acts:

(15) That was pretty silly wasn't it
     (*Older child to younger friend*)

Table 6.5 shows the overall distribution of tags in a corpus consisting

Table 6.5: Distribution of tag questions according to speaker's gender and function of tag in discourse (based on Holmes 1984: 54)

Type of meaning	No. of tag questions	
	Female	Male
Modal meaning	18	24
	(35%)	(61%)
Affective meaning		
Facilitative	30	10
	(59%)	(25%)
Softening	3	5
	(6%)	(13%)
Total	51	39

of equal amounts of female and male speech in matched contexts. Women and men do not differ greatly in total usage (but note that women do turn out to use more tags). However, the important point to notice is that 59 per cent of the tags used by women are facilitative (compared with 25 per cent for men) while 61 per cent of the tags used by men are modal, expressing uncertainty (compared with 35 per cent for women).

When the relationship between the participants in the interaction is taken into account, it emerges that **facilitators** are more likely to use tags than non-facilitators (Holmes uses the term *facilitator* to refer to those responsible for ensuring that interaction proceeds smoothly, e.g. interviewers on radio and television, discussion group leaders, teachers, hosts). Moreover, women are more likely than men to use tags when acting as facilitators. The significance of Holmes's findings will be taken up in the discussion of women and politeness (section 6.3) and of women and powerless language (section 6.4).

Cameron et al.'s (1989) study of tag questions supports Holmes's findings. They looked at gender differences in tag usage in both symmetrical and asymmetrical discourse. In asymmetrical discourse (i.e. in discourse where participants are not equal in status), the striking finding was that powerless participants *never* used affective tags. Table 6.6 gives the details.

Table 6.6: Tag questions in unequal encounters (Cameron, McAlinden and O'Leary 1989: 89)

	Women		Men	
	P'ful	**P'less**	**P'ful**	**P'less**
Modal	3	9	10	16
	(5%)	(15%)	(18%)	(29%)
Affective				
Facilitative	43	0	25	0
	(70%)	—	(45%)	—
Softeners	6	0	4	0
	(10%)	—	(7%)	—
Total		61		55

It seems that affective tags are associated with *powerful* speakers, a finding which challenges Lakoff's assumption that tags are intrinsically weak. This finding will be discussed further in the following section on Questions.

QUESTIONS

Fishman (1980a) analysed her transcripts of couples in conversation for questions as well as for *you know*. She looked at yes/no questions such as 'Did you see Sarah last night?' as well as at tag questions. The women in her sample used three times as many tag and yes/no questions as the men (87 : 29). During the twelve-and-a-half hours of conversation transcribed, a total of 370 questions was asked, of which women asked 263 (two-and-a-half times as many as the men). A survey of the linguistic behaviour of people buying a ticket at Central Station in Amsterdam also established that women ask more questions than men, especially when addressing a *male* ticket-seller (Brouwer et al. 1979). Why should this be so? Are men seen as repositories of knowledge, and women as ignorant? Perhaps women feel less inhibited about asking for information, since this does not conflict with the gender-role prescribed by society.

Fishman prefers to explain women's question-asking in linguistic terms. Questions are part of the conversational sequencing device Question + Answer. Questions and answers are linked together in conversation: questions demand a response from the addressee. In interactive terms, then, questions are stronger than statements, since they give the speaker the power to elicit a response. As we saw in the model of turn-taking in conversation presented in Figure 6.1, current speaker can exercise the option to select next speaker. Example (16) demonstrates that tag questions are also used to elicit a response (a minimal response rather than a full turn):

(16) A: Three and six a week I used to get – and me Mum used to give me money on top of that to keep me out of trouble didn't she

B: yes.

(Coates, Birkenhead survey, 1983)

Speaker A uses the tag *didn't she* to nudge B into an active role. In the following extract (taken from Pinter's *The Birthday Party*) note how Petey is forced into conversation by Meg's use of questions:

(17) (*Meg gives Petey a bowl of cornflakes. He sits at the table, props up his paper and starts to eat*)
Meg: Are they nice?
Petey: Very nice.
Meg: I thought they'd be nice. You got your paper?
Petey: Yes.
Meg: Is it good?
Petey: Not bad.
Meg: What does it say?
Petey: Nothing much.

Research findings so far suggest that women use interrogative forms more than men and that this may reflect women's relative weakness in interactive situations: they exploit questions and tag questions in order to keep conversation going.

However, as Cameron et al.'s (1989) research on tag questions demonstrates, some kinds of questions are associated with *powerful* speakers. Sandra Harris, in her study of the language of magistrates' courts, established that questions are a crucial resource for powerful participants, since questions oblige the addressee both to produce an answer, and to produce an answer that is conversationally relevant. In other words, questions control what the next speaker is able to say. Not only do powerful participants use many questions, but also participants *without* power are explicitly prohibited from using them in this situation:

(18) *Magistrate*: I'm putting it to you again – are you going to make an offer – wh – wh – to discharge this debt?
Defendant: Would you in my position?
Magistrate: I – I'm not here to answer questions – you answer *my* question
(Harris 1984: 5)

Research into other sorts of asymmetrical discourse, such as doctor–patient interaction (Todd 1983; West 1984b), or teacher–pupil interaction (Barnes 1971; Stubbs 1983) confirms this finding: questions are overwhelmingly used by powerful participants.

Thus, while it seems that in some situations women use more questions than men, in others the relevant variable is occupational status not gender. If we are to make sense of the way questions are used in speech, we have to distinguish between the different functions of questions, and we have to keep symmetrical and asymmetrical discourse separate. It is certainly true that questions are powerful linguistic forms: they give the speaker the power to elicit a response from the other participant(s). This characteristic of questions is exploited by powerful participants in asymmetrical situations; it is also exploited by women speakers who use questions and tag questions to keep conversation going.

COMMANDS AND DIRECTIVES

We can define a directive as a speech act which tries to get someone to do something. Goodwin (1980; 1988; 1990) observed the group play of girls and boys in a Philadelphia street, and noticed that the boys used different sorts of directives from the girls. The boys used explicit commands:

> (19) *Michael*: <u>Gimme</u> the pliers (*Poochie gives pliers to Michael*)

> (20) *Huey*: <u>Get off</u> my steps (*Poochie moves down steps*)

Michael, the leader of the group, often supported his commands with statements of his own desires:

> (21) *Michael*: <u>Gimme</u> the wire . . . Look man, <u>I want</u> the wire cutters right now.

The boys preferred directives explicitly to establish status differences between participants; Goodwin calls these 'aggravated' directives. The girls, by contrast, typically used more mitigated directives such as the following:

> (22) *Terry*: Hey y'all <u>let's</u> use these first and then come back and get the rest cuz it's too many of 'em.

> (23) *Sharon*: <u>Let's</u> go around Subs and Suds.
> *Pam*: <u>Let's</u> ask her 'do you have any bottles?'

The form *let's* is hardly ever used by the boys: it explicitly includes the speaker in the proposed action. The girls' use of *gonna* (see 24 below) exploits suggestions for future action as a form of directive:

> (24) *Sharon*: We <u>gonna</u> paint 'em and stuff.

The modal auxiliaries *can* and *could* are also used by the girls to suggest rather than demand action:

> (25) *Pam*: We <u>could</u> go around looking for more bottles.

> (26) *Sharon*: Hey maybe tomorrow we <u>can</u> come up here and see if they got some more.

Note the use of the adverbial *maybe* in (26) to further soften the directive.

While Goodwin demonstrates convincingly that the girls and boys use quite different linguistic means to express directives when playing in same-sex groups, she stresses that this does not mean that girls are incapable of using more forceful directives in other contexts (such as in cross-sex arguments). She argues that the linguistic forms used reflect the social organisation of the group: the boys' group is hierarchically organised, with leaders using very strong directive forms to demonstrate control, while the girls' group is non-hierarchical with all girls participating in decision-making on an equal basis.

Engle's (1980b) study of the language of parents when they play with their children revealed that fathers tend to give directions:

(27) Why don't you make a chimney?

(28) Off! Take it off!

Mothers, on the other hand, are more likely to consult the child's wishes:

(29) Do you want to look at any of the other toys over here?

(30) What else shall we put on the truck?

Not only were the fathers more directive than the mothers, they were also more directive with their sons than with their daughters. These linguistic differences again reflect a difference in organisation: mothers view interaction as an occasion to help children learn how to choose: fathers were less concerned with the children's desires and introduced new ideas. Differences in parents' speech to children will be taken up in Chapter 7.

Using Goodwin's definition of aggravated and mitigated directives, West (1990) looked at the directives used by male and female doctors to their patients. Male doctors preferred to use aggravated forms, such as imperatives:

(31) (a) Lie down
    (b) Take off your shoes and socks
    (c) Sit for me right there

They also used statements in which they told patients what they 'needed' to do, or what they 'had to' do. Female doctors, on the other hand, preferred more mitigated forms, phrasing their directives as proposals for joint action:

(32) Okay? well let's make that our plan

125

(33) So let's stay on what we're doing

They also used the pronoun *we* rather than *you* in their directives:

(34) Maybe what we ought to do is, is to stay with the dose . . . you're on

When a woman doctor used the pronoun *you*, the directive was typically mitigated by the addition of modal forms such as *can* or *could*:

(35) and then maybe you can stay away from the desserts and stay away from the food in between meals

The female doctors' mitigated directives are very similar to those used by the girls in Goodwin's Philadelphia study. Just as in example (26), the addition of the adverbial *maybe* in the two examples above softens the force of the directive.

West's discovery that male and female doctors issued directives in very different ways was followed by the discovery that patients reacted differently to these different directives. If the aim of giving a directive is to get someone to do something, then the directives used by women doctors were far more successful than those used by male doctors. Male doctors' bare imperatives (e.g. *lie down*!) elicited compliant responses in 47 per cent of cases, while their statements of patients' needs elicited only 38 per cent compliant responses. As West puts it, 'the more aggravated the directive, the less likely it was to elicit a compliant response' (West 1990: 108). Female doctors' proposals for joint action (using *let's*) elicited compliant responses in 67 per cent of cases, while suggestions for action (e.g. *you could try taking two every four hours*) had a 75 per cent success rate. Overall, the women doctors used far fewer aggravated directives than the male doctors, and their overall rate of compliant responses was 67 per cent, compared with the male doctors' 50 per cent.

SWEARING AND TABOO LANGUAGE

There is little hard evidence on male/female differences in swearing, though as we saw in Chapter 2 the folklinguistic belief that men swear more than women and use more taboo words is widespread. Jespersen (1922) claimed (see section 2.2.2) that women have an 'instinctive shrinking from coarse and gross expressions and a preference for refined and (in certain spheres) veiled and indirect expressions'. In his preface to the *Dictionary of American Slang*, Flexner claims that 'most American slang is created and used by males' (Flexner

1960: xii). Lakoff (1975) also claims that men use stronger expletives (*damn, shit*) than women (*oh dear, goodness*), but her evidence is purely impressionistic.

Kramer (1974) analysed cartoons from the *New Yorker*. She found that cartoonists make their male characters swear much more freely than the female characters. She asked students to identify captions taken from the cartoons as male or female. For most of the captions there was a clear consensus (at least 66 per cent agreement) on the sex of the speaker, and the students commented explicitly on the way in which swearing distinguished male speech from female speech. A second study (Kramer 1975) used cartoons from four different magazines (*New Yorker, Playboy, Cosmopolitan, Ladies Home Journal*). Students correctly identified the sex of the speaker in 79 per cent of cases. Analysis of the captions showed that, among other things, women used fewer swear words. Both these studies confirm the existence of a cultural stereotype but provide no evidence as to whether or not men actually *do* swear more than women.

The comments of contemporary sociolinguists on this area of linguistic usage are unsupported by data. Labov (1971: 207) says: 'In middle-class groups, women generally show much less familiarity with and much less tolerance for non-standard grammar and taboo'. Cheshire (1982a: 101) selects swearing as one of the measures to be included in her Vernacular Culture Index (see section 5.1.2), since, as she says, 'this was a major symbol of vernacular identity for both boys and girls'. This index was applied only to the boys in her sample (since the girls were said not to have a clearly defined system of cultural values) and there is therefore no comparative data.

Gomm (1981) recorded fourteen conversations between young British speakers: the participants were all female in five of these, all male in five, and mixed in four. An analysis of the transcripts of these conversations reveals no qualitative difference in the use of swear words, but Table 6.7 shows the difference in frequency between male and female usage. Clearly, the male speakers in Gomm's sample

Table 6.7: Incidence of swearing in single sex and mixed groups (based on Gomm 1981)

	Single sex groups	Mixed groups	Total
Men	21	4	25
Women	7	2	9

swear more often than the female speakers. Moreover, both women and men swear more in the company of their own sex; male usage of swear words in particular drops dramatically in mixed-sex conversations.

Gomm's findings are supported by a small-scale study reported in Hudson (1992). However, there is evidence that female speakers are familiar with – and increasingly ready to use – a wide range of taboo words (De Klerk 1992). Moreover, research which moves the focus to *working class* women in a deprived inner-city area (Hughes 1992) establishes that such speakers make frequent use of taboo language. As one of Hughes's informants said: "It's not swearing to us, it's part of our everyday talking".

COMPLIMENTS

Research in New Zealand, the United States and Britain suggests that women both give and receive more compliments than men. Holmes (1988) analysed a corpus of 484 compliment exchanges in New Zealand, and established that 51 per cent of these (248) were given by a woman to another woman, while only 9 per cent (44) were given by a man to another man; 23.1 per cent were given by a man to a woman, and 16.5 per cent by a woman to a man. This pattern has also been found in comparable American data (Wolfson 1983) and in Britain (Baptiste 1990).[1]

The compliments given by women to other women differ both in tone and topic from those given by men to other men. For women in the company of other women, giving and receiving compliments is unremarkable, an everyday occurrence. Women tend to compliment each other on appearance:[2]

(36) [in college]
Hi, Joanna, you look nice – your eye make-up is brilliant

(37) [in the office]
you've got such lovely eyes

Men, by contrast, prefer to compliment each other on possessions or skill:

(38) [on top deck of bus, South London]
Rasclat, man, your boots are wicked, know what I mean?

(39) [in pub]
you're very quick with witty one-liners – I would imagine you must have a very high IQ

Cross-sex compliments can be problematic, as the following examples illustrate. In example (40), the man's 'compliment' amounts to sexual harassment:

(40) [in office]
you look so sexy today, Faye – I must remember to have a cuddle with you later

Example (41), on the other hand, illustrates male uneasiness with a compliment from a woman:

(41) [in pub]
Woman: the thing I really like about you and the thing that makes our relationship into a special kind of friendship above all else is that you're always prepared to listen
Man: pardon? (sarcastic)

In some situations, compliments seem to function as **positive** politeness strategies, that is, they attend to the positive face needs of the addressee. As examples (36) and (37) illustrate, women tend to use compliments as signals of positive politeness. In other situations, however, as illustrated in example (40), compliments can be face-threatening, because they ignore the **negative** face-needs of the addressee. (See sections 4.4.5 and 6.3 for further discussion of the role of face.) Cross-sex compliments are clearly more face-threatening than same-sex compliments, and compliments seem to be more face-threatening to men than to women. Research findings indicate that people accept the majority of compliments they receive from someone of the same sex, but reject around 50 per cent of compliments offered by members of the opposite sex.

6.3 Politeness

It is part of folklinguistics, and has also been asserted by linguists, that women are more polite than men. In order to examine this claim, we need to look at what politeness is, and how it is realised linguistically in different societies.

Brown and Levinson (1978; 1987) define politeness in terms of the concept of **face**. (This term is introduced in section 4.4.5 on p. 84.) In British society, we try to satisfy the **negative face wants** of others by, for example, accompanying requests with apologies for the imposition: 'I'm awfully sorry to bother you but I've run out of milk – could you possibly lend me half a pint?' A request phrased like this makes it possible for the addressee to avoid cooperating. We try to satisfy the **positive face wants** of others by greeting them when we see them, asking them how they are, expressing admiration and approval for what they've been doing and for what they feel about things: 'You're looking marvellous!'; 'I know exactly how you feel'. To ask for something baldly, e.g. 'Give me some milk', or to ignore someone we know in any social setting, is to act impolitely in our culture. Politeness, then, can be defined as satisfying the face wants of others (while protecting our own), and linguistically this can be carried out in many different ways.

Brown (1980) studied the language of women and men in a Mayan community in Mexico, to test the hypothesis that women are more polite than men. She argues that the level of politeness appropriate to a given interaction will depend on the social relationship of the participants. This means that linguistic markers of politeness are a good indication of social relationships. If women *do* use more polite forms than men, what does this indicate? That women treat men as socially superior? That women treat men as socially distant? That women are involved in more face-threatening acts (that is, that for various reasons, when women address men, their requests etc. impose on men's negative or positive face)?

In Tzeltal, the language spoken by the Mayans, there is a class of particles which operate as adverbials and modify the force of the speech act. To put it simply, they either strengthen or weaken the force of what is said; either *I emphatically/sincerely/really assert/request/promise* . . . or *I tentatively/maybe/perhaps assert/request/promise* . . . In all languages, you can emphasise the force of your speech act to be positively polite, or hedge the force of your speech act to be negatively polite. In English, for example, the modal auxiliaries *may*, *might* and *could* and the modal adverbs *perhaps, possibly, maybe* can be used as hedges by speakers, and thus function as negative politeness strategies. According to Holmes (1984), it is when modals are used to express affective meaning that they show concern for the face needs of others, and are thus politeness markers. Examples (25), (26) and (35) illustrate such usage.

Brown tested three hypotheses: (1) women use more strengthening particles when speaking to women (that is pay a lot of attention to women's positive face wants); (2) women use more weakening particles when speaking to men (that is pay a lot of attention to men's negative face wants); (3) women speaking to women use more particles than men speaking to men. She compared the speech of male and female speakers in mixed and single-sex pairs, matched as far as possible (her data consisted of spontaneous conversation) for familiarity of participants, status of participants, and speaker's knowledge of the topic (all speakers hedge more when they know less about a topic). The analysis of particles used by members of same-sex pairs showed that Brown's third hypothesis was confirmed: women do use more particles (Table 6.8).

Table 6.8: Average number of particles for 100 speech acts in same-sex pairs (based on Brown 1980: 122)

	Strengtheners	Weakeners	Total particles
Mean for female pairs	25.2	34.1	59.3
Mean for male pairs	14.4	18.1	32.6

However, her data did not confirm her other two hypotheses, as Table 6.9 (for mixed-sex pairs) shows.

Table 6.9: Average number of particles for 100 speech acts in mixed-sex pairs (based on Brown 1980: 123)

	Strengtheners	Weakeners	Total particles
Mean for women speaking to men	35.7	24.4	60.2
Mean for men speaking to women	24.1	33.1	57.2

Tables 6.8 and 6.9 show us that the women did not use more strengthening particles when speaking to women; in fact, they used more when speaking to men (35.7: 25.2). Nor did women use more weakening particles when speaking to men; a comparison of the two tables shows, on the contrary, that women used more weakening particles when speaking to other women (34.1 : 24.4). Why is this?

Brown attempts to explain these results by arguing that conversation between two men in her Mayan community differs in terms of topic so much from conversation between two women that they are not strictly comparable (see discussion of topic pp. 118–9). She emphasises, however, that on the crude measure of gross use of particles women clearly use more, and thus particle-usage in this community is a crude index of politeness. It emerges, as expected, that women are more polite than men.

It seems to me that the most interesting fact thrown up by Tables 6.8 and 6.9 is the particle usage of men talking to men. The averages, in terms of total particles used, are not strikingly dissimilar for the other three possible combinations (men to women, women to women, women to men). In other words, men use a different style with each other, a style characterised by low particle usage; this style differs

Brown examined particle usage in Tzeltal to establish what was the full range of expression available to the individual speaker. She came to the conclusion that the usage of women and men differs systematically. Women seem to be alert to the fact that what they are saying may threaten face. This sensitivity to the face needs of others results in different linguistic usage. Women use the extremes of positive and negative politeness; men's speech is more matter-of-fact. Moreover, certain usages – such as the women's use of the diminutive [ʔala], or the men's use of the strengthening particle [melel] in public speaking – result in recognisable 'feminine' and 'masculine' styles.

6.4 Powerful and Powerless Language

Brown argues that negative politeness – where the speaker apologises for intruding, uses impersonal structures (such as passives), and hedges assertions – is found where people are in an inferior position in society. This deduction is also made by O'Barr and Atkins (1980) in their study of courtroom language. O'Barr and Atkins observed that manuals for lawyers on tactics in court often treated female witnesses as a special case. This led them to wonder if female witnesses differed *linguistically* from male witnesses. They analysed transcripts of 150 hours of trials in a North Carolina superior criminal court, looking at features which they call Women's Language or WL (and which are largely based on Lakoff 1975). These ten features are listed below.

1. Hedges e.g. *sort of, kind of, I guess;*
2. (Super) polite forms e.g. *would you please . . ., I'd really appreciate it if . . .;*
3. Tag questions;
4. Speaking in italics, e.g. emphatic *so* and *very*, intonational emphasis equivalent to underlining words in written language;
5. Empty adjectives, e.g. *divine, charming, sweet, adorable;*

6. Hypercorrect grammar and pronunciation;
7. Lack of a sense of humour e.g. poor at telling jokes;
8. Direct quotations;
9. Special vocabulary, e.g. specialised colour terms;
10. Question intonation in declarative contexts.

Each witness was given a score arrived at by dividing the total number of WL features used by the number of utterances. Scores varied from 1.39 (indicating an average of more than one WL feature per utterance) to 0.18 (indicating very infrequent use of WL features). The following is an example of speech high in WL features:

(42) *Lawyer*:　What was the nature of your acquaintance with the late Mrs. E.D.?

　Witness A:　Well, we were, uh, very close friends. Uh, she was even sort of like a mother to me.

This witness gained an overall score of 1.14. The following is an example of speech low in WL features:

(43) *Lawyer*:　And had the heart not been functioning, in other words, had the heart been stopped, there would have been no blood to have come from that region?

　Witness C:　It may leak down depending on the position of the body after death. But the presence of blood in the alveoli indicates that some active respiratory action had to take place.

Witness C gained an overall score of 0.18.

Both these examples are taken from the speech of *female* witnesses, and they show that the use of WL features (as defined by O'Barr and Atkins for this study) does not correlate with speaker's gender. They found that not only did some female witnesses use very few WL features, but also some male witnesses used a high proportion of WL features. The example below comes from the speech of witness D, a man:

(44) *Lawyer*:　And you saw, you observed what?

　Witness D:　Well, after I heard – I can't really, I can't definitely state whether the brakes or the lights came first, but I rotated my head slightly to the right, and looked directly behind Mr Z, and I saw reflections of lights, and uh, very, very, very instantaneously after that, I heard a very, very loud explosion – from my standpoint of view it would have been an implosion because everything was forced outward

like this, like a grenade thrown into a room. And,
uh, it was, it was terrifically loud.

Witness D's score for WL features was 1.39 – higher than that of
witness A.

O'Barr and Atkins' findings can be summarised as follows:

1. WL features are not characteristic of the speech of all women (see
   for example witness C).
2. WL features are not restricted to the speech of female speakers
   (see for example witness D).
3. The scores of speakers can be placed on a continuum (from high
   to low) – more women have high scores while more men have low
   scores.

O'Barr and Atkins argue that Lakoff's description of such features as
'Women's Language' is inaccurate. They show that the frequency of
WL features in the speech of the witnesses in their study correlates
not with sex, but with two other factors – first, with the speaker's
social status, and second, with the speaker's previous courtroom
experience. Witness C is a pathologist who often has to appear in
court as an expert witness; she is a highly educated, professional
woman. Her low score for WL features correlates with her high
social status and her courtroom experience. Witnesses A and D, on
the other hand, who both have high scores, have low social status and
little courtroom experience (A is a housewife; D is an inexperienced
ambulance attendant).

On the basis of this correlation, O'Barr and Atkins rename the
linguistic features normally associated with women's speech **Powerless
Language**. They argue that powerless language has been confused
with women's language because, in societies like ours, women are
usually less powerful than men. Many women therefore typically use
powerless language, according to O'Barr and Atkins, but this is the
result of their position in society rather than of their gender.

O'Barr and Atkins's findings are not supported by more recent
sociolinguistic work which keeps the non-linguistic variables of gender
and social status apart. Both Candace West and Nicola Woods investigated whether women in powerful positions in society take on a
dominant role in interaction. West (1984a; 1984b) analysed doctor–
patient interaction in a local clinic and discovered, among other things,
that doctors regularly interrupt their patients, except when the doctor
is female and the patient white and male (when it is the doctor who
gets interrupted). This unexpected finding suggests that even when a
woman is in a position of power (in the role of doctor), it is her gender,

not her status, which enables us to predict who interrupts whom. The finding that gender overrides status is confirmed by Woods (1989), who made recordings of three-party conversations between work colleagues of differing occupational status. In some cases, a male speaker held the 'boss' position, and in others, a female speaker was the most powerful. While occupational status did have some influence on floor-holding, it was men who dominated, whether they were boss or subordinate; being the boss did not lead to women holding the floor more than men.

O'Barr and Atkins claimed that low-status speakers with little courtroom experience used 'powerless' language. West's and Woods's studies, on the other hand, show that low status *males* do not use powerless language, but on the contrary try to dominate interaction through the use of powerful forms such as interruptions. These latter two studies show that, where status and gender are in conflict, as in the case of female doctors or women 'bosses', then gender seems to override status.

One of the problems with O'Barr and Atkins's work is their unquestioning acceptance of Lakoff's claims. In particular, their relabelling of Lakoff's 'Women's Language' features as 'Powerless Language' perpetuates the myth of the intrinsic *weakness* of women's language. As we have already seen in this chapter, some of these linguistic features can be very powerful. We must avoid labelling linguistic forms in a simplistic manner as 'powerful' or 'powerless'. We must also fight against the androcentric tendency to assume that, because certain linguistic forms are characteristic of women's talk, they must inevitably be weak. As the next section should make apparent, this is far from the case.

6.5 Women Talking to Women

Interest is growing in all-female discourse. Deborah Jones's paper, 'Gossip: notes on women's oral culture' (1980), was a landmark, because it put the subject of women talking to women firmly on the sociolinguistic agenda. 'Gossip' is a term used almost exclusively of women's talk; it usually has pejorative connotations ('idle talk . . . tittle-tattle', *Concise Oxford Dictionary*). Jones (1980) accepts it as a term describing women's talk, but redefines it in a non-pejorative way as 'a way of talking between women in their roles as women, intimate in style, personal and domestic in topic and setting'. Using a term such as *gossip* draws attention to the fact that the language women use when talking to each other has not traditionally been treated as serious linguistic data; by contrast, men's talk is seen as 'real' talk and has always been taken seriously.

Jones's use of the term *gossip* is not original: it is used in anthropological work to refer to informal communication between members of a social group. Anthropologists stress, among other things, the social function of gossip – it maintains 'the unity, morals and values of social groups' (Gluckman, as quoted in Jones 1980). This is clearly an important function. According to Emler (forthcoming), gossip is, perhaps, *the* basic process in the social psychology of everyday life, since gossip 'provides people with information essential to their capacity to cope with their social worlds, to solve the various problems they face, and to deal with the people around them'.

Using the sociolinguistic framework established by Ervin-Tripp (1972), Jones describes gossip in terms of the relations between setting, participants, topic, formal features and functions. The setting for women's talk is typically the home, and also sometimes shops, supermarkets and hairdressers. The home is a setting which can be labelled private rather than public. The participants are, self-evidently, women. The topics stem from women's chief roles as wife, mother and housewife, and thus range from husbands and child-rearing to housework. Clearly, discussion of such topics can vary widely, from a simple exchange of recipes to an intense interaction involving women in mutual self-disclosure.

Her most significant observation is that, where men disagree with or ignore each other's utterances, women tend to acknowledge and build on them. In other words, it seems that men pursue a style of interaction based on **power**, while women pursue a style based on **solidarity** and **support**. At a purely descriptive level, Stone's (1983) account of how he, a man who chose to stay at home and look after his children, experienced women's mode of discourse confirms Jones' work. He describes men's talk as follows:

> From football to sex, from politics to literature, talk had one thing in common; it knew where it was going. It wasn't baffled, it wasn't awed, it wasn't speculative . . . as a rule these conversations were gladiatorial, a contest in language with a familiar topic the arena.

He goes on: 'while I still miss the stimulation of battling wit against wit. I am beginning to be satisfied by a different sort of language'. He then sketches a description of this different sort of language, that is, women's language:

> What do we talk about? It's obvious. We talk about ailments, bowel and bladder functions and household chores. . . . Most of all we talk about

children . . . expressed in short and perfunctory statements that are accommodated with humour and concern by people whose common experience lends an intimacy to their understanding. . . . The constant care of children imbues those involved with . . . a need *to cooperate rather than compete*, . . . a willingness to accept confusion and speculation as an end rather than rely on the dogma of formulae. (Stone 1983, my italics)

Kalcik (1975), who studied personal narrative in all-women groups, also argues that the prime pattern of interaction in such groups is cooperative rather than competitive, and this is confirmed by Aries's (1976) work on mixed and single-sex groups. Aries analysed the interaction patterns of six experimental groups: two all-female, two all-male, and two mixed. The all-male groups were concerned to establish where each member stood in relation to other members and in these groups a hierarchy emerged with some members holding dominant positions and others more submissive positions. The two women's groups, on the other hand, were more flexible: active speakers were concerned to draw out more reticent speakers and the women developed ways to express affection and interpersonal concern.

Cooperative linguistic behaviour is the subject of Marie Wilson Nelson's (1988) study of five successive teams of teachers working at a university writing centre. The teams consisted almost entirely of female graduate assistants, and the working practices they established were explicitly collaborative. One of the rare male graduate assistants involved commented:

I just love being in here with all you women. You make it such a nice place to work. You're so warm and supportive that I never feel stupid when I make a mistake. It's different in here from how I've seen people do things before. Most graduate students are so competitive.

The work referred to in this section is all based on white, middle-class speakers. However, Goodwin's (1980) work on the street play of Black children in Philadelphia (described in section 6.2.2) established that the linguistic forms used by the children reflected the social organisation of their social groups: the non-hierarchical nature of the girls' group resulted in the use of co-operative rather than competitive forms. Wodak (1981) also included working-class speakers in her work on the discourse strategies of women and men in group therapy. She noted interesting class differences: in particular, working-class *men* are considerably more emotional than many middle-class *women*, and working-class speakers in general differ significantly from lower middle-class speakers and from middle-class *men* in their presentation of their problems. However, she also noted significant gender differences.

The men and women talked about their problems in different ways: the men tended to use circumstantial descriptions while the women were more personal.

In my own research (see Coates 1989a; 1991; forthcoming a & b), I have tried to establish which linguistic features are characteristic of all-female discourse. My data suggest that the following are some of the relevant categories for understanding how women's cooperative discourse is achieved.[3]

1. *Topic and topic development*

   Talk is central to women's friendships, and women typically choose to talk about people and feelings, rather than about things (see pp. 118–19). These topics are developed slowly and accretively, with participants building on each other's contributions and arriving at a consensus.

2. *Minimal responses*

   Women use minimal responses to signal their active listenership and support for each other. They also use them to mark their recognition of different stages of a conversation, e.g. to accept a new topic, or to acknowledge the end of a topic.

3. *Hedges*

   Hedges are used to respect the face needs of all participants (see section 6.3), to negotiate sensitive topics, and to encourage the participation of others. Mitigated utterances encourage discussion because they prevent speakers taking a hard line.

4. *Questions*

   Questions often function as information-seeking devices and in conversation, a speaker can take on the role of 'expert', while other participants ask the expert questions. Women avoid the role of expert in friendly conversation (since this would disturb the symmetry of the group); information-seeking questions are consequently rare in all-female discourse. Instead, interrogative forms are used to invite others to participate, and to check that what is being said is acceptable to everyone present.

5. *Turn-taking*

   Simultaneous speech (that is, two or more people speaking at the same time) is common in all-female discourse, yet it is rarely a sign of conversational malfunction (see section 6.2.1). It seems that female speakers use a turn-taking model where the rule of one-person-at-a-time does not apply. Co-conversationalists ask questions or make comments *while another participant is speaking*; these questions and comments are, like minimal responses, signals of active listenership, but they contribute more substantially to the production of joint text. Simultaneous speech also occurs when speakers complete each other's utterances, or repeat or rephrase each other's words. Finally, overlapping speech is found when two or more speakers pursue a theme simultaneously; this does not threaten comprehension, but on the contrary permits a more multi-layered development of topics.

The talk of single-sex groups is still under-researched, but, as the studies referred to in this section show, we are beginning to understand the conversational patterns of all-female discourse. Not only that, we are beginning to reassess the linguistic features associated with women's talk which were previously described as 'weak'. Where the chief goal of talk is the maintenance of good social relationships, then cooperative discourse strategies are highly functional. There are situations where a more competitive style of interaction may be more appropriate; but it is surely not radical to claim that in other situations a more cooperative style will be more appropriate. The ideal (androgynous) speaker would be competent in both.

6.6 Conclusion

In this chapter we have looked at work which reveals gender differences in communicative competence. The evidence at present suggests that women and men do pursue different interactive styles: in mixed-sex conversations this means that men dominate conversation by interrupting women, controlling topics of conversation and also by becoming silent. Women make greater use of minimal responses to indicate support for the speaker. It also seems that women use more hedges, while men talk more, swear more and use imperative forms to get things done. Women use more linguistic forms associated with politeness. These clusters of linguistic characteristics are sometimes termed 'men's style' and 'women's style'. This terminology is disputed by O'Barr and Atkins, who claim that the linguistic features found in the speech of many women are typical of people of low status in society, both women and men, and should more accurately be called 'Powerless Language'. Subsequent studies of asymmetrical discourse, however, have shown that low status *men* do not use powerless language, but attempt to dominate interaction.

The cluster of 'women's' linguistic features is shown in a more positive light when examined in the context of women talking to other women. In woman-to-woman interaction, these 'powerless' forms can be used as a powerful sign of mutual support and solidarity. When used reciprocally, then, it seems that 'powerless' language approaches the ideal form of cooperative discourse – what those who work in the counselling professions call 'co-counselling'. (Note that some dissatisfaction with the male style is implied by Aries's finding that the men she studied became less and less interested in attending the all-male sessions and looked forward to the meetings of the mixed groups; the women, on the other hand, preferred the all-women sessions.)

Labov defined the speech community in terms of 'participation in a set of shared norms' (Labov 1972: 121). It seems that women and men have different sets of norms for conversational interaction, and we have already seen (in Chapters 4 and 5) that we cannot assume that male and female speakers share grammatical and phonological norms. It seems, then, that women and men may constitute distinct speech communities. In the final part of this book (Part III), we shall see how this comes about, and examine the linguistic and social consequences of such a distinction.

Notes

1   It should be noted that in all these studies, female fieldworkers outnumbered male. An empirical study of compliments carried out by a male fieldworker (Bevan 1990) found a higher proportion of male–male compliments, a result which suggests that the gender of the fieldworker is a significant variable.
2   All the examples are taken from Baptiste (1990).
3   My data consist of recordings of spontaneous conversation between women friends. These friendship groups represent a range of ages (from 12-year-old girls to middle-aged women) and come from different social backgrounds and from a variety of regions (London, the Midlands, Belfast, Merseyside).

Part Three

Causes and Consequences

CHAPTER 7

The acquisition of gender-differentiated language

7.1 Children and Gender Identity

The last three chapters have established that women and men differ linguistically in a wide variety of ways. In this chapter I shall look at the way these different repertoires are acquired. Work on child language acquisition is relatively recent, and it tends to concentrate on how the (undifferentiated) child acquires his (*sic*) language. Language is often interpreted in the narrow sense of grammar, phonology, and lexicon, with particular emphasis on the development of syntax. Classic studies in this field are Bloom (1975), Brown (1976), Dale (1976), Fletcher and Garman (1986), Ingram (1989). More recently, with increased awareness of language as social behaviour, researchers have widened the scope of their enquiries. They still aim to discover how a child becomes linguistically competent, but 'linguistically competent' has been redefined. As was pointed out in Chapter 6, a knowledge of grammar, phonology and lexicon is not enough – it does not make the child competent; children need to master not only the formal rules of language, but also rules for the appropriate use of language. Linguistic competence is now taken to include a knowledge of the cultural norms of spoken interaction. The best work using this new framework is Ochs and Schieffelin's (1983) study of children's acquisition of conversational competence.[1]

Works such as the latter are based on the premise that learning to speak is learning to be a member of a particular culture. The social order, in other words, is reproduced through speech. This being so, and since it seems to be common to all cultures that women's and men's roles are distinguished, it is reasonable to assume that when children learn to speak, one of the things they learn is the cultural role assigned to them on the basis of their sex. This is a two-way process:

in becoming linguistically competent, the child learns to be a fully fledged male or female member of the speech community; conversely, when children adopt linguistic behaviour considered appropriate to their gender they perpetuate the social order which creates gender distinctions.

In Chapter 1 we discussed women and men as social groups, and argued that, despite their greater numbers, women constitute a minority group (see sections 1.3 and 1.4). Girls and boys learn during childhood to identify with one group or the other. They demonstrate their membership of the group by their use of gender-appropriate behaviour, and this includes gender-appropriate *linguistic* behaviour. Social psychologists refer to this process of learning how to be a 'proper' girl or a 'proper' boy as the acquisition of **gender identity.**

In this chapter I shall describe work which demonstrates that gender differences are found in the speech of children. This work is of two kinds. First, there is work which aims to test the belief that girls acquire language at a faster rate than boys; this work will be described briefly. Second, there is work which explores children's acquisition of gender-differentiated language in terms of both formal features and communicative competence; this work will be described in some detail. In this second group I shall include work which analyses the ways in which adults – particularly parents – interact with children, as well as work which analyses the ways in which children interact with each other in same-sex peer groups.

7.2   Gender Differences in Early Language Learning

One of the most well-known and best established generalisations in the area of gender differences is girls' superiority over boys in the acquisition of speech. On measures such as the onset of babbling, the first word, number of words used at 18 months, girls tend to do better than boys. This contrast between girls and boys seems to have been exaggerated in the past, although it has been suggested that differences between male and female children might be diminishing as a reflection of less polarised gender roles and less sexist modes of child care in contemporary societies. However, Maccoby and Jacklin's (1974) authoritative survey of all extant research in the area concluded that the generalisation still holds good. For pre-school children, the research findings indicate that where a gender difference is found, it is nearly always girls who are ahead. Not all these differences achieved statistical significance, but the combined results of all the studies amount to a significant trend. For the early school years, on the other hand, no consistent differences emerge from the research literature, but from the age of 10 or 11, girls again outscore boys on a variety of measures of verbal competence. Some examples of these findings are described below.

Clarke-Stewart (1973) observed American mothers and first-born children for 9 months, from when the children were 9 months until they were 18 months. She found that the language skills of girls in the sample in terms of both comprehension and vocabulary were significantly higher than those of boys; this was paralleled by the girls' more positive involvement with the mother. The girls' mothers differed from the boys' mothers in that they spent more time in the same room as their daughters, had more eye contact with them, used a higher proportion of directive and restrictive behaviours, and a higher ratio of social to referential speech. (Social speech includes greetings, *thank you*, apologies, etc. while referential speech, as its name implies, means speech which refers to things: *What's this?*; *Give me the red brick*, etc.)

Nelson (1973) studied the acquisition of vocabulary by eighteen children between 1 and 2 years of age (again in the USA). She divided her sample into two groups according to the rate at which they acquired vocabulary (the index was the age at which the child had acquired fifty words). All the boys fell into the group with a slower acquisition rate. The mean age for fifty words was 18.0 months for the girls and 22.1 months for the boys.

Perkins (1983) reports a study of modal expressions (*can, will, have to, probably*, etc.) used in spontaneous speech by children aged between 6 and 12. His subjects were the ninety-six children taking part in the Polytechnic of Wales Language Development project. All the children were monolingual English speakers, and the sample was balanced in terms of age, gender, and social class. Perkins discovered that frequency of use of modal expressions varied in relation to the child's gender, with girls using modal expressions more frequently than boys (though this difference was too small to be statistically significant). Interestingly, Perkins found that social class was significantly correlated with modal usage: children from middle-class homes used modal expressions more frequently. This parallelism between girls and the middle class on one hand and boys and the working class on the other is something that has been noted earlier (see section 4.4.3). In fact, linguistic gender differences seem to be more marked in poorer families: two studies of disadvantaged children (Shipman

1971; Stanford Research Institute 1972) found girls clearly ahead on a number of language measures.

These studies are representative of the many that have been carried out on child language and show a general pattern of girls acquiring language faster than boys. This means that at any given age, girls will be found to be superior in terms of comprehension, size of vocabulary, reading ability, handling of complex expressions such as the modals, etc. While such findings are of interest, they are not necessarily relevant to the linguistic differences we find between women and men (many just reflect slower maturation). In the next section, I shall describe work which, it can be argued, shows children developing gender-differentiated language. The linguistic differences described below show girls and boys acquiring the gender-roles prescribed by society.

7.3   The Development of Gender-Appropriate Speech

In this section I shall look first at work which describes gender differences in children's language which anticipate formal differences in adult language of the kind described in Chapters 4 and 5. Secondly, I shall look at work where children's language usage anticipates adult communicative competence differences of the kind described in Chapter 6.

7.3.1   Formal Differences

Before puberty, children's vocal tracts differ only in relation to the child's size and not in relation to the child's gender. But work on *pitch* has revealed that gender differences emerge before the onset of puberty. Liebermann's (1967) study suggests that, even before they can talk, babies alter the pitch of their voices depending on the gender of the addressee: their average fundamental frequency is lower when they 'talk' to their fathers than when they 'talk' to their mothers.

Several projects (e.g. Sachs et al 1973; Meditch 1975; Fichtelius et al 1980) have tested the ability of adult judges to identify a child's gender from recorded samples of speech. These projects find that judges identify children correctly as male or female at well above chance level. Further analysis of the child speech samples suggests that it is **formant** patterns which identify speakers as male or female. (A formant is a concentration of acoustic energy, reflecting the way air vibrates in the vocal tract as it changes its shape; most sounds can be described on the basis of three main formants.) 'The child would be learning culturally determined patterns that are viewed as appropriate for each sex. Within the limit of his (*sic*) anatomy, a speaker could change the formant pattern by pronouncing vowels with phonetic variations, or by changing the configuration of the lips' (Sachs et al 1973: 80). So even at an age when their articulatory mechanisms are identical, girls and boys are learning to speak appropriately, that is, to produce higher or lower formants respectively.

Fichtelius et al (1980) showed that both adult and child judges could still guess the gender of a child speaker even when the tapes had been submitted to a process which affects the sound so that individual words and syllables are no longer discernible but rhythmic patterns and intonation are still apparent. Older children were more easily identified than younger ones, since as girls and boys get older, their speech becomes *prosodically* differentiated. Boys begin to employ a more rapid tempo, while girls use a greater variety of intonation patterns.

Children's acquisition of *intonation* has also been investigated by Local (1982) as part of the Tyneside Linguistic Survey. The children were aged between $5^{1}/_{4}$ and 6 by the end of the study. Taped extracts of their speech were abstracted from a larger corpus collected over a period of about a year. Adults on Tyneside use a system of nuclear tone which differs markedly in its frequency distribution from the system used by adult speakers of Standard English. Figure 7.1 pictures these differences and shows the gross percentage distribution of each tone in two samples (one of Tyneside speakers, and the other of speakers of Standard English). Note especially the difference in the relative frequency of falls ($\diagdown$), rise-falls ($\diagup\diagdown$), and levels (—) between the Tyneside and Standard speakers. These differences reflect dialectal differences which enable us to say of a speaker using Tyneside intonation pattern 's/he comes from Tyneside'.

Local shows how the children's tone system altered over the period studied. Most importantly, there was a shift in the relative frequency of falls, rises, and level tones in the children's speech. Further, there was a *decrease* in the frequency of nuclear falls, and an *increase* in the frequency of nuclear levels in the children's speech throughout the period studied. In other words, during the year all the children shifted their speech in the direction of adult Tyneside English. However, the relative frequency of these tones was not the same for all children, and Local identified three different patterns:

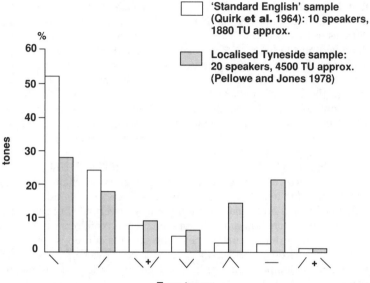

Figure 7.1 Gross percentage distribution of tones for two samples – Tyneside speakers and Standard English speakers (Local 1982: 89)

Pattern 1: More falls than rises and more levels than rises (Paul, Peter, James, Colin, Robert, Allan)

Pattern 2: More falls than rises and more rises than levels (Keith, Derek, Cath, Eunice, Kate, Judith)

Pattern 3: More rises than falls and more rises than levels (Claire, Angela, Sheila, Janice, Elaine, Anne)

These patterns reveal that the children's speech varies on the basis of speaker's gender. Pattern 3 (more rises than falls or levels) is typical of girls' speech; pattern 1 (falls and levels more frequent than rises) is typical of boys' speech; while pattern 2 is ambiguous, being realised by both girls and boys. Patterns 3 and 1 are also found in adult speech on Tyneside, with adult females using more rises than falls or levels and adult males using more falls and levels than rises. Thus Local's analysis reveals children acquiring not just Tyneside intonation, but Tyneside intonation appropriate to their gender.

Work on *phonological variation* in children's speech also confirms that gender differentiation is present from an early age. In the course of a study of child-rearing in a semi-rural New England village, Fischer

(1964) was struck by differences between the pronunciation of girls and boys. Using his tapes of interviews with the twenty-four children in the sample, he carried out a quantitative analysis of the variable (ing). In this community, (ing) has two variants: the standard variant [ɪŋ] and the non-standard variant [ɪn]. The twenty-four children in the sample consisted of two equal age groups (3–6 year olds and 7–10 year olds), each group containing equal numbers of girls and boys. Fischer's analysis of his data revealed that the girls used the standard variant [ɪŋ] more frequently, while the boys preferred the non-standard variant [ɪn] (see Table 7.1).

Table 7.1: Gender differences in the use of (ing) (based on Fischer 1964: 484)

	More [ɪŋ]	More [ɪn]
Girls	10	2
Boys	5	7

These differences are statistically significant. It seems likely that the children have learned that in their speech community [ɪŋ] is a marker of female speech and [ɪn] is a marker of male speech.

I have already discussed Romaine's (1978) study of primary school children in Edinburgh (see section 4.3.4), where Romaine found that speaker's gender was the single most important factor correlating with use of the phonological variable (r). In a survey of gender differences in the language of children and adolescents, Romaine (1984) compares her results for 10 year olds in Edinburgh with Macaulay's results for 10 year olds in Glasgow (Macaulay's work on *adult* gender differences in Glasgow was discussed in section 4.3.2). Although the scoring procedures used in the two studies were slightly different, the results are very similar. Both Romaine and Macaulay investigated the variables (gs) (the glottal stop), (i), (au) and (a), which occur in words like *butter, hit, house,* and *bag*. For all these variables, there is clear gender differentiation in both Edinburgh and Glasgow (though for (a) in Glasgow the differences in girls' and boys' scores is not large enough to be significant). In other words, girls obtained lower scores than boys for all these variables; their lower scores reflect less frequent use of non-standard variants.[2] The pattern of gender differentiation found among children in Edinburgh and Glasgow is the same as that found in the adult population: the girls consistently prefer forms which are closer to standard pronunciation, while the boys prefer forms which are more non-standard.

It's even possible that these findings greatly underestimate the variation in children's speech. The results discussed here are for 10 year olds; as children get older and move through primary school, their use of non-standard forms appears to diminish, so 10 year olds have lower scores on average than 6 year olds. If we look at the variable (au) in Edinburgh, as used by three different age groups, we can see how the scores get lower, apparently reflecting diminished use of the stigmatised non-standard variant [u:] (as in *hoos*) and increased use of the standard variant [au] (as in *house*) (see Figure 7.2).

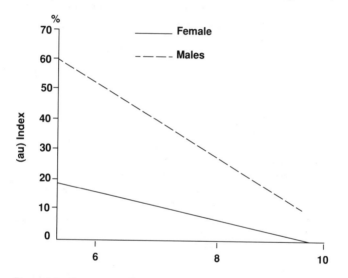

Figure 7.2 Percentage of non-standard [u:] in the usage of girls and boys in three age groups in Edinburgh (Romaine 1984: 101)

At the age of 6, the difference between boys' and girls' use of (au) is very marked – boys are shown to choose the non-standard variant [u:] more than 50 per cent of the time (that is they tend to say *hoos* rather than *house*). Girls at 6, on the other hand, use the non-standard variant less than 20 per cent of the time. As the children get older, both girls and boys are recorded as using fewer stigmatised forms, and the difference between girls' and boys' usage gets smaller.

Romaine (1984) suggests that what these figures might actually show is children's growing ability to code-switch, that is, to use different forms in different contexts. She observes that while use of the stigmatised variant certainly decreases in the interview situation as children get older, it is still much in evidence when children are talking among themselves in the playgrounds. So these children can be seen to be acquiring competence in style-shifting (they are learning which styles are appropriate in which contexts), as well as acquiring competence in gender-appropriate linguistic behaviour.

Eisikovits's study (1987; 1988) of adolescent speech in Sydney, Australia, provides very interesting evidence of the way children's usage shifts as they acquire gender-appropriate speech. She obtained data from two groups of working-class adolescents, interviewed in self-selected pairs (to reduce the formality of the situation). The twenty subjects in the first group had an average age of 16 years 1 month; the twenty subjects in the second group had an average age of 13 years 11 months. As we saw in section 4.3.5, the results for the 16 year olds showed the expected pattern, with male speakers using consistently more non-standard forms than female speakers. But if we compare these results with those for the 13 year olds, we can see that there

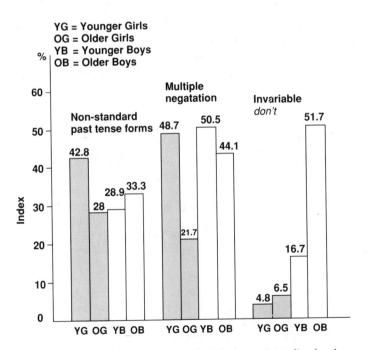

Figure 7.3 Age and gender differences in Sydney, Australia, for three non-standard grammatical features (based on Eisikovits 1988)

151

are significant differences between the two: the younger speakers do not conform to the expected pattern. As Figure 7.3 shows, the younger girls use a *higher* proportion of non-standard past tense forms than any other group, while their use of multiple negation is very similar to that of the younger boys. Invariable *don't* is the only non-standard grammatical feature which shows clear gender variation for both age groups; moreover, the boys increase their usage of this feature significantly as they get older.

What we see here is declining usage of non-standard forms among the girls, and stable or increasing usage among the boys. It looks as if many of the non-standard features of Sydney vernacular speech have prestige for young adolescents of both sexes. But as they get older, the girls learn to modify their speech in the direction of the standard, while the boys seem to consolidate their perception of non-standard forms as having positive value. In discussion with the interviewer, the older informants displayed divergent attitudes: the girls became increasingly conservative, the boys increasingly non-conformist. For example, the girls said they didn't like swearing any longer, and objected to their boyfriends swearing, while for the boys swearing is a normal part of everyday life: 'If I swear in front of me mother now, she don't say nothing'. It seems that a growing awareness of gender norms is matched by a shift in linguistic usage so that, by the age of 16, these speakers have adjusted their speech to be more congruent with adult patterns.

7.3.2 *Differences in Communicative Competence*

So far I have looked at work which shows children acquiring the formal features of language. Now I shall examine children's acquisition of gender-differentiated communicative competence. I shall look at work on verbosity and conversational dominance, interruptions and simultaneous speech, question-and-answer sequences, and politeness.

As far as *verbosity* is concerned, Smith and Connolly (1972) conclude that girls are both more talkative and more fluent. They talk more, both to their mothers and to other children, before the age of 4, but after that such quantitative differences disappear. These results could be the product of different expectations on the part of parents. Our culture expects girls and women to talk more and early research in this area, with crude measures and small samples, seemed to confirm the talkativeness of pre-school girls. However, as we saw in section 6.2.2, work on adult language indicates that women talk *less* than men in mixed company.

THE ACQUISITION OF GENDER-DIFFERENTIATED LANGUAGE

Certainly, recent research suggests that boys dominate mixed conversation from an early age. Adelaide Haas (1978) analysed the amount of speech produced by girls and boys aged 4, 8 and 12 in mixed-sex pairs: she found that boys used longer utterances than girls. Joan Swann's (1989) analysis of classroom talk (using 9–11 year olds) showed convincingly that boys talked far more than girls, both in terms of the number of turns taken and the number of words uttered. (This research will be described in greater detail in section 9.3.) She also demonstrates that *all* participants in the classroom collaborate to achieve male dominance: the teacher by paying more attention to the boys; the boys by using the interactional resources available to contribute more; the girls by using the same resources to contribute less.

This pattern of differential usage of interactional resources can also be seen in the context of the family. Male children are socialised to dominate conversation with the active support of female participants. Frederick Erickson (1990) analysed the dinner-table conversation of a large Italian-American family: mother, father, four sons (aged 7–14 years) and a daughter (aged 9 years). A female researcher was also present at the meal. The conversation consisted of a series of narratives. One set of narratives focused on accidents or near-misses experienced by members of the family when riding their bikes. The initial story was told by the youngest boy. This was followed by stories from the older boys. Finally, the father told a dramatic story about his own experience of nearly crashing his motor-bike, which capped the previous stories. The stories were recounted almost exclusively by the male members of the family (the daughter started one but didn't succeed in sustaining it), and celebrate the bravery and skill of the riders. The mother, daughter and female guest acted as an attentive audience for the story-tellers. These stories not only establish the relative status of male family members; they also function as a display of male dominance which is achieved collaboratively by the whole family.

Research on *interruptions* and *simultaneous speech* has found no significant differences between girls and boys. Parents, however, apparently do differ significantly on both these measures. Greif (1980) studied sixteen middle-class children, aged between 2 and 5, in conversation with (1) their mothers and (2) their fathers. Her results show that fathers interrupted more than mothers (though this difference was not quite large enough to be statistically significant), and that both parents interrupted girls more than boys. In terms of simultaneous speech (that is both speakers starting to speak at the same time), parents were significantly more likely to continue talking than were children, father-and-child pairs were more likely to engage in simultaneous speech than mother-and-child pairs, and finally both fathers and mothers were more likely to engage in simultaneous speech with daughters than with sons.

As we have seen (section 6.2.1), the use of interruptions and simultaneous speech can be interpreted as a way of controlling conversation. It seems that fathers try to control conversation more than mothers (which fits the research results for adult conversations), and both parents try to control conversation more with daughters than with sons. The implicit message to girls is that they are more interruptible and that their right to speak is less than that of boys.

When equals, as opposed to asymmetrical pairs such as father–child, engage in simultaneous speech, then such linguistic behaviour is likely to symbolise solidarity and cooperation rather than dominance (see section 6.5). In his study of the gender politics of an elementary school classroom in San Diego, California, Jurgen Streeck (1986) describes an episode where the girls' ability to talk in unison becomes a powerful strategy for demonstrating to the boys the unity of the girls' coalition.

(1)   [The teacher has given the group a task to do]

    Leola: I know y-you gotta make some wo:rds out of these

    Wallace: you don't

    { *Leola*:   yes ⌈you do
    { *Wallace*:   ⌊you don't

    { *Leola*:   you see, here it s ⌈ay–   how man–
    { *Carolyn*:   ⌊it say–

    { *Leola*:   ⌈how many words can you make out of those
    { *Carolyn*: ⌊how many words can you make out of those

    { *Leola*:   five letters
    { *Carolyn*: five letters

Given that talk in unison is not easy to accomplish, we have to admire the girls' interactive skills, which clearly prefigure women's later skills in contrapuntal talk.

Question-and-answer sequences are the focus of Hasan and Cloran's (1990) research on mother–child interaction. They studied twenty-four Australian mother–child dyads and found that the semantic features of question-and-answer sequences between mother and child differed depending on the social class of the family and the gender of the child.[3] There was overlap between patterns typical of mother–daughter dyads and middle-class dyads, an overlap we have remarked on before (see sections 4.4.3 and 7.2).

Politeness is another dimension of communicative competence where we find gender differences (see section 6.3). Research on child language has concentrated on the way parents teach polite language, for example, formulae like greetings and *thank you*. Gleason (1980) studied parents and children in both natural and laboratory settings. She was interested in finding out how much *explicit* teaching of such formulae goes on. She found parents very consistent in prompting their children to respond with socially appropriate items, particularly *thank you*. Parents treated girls and boys similarly, but provided different models: the mothers used far more polite speech than the fathers. Thus, while girls and boys are both urged to use polite forms, the children observe that it is predominantly adult females who use them themselves. The one significant difference observed of the children was that the boys were more likely than the girls to greet the researcher spontaneously (41 per cent : 18 per cent). This may also result from the children's observation of adults: adult male speakers tend to take the initiative in conversation.

Politeness is a relevant dimension for the speech act of requesting. A request may vary from the blunt imperative *Give me a pound* to the more polite (because sensitive to the face needs of the addressee – see section 6.3) *Would you lend me a pound?* Walters (1981) observed the requests of thirty-two bilingual children in four different contexts. He found no significant differences in terms of speaker's gender, but the gender of the addressee was significantly correlated with the politeness of the request. The children in the study were more polite when the addressee was female, and less polite when the addressee was male.

It seems that adult interaction with girls and boys may be significantly affected by *context*. In a long-term study of children in Bristol, Wells (1979) examined all conversations occurring when the children were 3¼ years old, and categorised them according to who initiated them (the child or the adult) and according to the context (mealtime, watching television, playing with another child, etc.). 30 per cent of conversation sequences were initiated by an adult (usually the mother), and an analysis of these revealed significant differences in the context in which adults addressed girls or boys. Table 7.2 gives the figures. This table shows that over half the sequences initiated with girls were in helping or non-play contexts – a ratio of 2:1 compared with the boys. Sequences initiated with boys, on the other hand, were overwhelmingly in the context of play. 'This suggests that adults emphasize more useful and domestic activities in their interaction with girls, whilst the emphasis with boys is towards a more free-ranging, exploratory manipulation of the physical environment' (Wells 1979: 392).

Table 7.2: Proportions of conversations initiated by adults with girls and boys in different contexts (based on Wells 1979: 391)

	Girls (%)	Boys (%)
Helping/non-play activity	56.8	28.8
Talking and reading	19.0	22.5
Playing with adult	5.2	18.1
Dressing, meals, toileting	12.1	14.4
Playing alone	3.4	8.1
Watching TV	0.9	5.4
Playing with another child	2.6	2.7
Total	100	100

Children are acquiring not only gender-appropriate behaviour, but also a knowledge of the folklinguistic beliefs of our society. At what age do children learn that in our culture swearing, for example, is considered 'masculine'? Edelsky (1976) tested this by selecting twelve language variables conventionally associated with 'women's language' or with 'men's language' and presenting them, embedded in utterances, to adult and child judges. The judges were asked to rate each sentence as probably made by a woman, probably made by a man, or no preference. Her child judges (aged 7, 9 and 12 years) demonstrated a growing ability to recognise certain linguistic forms as appropriate to speakers of a particular gender. At 7 years, only two variables get a consistent response: *adorable* is judged to be female, and *Damn it!* is judged to be male. At 9 years, this has increased to eight variables: *adorable, oh dear, my goodness, won't you please* are judged to be female, *and damn it!, damn* + adjective, *I'll be damned* are judged to be male (tag questions get a neutral response). At 12 years, the child judges agree on assigning every one of the twelve variables to one sex or the other: tag questions, *so, very, just* are added to the female list, and commands to the male list.

We can see that children are gradually acquiring a knowledge of adult norms, and internalising the folklinguistic beliefs of our society (the fact that some of these beliefs are false – see section 6.2 – is irrelevant). Edelsky gives a more delicate analysis of her findings to show that there are two clear patterns of acquisition. Variables in her first group – *adorable, oh dear, my goodness, so, just*, tag questions – show a steady increase with age in the number of people able to interpret them as being appropriate to a particular sex. Variables in the second group – *I'll be damned, damn* + adjective, *damnit, won't you please, very*, command as male – show a different pattern: there is an increase in 'correct' answers peaking at 12 years old and decreasing in adulthood. It seems that the variables in this second group are features of language which are explicitly commented on through proverbs or admonishments. Expressions such as 'Little girls don't say that' mean that children are *taught* the gender-appropriateness of some linguistic terms. As happens with other features of child language, when a rule is learned it is frequently over-generalised. Just as children add *-ed* to all verbs to form the past tense, once they've grasped this rule, producing forms like *goed, eated, singed* (even though they earlier used forms like *went, ate, sang* – and of course subsequently do so again), so it seems they over-generalise the rule for gender-appropriate language and treat such differences as *gender-exclusive* rather than *gender-preferential*. As a result, they have to modify their rules later to conform to adult norms.

7.3.3 Subculture and Conversational Style

The focus of much recent work on children's communicative competence is child–child talk rather than adult–child talk. It is now widely accepted that the peer group is of vital importance in a child's sociolinguistic development. Girls and boys tend to play in same-sex groups; gender is the organising principle that structures their activities. Streeck, for example, describes the behaviour of the children he observed in primary school: the girls and the boys huddled on opposite sides of the table, their posture and position clearly signifying two separate camps; when joint activity was required, talk between the two groups was antagonistic (Streeck 1986).

One of the chief reasons that girls and boys develop different styles of talk is that the all-girls and all-boys groups to which they belong interact in vastly different ways. Boys play in larger, more hierarchical groups, while girls play in small groups, often in pairs. Boys' friendships tend to be based on joint *activity*, while girls' friendships are based on *talk*. In their seminal article on gender-specific subcultures, Daniel Maltz and Ruth Borker (1982) argue that girls learn to do three things with words:

1. to create and maintain relationships of closeness and equality
2. to criticise others in acceptable ways
3. to interpret accurately the speech of other girls.

Boys, on the other hand, learn to do the following when they speak:

1. to assert a position of dominance
2. to attract and maintain an audience
3. to assert themselves when another speaker has the floor.

Maltz and Borker (1982) characterise girls' talk as **collaboration-oriented**, boys' talk as **competition-oriented**.

These gender-specific patterns of interaction develop very early. Girls and boys deal with conflict, for example, in very different ways. In a study of quarrels between children aged 5–7, Miller et al (1986) found that boys used a more heavy-handed style, their priority being to get their own way, while girls used more mitigating strategies (such as compromise, evasion or acquiescence) and were more concerned to maintain interpersonal harmony. Boys were more likely to resort to physical force to resolve conflicts. Similar findings emerged from a study of talk among 3-year-old friends in same-sex triads, carried out by Amy Sheldon (1990). She analyses in detail two disputes over a plastic pickle which arose when the children were playing in the home corner (with a toy cooker, pots and pans, a sink, and plastic items of food). One of the disputes occurred in a group of girls, the other in a group of boys. The girls succeeded in negotiating a resolution and maintained interconnectedness among members of the group. They also sustained their fantasy play, pretending to prepare food for the dolls. The boys, by contrast, adopted a more adversarial style, and since neither of the main protagonists was prepared to give in, the conflict escalated (and lasted considerably longer than the girls': 5 minutes compared to 1 minute 45 seconds for the girls). Moreover, this conflict disrupted the boys' fantasy play.

Disputes between boys at nursery school in Italy (Corsaro and Rizzo 1990) deal not only with issues of ownership and protection of territory, but also of who is 'il capo', the boss. In the following example, Matteo and Luigi are making a space ship; Nino approaches and tries to join in.

(2) *Nino*:   Anch'io posso?
              I can also?
    Luigi: si, puoi giocare
              yes, you can play
    Matteo: no, io sono il capo
              no, I'm the boss
    Nino: si, e vero
              yes, it's true
    Luigi (to Matteo):   Lui – puo giocare?
                           him – can he play?
    (Nino reaches over and picks up some building materials near
    Matteo)
    Matteo: no non puoi, ma, non puoi!
              no you can't, but, you can't!

Girls in this nursery school also get involved in disputes over
ownership and in excluding third parties from their play, but they
demonstrate an ability to work *together* to achieve their aims. For
example, in one incident observed by the researcher, Rosa and
Grazia work as a team to get a piece of building material back from
an intruder, Sara.

Goodwin's research on Black children's street play has been described
in some detail (p. 124). Analysis of the way arguments among the
children were structured shows that girls and boys use many common
strategies (Goodwin and Goodwin 1987). They organise their talk to
emphasise disagreement or opposition. This is true both of same-sex
and mixed talk.

(3) [talking about Sharon's hair]
    Eddie: wet it!
    Sharon: no, I don't *wanna* wet it
(4) [talking about slings]
    Chopper: I don't want these big thick ones
    Michael: you is crazy boy. I swear to god. You need that –
              thick like that.

However, there was one strategy which was used only by the girls,
labelled 'he-said-she-said'. This strategy only indirectly challenges
another participant, and opens the dispute to a wider group
of participants. Examples (5) and (6) are typical he-said-she-said
accusations:

(5) *Darlene*:   and *Step*hen said that *you* said that *I* was showin off
               just because I had that *blouse* on

159

(6) *Pam*:   Terri said you said that . I wasn't gonna go around
              *Pop*lar no more

Framing accusations in this way allows both the accuser and the accused to save face. The accuser focuses attention on somebody not present (Stephen in example (5); Terri in example (6)). The accused can deny responsibility (*I ain't say anything*), or can blame someone else (*that was Vincent said*), or can blame the third party referred to by the accuser (*well I know that they telling a lie cuz I know I ain't say nothin about you*). The he-said-she-said strategy allows for much more complex talk, involving many speakers and a longer time-span, than the two-party adversarial disputes typical of all-boy and of mixed talk.

Studies of older *male* children have found that most conflict exchanges are not resolved. In fact, resolution does not seem to be a primary goal. Some conflict is highly ritualised: what is most important is the display of verbal skill. The following example comes from Labov's famous study of pre-adolescent and adolescent boys in Harlem (Labov 1972b).

(7) C1:   your mother got on sneakers!
    C2:   your mother wear high-heeled sneakers to church!
    C3:   your mother wear high-heeled sneakers to come out
          and play on the basketball court!

A second function of the exchange of ritual insults such as these is to create and maintain status differences among the boys. Girls are far less likely to engage in ritual exchanges of this kind (see Goodwin 1980). When they do, they seem more concerned with establishing normative behaviour than with status distinctions. Girls aged 10–14 were observed by Donna Eder (1990); in their conflicts they focused on resolving issues such as what does it mean to be someone's best friend, or what constitutes flirting. The trick is to respond to insults with a clever remark or a counter-insult, and not to take them seriously. The girls show some skill at defending themselves against insults from each other, but at other times their inability to joke about certain topics shows how significant such issues are for them.

Goodwin's work on directives has been described in 6.2.2. She showed how boys' strategies for getting someone to do something reinforce the hierarchical organisation of the boys' group. Dominant members use bare imperatives (*Gimme the pliers*), while subordinate members use mitigated requests (*can I be on your side Michael?*). Girls prefer to use forms such as *let's* which minimise status differences between participants and which emphasise joint action. Jacqueline Sachs (1987) looked at similar strategies in the talk of much younger children in a pre-school playgroup. Same-sex dyads were videotaped while they played at doctor-and-patient. Sachs analysed the use of 'Obliges', a category wider than directives which includes any utterance that demands a response from the addressee. The following are different sorts of Obliges:

1. imperatives (a) positive, e.g. *bring her to the hospital*
   (b) negative, e.g. *don't touch it*
2. declarative directive, e.g. *you have to push it*
3. pretend directive, e.g. *pretend you had a bad cut*
4. question directive, e.g. *will you be the patient?*
5. tag question, e.g. *that's your bed, right?*
6. joint directive, e.g. *now we'll cover him up*
7. state question, e.g. *are you sick?*
8. information question, e.g. *what does she need now?*
9. attention-getting device, e.g. *lookit*

Sachs used as her data the fantasy play of four 5-year-old girl dyads and four 5-year-old boy dyads. She found that girls and boys used roughly the same number of Obliges, but they varied significantly in terms of which type they preferred. Table 7.3 gives the results.

Table 7.3: Distribution of Obliges by category and gender (Sachs 1987: 182)

Category	Girls (%)	Boys (%)
Imperative	12	36
Declarative directive	5	6
Pretend directive	11	4
Question directive	2	0
Tag question	35	16
Joint directive	15	3
State question	2	11
Information question	16	22
Attentional device	2	2
Total	100	100

Notice the boys' preference for imperative forms, and the girls' for tag questions. Overall, the girls preferred more mitigated strategies than the boys: 65 per cent of the girls' Obliges were mitigated, compared with only 34 per cent of the boys'. These findings are summarised in Table 7.4. The girls softened their Obliges, and seemed more concerned to include the other child in planning what they were going to play.

Table 7.4: Distribution of mitigated and unmitigated Obliges (Sachs 1987: 183)

Category	Girls (%)	Boys (%)
Mitigated	65	34
Unmitigated	17	42
Other	18	24

The question of topic is addressed in Haas's (1978) study of child language. Adelaide Haas analysed the speech of 4-, 8- and 12-year-old children in same-sex and mixed-sex pairs. In same-sex pairs, the main difference between girls and boys was that boys talked significantly more about sports and location, while girls talked significantly more about school, identity, wishes and needs. Haas's comparison of mixed-sex pairs also found a difference related to topic – the subject of sport was significantly associated with boy speakers. Boys also used more sound effects (e.g. *brrmm brrmm goes the car*) and more direct requests. The girls laughed more and used more compliant forms (e.g. *okay that's a good idea*). The girls' use of laughter was far more prominent in their interaction with boys than in same-sex interaction – they laughed only half as much when talking to each other. Haas comments that boys seemed to be the initiators of humour, and laughter was the girls' response to this. Laughter may also be seen as appropriately deferential behaviour by the girls, and therefore occurs more with the boys.[4] Both girls and boys adapted their linguistic behaviour when in mixed pairs, but girls accommodated to boys more than vice versa.

Tannen (1990a; 1990b) analysed the conversation of pairs of best friends (conversations which had been video-recorded for research purposes by a psychologist, Bruce Dorval). These children were asked by the researcher to talk about something serious or intimate, and were then left alone in front of a video camera. The youngest boys (8 years old) squirmed in their chairs, kicked their feet, made faces at each other and at the camera. Their conversation jumps from topic to topic, and consists of very short turns. They rebel against the researcher's instructions: they tell jokes, fool around in front of the camera, and conduct mock interviews. The following extract is typical of their conversation:[5]

(8) *Sam*: did you see Star Wars
    (0.8)
    Jeff: no, hey, guess *what?* (1.1) ahm=
    Sam: =you have HBO? (0.6) do you?=
    Jeff: =no [shakes head]
    (0.4)
    Sam: neither do we (1.5) you saw Star Track?
    (0.3)
    Jeff: yeah::= [enthused tone, head motion]
    Sam: =I like the part when they um, .hh when they
        ⌐were having that:: battle=
    Jeff: ⌊I, I, I,   =at the en', hah
    (0.5)
    Sam: Un hn
    (0.7)
    Jeff: that's *goo::d*

Girls of the same age carried out the researcher's instructions to the letter, and talked seriously for twenty minutes with no sign of discomfort.

(9) *Ellen*: Remember what when I told you about my uncle?
        He went up the ladder after my grandpa?
        And he fell and um cracked his head open? He's and
        you know what? it still hasn't healed
    Jane: one time, my uncle, he was uh he has like this bull
        ranch? in Millworth?
        and the bull's horns went right through his head
    Ellen: that's serious

Note how Ellen's comment on her friend's anecdote is supportive, and explicitly orients it to the instructions they've been given.

Pairs of male friends at all ages seemed less comfortable with the task assigned to them. They avoided eye contact and sat parallel rather than facing one another. Older pairs were able to sustain topics for longer, but preferred to remain at an abstract level of discussion and avoided personal details. The only pair who became involved in a personal discussion (16 year olds) did not respond to each other's revelation of anxiety or unhappiness with support, but played down the significance of what the other had said.

(10) [talking about who to take to the dance]
    Tim: I don't want to ask Bar– , I just don't feel like

> asking anyone, and I don't know why, and I don't
> want to ask Janet, and I felt so bad when she came
> over and started talking to me last night

(0.1)

Robert: why?

(0.9)

Tim: I don't know, I felt uncomfortable I guess

(2.3)

Robert: I'll never understand that [laughs]

(0.7)

Tim: why?

(1.1)

Robert: ((x)) well I can't seem to just do that, ah, I mean, I
know that's what you do, but I mean, I just could
never do that

The girls, on the other hand, sit closer to each other and look at each
other directly. They talk about serious topics and self-disclose that
about feelings. Even the youngest girls can sustain a topic over several
turns. Individual turns are longer, as the following example shows. It
is taken from the conversation of the pair of 12-year-old friends.

(11) *Susan*: too bad you and Lesley are not good good friends
anymore

Jane: I know. God, it's– she's so *mean* sometimes because
.h I mean– she/jus'gets you sta:rted in something
nice, she says, um, she's so *ni:ce* today, that's why
I wanted to be her best friend, I mean, I wasn't tryin'
to to take her away from you or anything, .h but I
mean she's so ⌈*ni:ce*=

Susan: ⌊*ni:ce*=

Jane: =like I just couldn't (let) her down or anything,
.h an' so I just wanted to BE her friend, I mean–
I wanted to be ⌈her best friend

Susan: ⌊(I know)

Jane: .h and then– what was so sad she just gets mad at
you all of a sudden .h an like if she does somethin
I don't like (0.3) I mean, I jist (0.5) I don't *li:ke* it, I
mean I don't get *ma:d* at her!

(0.7)

Susan: she tries to upset people

(0.5)

Jane: she *doe:s*, and she just sees me crying an everything
(0.5) she just lets me suffer=

Susan: =and she loves it
Jane: I know

Note how the girls work together to try to understand a problem. Their talk involves longer turns than that of boys of the same age, and their turns follow very closely one after the other, with only occasional pauses. Moreover, when a girl told a story like this, her friend invariably responded with concern, rather than belittling the problem (compare Tim and Robert in example 10). The girls' body posture, their patterns of eye contact, and the topics they choose, all emphasise closeness. The boys, on the other hand, choose patterns of physical alignment and eye contact which symbolise separateness, and their choice of impersonal topics and lack of engagement in each other's problems reinforce the impression of separateness.

All the studies referred to in this section demonstrate significant differences in the conversational strategies of girls and boys. Girls prefer a more mitigated style; they use linguistic forms which minimise differences between participants and which are sensitive to speaker's and hearer's face needs. Boys, on the other hand, prefer a more adversarial style and pursue their own agenda without reference to other participants. For boys, winning is all-important. Girls, by contrast, seem aware that where there are winners there are also losers; they prefer jointly negotiated outcomes. However, several of these studies show that, both when interacting with boys, or when taking on roles such as mother in pretend play, girls are perfectly competent at the more adversarial style typical of boys (see Goodwin 1980; 1988; 1990; Maynard 1986; Miller et al 1986; Goodwin and Goodwin 1987; Sheldon 1992). Girls, in other words, can style-shift to suit the sociolinguistic context; boys, on the other hand, tend to be mono-stylistic.

These studies encompass children as young as 3 years old, and include both Black children and white children, working-class children and middle-class children, in both natural and experimental situations. This research is unanimous in showing that the gender-specific subcultures which children belong to generate different linguistic subcultures. These anticipate the gender-differentiated talk of adult women and men.

7.4   Conclusion

As we have seen, various studies show differences in male and female children in a wide range of linguistic forms. What emerges is a picture of girls acquiring linguistic skills at a faster rate than boys (though this superiority is not as marked as was claimed in the past), and acquiring patterns which differentiate them from boys. In the past, researchers believed that such differences arose from innate biological differences, but now differences in linguistic usage are explained by differences in the linguistic environment of girls and boys. Work on the development of differential communicative competence illustrates particularly clearly the crucial role played by environmental factors.

Language is an important part of the socialisation process, and children are socialised into culturally approved gender roles largely through language. Learning to be male or female in our society means among other things learning to use gender-appropriate language. This survey of work on children's acquisition of language suggests that socialisation is achieved in a variety of ways:

1. through explicit comment on certain aspects of linguistic behaviour (e.g. swearing, taboo language, verbosity, politeness);
2. through adults providing different linguistic models for children to identify with (see also Chapters 4, 5 and 6);
3. through adults talking to children differently depending on the sex of the child (e.g. adults are more likely to interrupt girls, and lisp more when talking to little girls);
4. through adults having different preconceptions of male and female children (e.g. adults expect female infants to be more verbally able than male infants);
5. through adults responding differently to girls and boys using the same linguistic strategy (e.g. boys arguing or talking assertively are more likely to get a positive response than girls);
6. perhaps most importantly, through children's participation in gender-specific subcultures which create and maintain distinct male and female styles of interaction.

It is often suggested that child language may be the locus of linguistic change: that is, a comparison of the variety of language acquired by children with the variety used by adults of the same ethnic group, social class, etc. will reveal linguistic change in progress. I shall turn now from this survey of child language and the acquisition of gender-preferential differences to an examination of the role these gender differences play in the process of linguistic change.

Notes

1   Other good work using this framework includes Ochs and Schieffelin 1979; McTear 1985; Foster 1990; Schieffelin 1990.
2   Both Romaine and Macaulay adopted scoring procedures which represent RP with a score of 0.
3   Hasan and Cloran (1990) assigned class position according to the autonomy experienced by the main breadwinner of the family in his (*sic*) profession (all main breadwinners in the sample were male). Families were assigned to one of two groups: LAP (Lower Autonomy Profession) or HAP (Higher Autonomy Profession).
4   See Pizzini (1991) for an analysis of the way humour is used to reinforce existing power relationships between women and men in the obstetrical/gynaecological setting.
5   Examples (8), (10) and (11) are taken from transcripts given in the Appendix of Dorval (1990). Example (9) comes from Tannen (1990a).

CHAPTER 8

The role of gender differences in linguistic change

8.1 Introduction

One of the linguistic consequences of gender differentiation in language seems to be linguistic change. Certainly, differences in women's and men's language are regularly associated with changes in language.

Yet it is only recently that sociolinguistic factors have been taken into consideration by linguists studying language change. Linguists have traditionally preferred to treat language as a closed system which could be studied without reference to 'external' factors. Linguistic study, in other words, has until recently been a-social. The neogrammarians – nineteenth-century comparative philologists – argued that linguistic change was caused by the twin mechanisms of sound change and analogy: sound change altered the system, and analogy made the system regular again. The functionalists on the other hand – linguists who treated the notion of function as central – argued that change occurs because of the opposing demands of the need to communicate and the desire to make as little effort as possible.

The most striking thing about this debate is the way it *reifies* language, that is, treats language as a *thing*, existing in its own right. But language does not exist apart from language users; speech does not exist independently of speakers. So we need to make a distinction between linguistic change, which is change in the language system, and speaker innovation, which describes the role played by speakers in initiating linguistic change (for an illuminating discussion of this distinction, see Milroy and Milroy 1985). The study of linguistic change has a long history, but our understanding of the role played by individual speakers is still in its infancy.

Linguistic change occurs in the context of linguistic heterogeneity. Linguistic variation exists in all known societies: it distinguishes the speech of different social groups (**social variation**), and it distinguishes the speech of a given individual in different contexts (**stylistic variation**). Linguistic change can be said to have taken place when a new linguistic form, used by some sub-group within a speech community, is adopted by other members of that community and accepted as the norm. Our understanding of the interaction of groups within society is still poor, but we are beginning to see that the linguistic variation which characterises the differentiation of social groups is crucially associated with the rise and fall of linguistic forms.

In this book, I have focused on the linguistic variation associated with speaker's gender. Sociolinguistic research is beginning to improve our understanding of linguistic change, and it now seems that gender differentiation in speech plays an important role in the mechanism of linguistic change. More accurately, the gender of the speaker plays a significant part in innovation – sometimes women and sometimes men are said to be the group which typically initiates change. This debate parallels that described earlier in dialectology (section 3.5.1) on whether women or men are more conservative linguistically. I shall return to this issue later. In this chapter I shall look at work demonstrating (or claiming to demonstrate) a link between gender differences in language and linguistic change. I shall look first at earlier (dialectological) work, and then, in greater detail, at some recent sociolinguistic studies. In this latter section I shall refer back to studies already discussed in Chapters 4 and 5.

8.2 Dialectological Evidence

Dialectologists discussed linguistic change in the communities they studied, sometimes in terms of changing patterns of bilingualism, sometimes in terms of changes in vocabulary or pronunciation within one language system. Since they were often trying to make a record of rural dialects before they died out, they were very aware that linguistic change was taking place, and their comments on the social background of such changes are of great interest.

Auguste Brun, a specialist in the language known as Provençal, discusses the relative roles of Provençal and French in one particular community (Brun 1946). He observes that older people (over 50) speak mainly Provençal, as do younger men, but *women* under 45 speak mainly French. He claims that younger women do not speak Provençal at all among themselves ('je n'ai jamais entendu une phrase de provençal dans une groupe de jeunes filles ou de jeunes femmes'), nor do they speak Provençal to their children, but only occasionally to the old people. As a result, children of both sexes speak French: they don't speak Provençal to each other or to adults (Brun, as quoted in Pop 1950: 281). If Brun's observations are accurate, we see that in three generations this community has switched from being bilingual but mainly Provençal-speaking to being bilingual but mainly French-speaking, with the use of Provençal diminishing rapidly. Women are portrayed as having a crucial role, since it is they and not the men who adopt French as their main language, and they who use it when bringing up the next generation. At all events, the difference between male and female usage is clearly a crucial factor in the linguistic change described here.

Pée's (1946) account of changing linguistic usage in Flanders is interesting because he is able to give the background to the change described. The older generation, according to Pée, speak patois (varieties of Flemish); Pée found the women particularly good as informants because of their lack of mobility – they hardly ever left their village and so had little contact with other linguistic varieties. But the First World War resulted in an improved standard of living for many peasants, some of whom sent their daughters to French boarding schools. These girls became 'francisées' (Frenchified/Francophile) and insisted on speaking French instead of Flemish when they returned home. Only those who then worked on the land reverted to Flemish. Pée reports that the girls back from boarding school asked for the sermon at least to be in French at Mass on a Sunday. Clearly the girls in this community were initiating change, and the balance between Flemish and French was changing as a result of their influence.

Gilliéron studied a monolingual French community, and he comments on changes taking place in vocabulary there. He quotes the Torgon peasant who told him: 'In the past the room where we are was called *le pailé*, now we call it *la tsābra*, and my wife, who wants to be more refined than us, calls it *kabiné*'.[1] This remark by one of Gilliéron's informants reveals three stages in the linguistic evolution of a lexical item: an old form – *pailé*; a current form – *tsabra*; and a new advanced form – *kabiné*. It is women again who are innovating, using the most advanced form (for status reasons, according to the peasant).

Gauchat's (1905) study of the dialect of Charmey, a remote village in Switzerland, shows a great sensitivity to the social context in which linguistic evolution takes place. He observed that the old inhabitants of the village used forms which were phonetically older than those beginning to be used by the young people. He noted that among people of the same age, the women's pronunciation was more advanced. In other words, there were gender differences as well as age differences in the language of the community (he had chosen Charmey to try to avoid linguistic variation!). He argues that changes have occurred in French because of women's innovativeness ('women welcome every linguistic novelty with open arms')[2] and that these changes are disseminated by women in their role as mothers: 'Once the woman has accepted the innovation, it is from *her* language that this will pass into the language of the young, because children tend to follow their mother's example'.[3] As this extract shows, Gauchat was one of those dialectologists who believed that women were an innovatory rather than a conservative force. It is clearly a logical extension of this position to argue that women, in their role as primary caretakers of children, initiate linguistic change. I shall pursue this argument in section 8.4.

As these four examples from dialectology show, women are frequently portrayed as playing a crucial role in initiating and furthering linguistic change. However, as the following sociolinguistic examples will demonstrate, this is an over-simplistic picture, as some innovations are clearly associated with male rather than with female speakers.

8.3 Sociolinguistic Studies Showing Change in Progress

Linguists used to think that linguistic change was something which could not be observed: 'such observation . . . is inconceivable' (Bloomfield 1933: 347). This misconception was partly the result of de Saussure's division of linguistic study into **synchronic** and **diachronic**: synchronic study took language at one point in time, while diachronic study took language *through* time, comparing language at different points in time to see how it changed. The study of change, then, was firmly linked with **diachronic** linguistics. It is only with the advent of sociolinguistics, specifically with the work of William Labov, that linguists have demonstrated that linguistic change is amenable to analysis. Quantitative studies, analysing synchronic variation in language, have the capacity to reveal change in progress.

The best-known diagram of change in progress is Labov's diagram for post-vocalic (r) in New York City which is reproduced in Figure 8.1. I have already discussed this briefly in section 4.2.2. Note again

Figure 8.1 Social stratification of a linguistic variable undergoing change – post-vocalic (r) in New York City (Labov 1972a: 114)

the hypercorrect pattern of the lower middle class, with very low scores for (r) usage in Casual Speech, rising to extremely high scores (higher than the upper middle class) in the two most formal styles. The crossover pattern this produces is said by Labov to be typical of a variable undergoing change. 'The hypercorrect behaviour of the lower middle class is seen as a synchronic indicator of linguistic change in progress' (Labov 1972a: 115).

In his earlier work, Labov reflected the prevailing view that women were innovators. He included a section on 'The Role of Women' in a chapter of his book *Sociolinguistic Patterns* (Labov 1972a: 301–4), where he claimed that women played an important part in linguistic change. However, more recently he has modified his views, and now argues that change is precipitated by linguistic differences between men and women rather than being associated with one particular gender. As we shall see, this latter view accords far better with his own findings.

I shall therefore look first at the work of Labov himself in this field, both his analysis of the variable (a) in New York City and his study of centralised diphthongs on Martha's Vineyard. I shall then re-examine the work of Trudgill in Norwich and Milroy in Belfast (as discussed in Chapters 4 and 5), paying particular attention this time to the relationship between gender differences in language and linguistic change. Finally, we shall look at two pieces of research from further afield: Gal's study of a bilingual community in Austria, and Nichols' study of linguistic patterns in South Carolina.

8.3.1 New York City and Martha's Vineyard

Many of the variables studied by Labov in New York City were in the process of change, and he was able to show significant gender differences in their usage. With the variable (a)[4] (the short vowel found in words like *bag, ham, cab*), for example, Labov found that men's pronunciation varied very little between formal and less formal contexts, while women's pronunciation varied a great deal. Style-shifting, then, was typical of female speakers. Moreover, it was women rather than men who were using the new advanced forms [i <:ə] and [e <:ə] in casual speech; women, in other words, are leading in the raising of this vowel and are thus initiating change.

It seems then that linguistic change in New York City is crucially associated with women. However, in his work on Martha's Vineyard (an island off the coast of Massachusetts), Labov found a different pattern: men, not women, were initiating change. The two variables investigated by Labov were both diphthongs: (aw) as in *house*, and (ay) as in *white* (diphthongs are glides from one vowel to another vowel). In these two diphthongs, the initial element [a] was becoming centralised to something like [ə] in the speech of many of the people on the island. In other words [au] was shifting towards [əu], and [ai] towards [əi].

Labov conducted interviews with sixty-nine informants; he included only members of the permanent population and excluded the summer visitors. He realised that there was no conscious awareness among the islanders that these sounds were fluctuating, since he found no *stylistic* variation – individuals' pronunciation of the diphthongs was consistent in different styles of speech. He established that the centralised variants were used mostly by *men* (specifically fishermen) aged between 31 and 45 from an area at the western end of the island called Chilmark. It seems that the centralised diphthongs were used by the Chilmark fishermen as a sign of solidarity; use of these variants symbolised their identification with the island and its values, and their rejection of the summer visitors.

These centralised diphthongs are actually very old. They were conservative features of the fishermen's speech which are now spreading to the speech of other islanders. In other words, an older form, which was in the process of dying out, has now become a significant feature of the island phonology; a linguistic change has reversed direction.

What quantitative studies such as this reveal is **change in apparent time,** that is fluctuating usage at one particular point in time. By consulting the Linguistic Atlas of New England and other earlier surveys of pronunciation in this region, Labov was able to confirm that this is actually a **change in real time** (diachronic change). As we shall see, this practice of testing findings against earlier historical records is common in sociolinguistic work charting change in progress.

Linguistic change on Martha's Vineyard, then, has been initiated by a group of *male* speakers, the Chilmark fishermen. Their speech, with its centralised diphthongs, was once seen as old-fashioned, but at some stage, as local feeling grew stronger in the face of the invading 'outsider' (the summer visitors), this type of speech became symbolic of belonging to the island, of being an 'insider'. Note that it is still primarily male speakers who use these centralised diphthongs. Thus the change begins with, and is imitated by, men.

Labov's New York survey shows *women* in the vanguard of linguistic change, while the study of Martha's Vineyard reveals a linguistic change in progress which originated with *male* speakers. As we shall see in the following sections, these two contrasting patterns are found in other studies of linguistic change in progress.

8.3.2 Norwich

Some of the variables investigated by Trudgill in Norwich displayed irregularities of class or style variation which indicated that change was taking place. I shall look at two of these, where gender as well as class and style variation is involved.

The variable (e) displays a very unusual pattern of class differentiation, as can be seen in Figure 8.2. Index scores measure the centralisation of the vowel in words like *tell, well, better*. A score of 200 represents consistent RP pronunciation: [ɛ]; a score of 0 represents consistent non-standard pronunciation: [ʌ].[5] There are two points to notice here. First, in Casual Style the *upper* working-class group has a *lower* score than the other working-class groups, that is upper-working-class speakers use more of the non-standard centralised variant. Second, in *all* styles the upper- and middle-working-class groups use more of the non-standard variant than the lower working class. So while the stratification of the middle class as a whole and the working class as a whole is as expected, the pattern of groups *within*

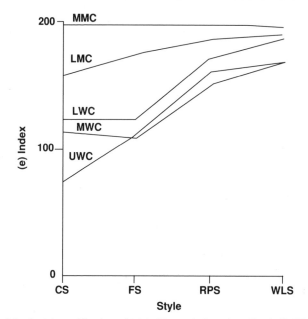

Figure 8.2 Social stratification of (e) in Norwich (based on Trudgill 1974a: 105)

the working class is upside down, with the upper working class using the highest proportion of non-standard variants.

Trudgill observes that centralisation of (e) is increasing in Norwich, and this change is being innovated by the upper working class. He notes that the use of centralised variants is associated not only with upper-working-class speakers but also with *male* speakers under 30. Younger speakers have much lower scores than older speakers, and male speakers have lower scores than female speakers. In the youngest age group studied by Trudgill (10–19), male and female speakers differed significantly: the average score for the young male speakers was 0 indicating consistent use of the centralised vowel.

We can summarise these findings by saying that the variable (e) in Norwich is undergoing change, this change is manifest in the irregular pattern of class stratification, and the change is being innovated by young *male* upper-working-class speakers in particular.

The variable (o), the vowel occurring in words like *top, fog, lorry*, is also involved in change. Figure 8.3 gives the results for class, gender and style variation: index scores measure the degree of lip-rounding in the pronunciation of the vowel (o). A score of 100 represents

Figure 8.3 Stratification of (o) in Norwich by social class and gender (based on Trudgill 1972: 189)

consistent RP pronunciation: [ɒ]; a score of 0 represents consistent non-standard pronunciation [ɑ].[5] Figure 8.3 reveals a striking irregularity in the stratification of speakers. Middle-class women use a virtually consistent RP pronunciation of (o); they score higher than middle-class men in all styles. Working-class women, on the other hand, consistently score *lower* than working-class men; in all styles the diagram shows that working-class women used a higher proportion of the non-standard variant [ɑ]. What is the explanation for this unusual pattern? (compare it with the expected pattern shown in Figure 4.5, p. 68). It seems that working-class *men* are innovating with the pronunciation [ɒ], imitating local Suffolk working-class speech (Norfolk speech has traditionally used the unrounded vowel [ɑ]). This change happens to coincide with the standard (RP) form, which is used predominantly by middle-class *women*. Thus, middle-class women are conforming to the prestige norm, while working-class women are conforming to an older vernacular norm; working-class men, however, are innovating with a new vernacular norm. The coincidence of this Suffolk vernacular form with the prestige form means that working-class men's scores are closer to those of the middle class. With this variable, it is the irregularity in the pattern of gender differentiation which signals change in progress.

8.3.3 Belfast

Several of the variables studied by the Milroys in Belfast are in the process of change. I shall look at two of them – (ε) and (a) – since in both cases linguistic change is associated with gender-differentiated usage.

The variable (ε) occurs in words like *step, peck, bet,* and variants range from [a] to [ẹ]. The variable is undergoing raising, and the new prestigious raised variants of (ε) are being introduced by women, particularly younger women. Figure 8.4 shows the distribution of (ε) in 'short' phonetic environments, that is, where the vowel is followed by a voiceless stop: [p, t, k].

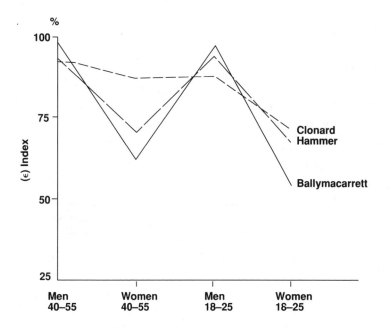

Figure 8.4 The distribution of (ε) by age, gender and area in Belfast (Milroy and Milroy 1978: 30)

Note the clear gender-differentiation involved in the use of this variable; this is particularly marked in Ballymacarrett. For many male speakers, the low short variant [a] or [æ] is categorical before voiceless stops. Both older and younger men in Ballymacarrett score 100, that is, use the low short variant consistently. The younger women in all three communities have much lower scores than the men, reflecting their preference for raised variants. Comparison with historical records leads the Milroys to conclude that the raising of (ɛ) is a change in real time. Change is being initiated by younger female speakers who are introducing a new high-status variant into inner-city Belfast.

The variable (a) is also undergoing change, but here the pattern is different. Backing of (a) is in progress, and backed variants are typical of Ballymacarrett speakers and typical of *male* speakers. In other words, men are more likely than women to pronounce *man* [mɔ.ən]. Figure 8.5 shows the distribution of (a) in the three communities.

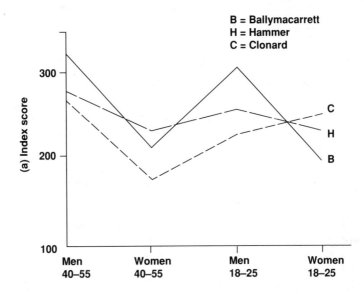

Figure 8.5 The distribution of (a) by age, gender and area in Belfast (Milroy 1980: 124)

The Milroys' data enable us to see how a changing pattern of pronunciation – backing of (a) – is introduced into working-class speech by the Ballymacarrett men (note that Ballymacarrett is a stable and prestigious community.) This new vernacular variant is then adopted by another sub-group, the Clonard young women. As Figure 8.5 shows, young women in the Clonard score higher than the young men of their community and also higher than the Ballymacarrett young women. This produces the crossover pattern typical of a linguistic change in progress. The young Clonard women, then, are introducing into their own community a variant of (a) borrowed from a higher ranking community. (In Belfast, Protestant ranks higher than Catholic.) Backing of (a) is spreading from East to West Belfast, from a high-ranking to a low-ranking working-class community.

By consulting early records of Belfast pronunciation (Patterson 1860), the Milroys have established that (a) was not normally backed in 1860. Thus we have evidence, in both apparent and real time, that a linguistic change is taking place, and again we find that the variable in question is involved in gender differentiation. It seems that backing of (a) has the status of a vernacular norm and is typical of speakers belonging to close-knit working-class groups; the young Clonard women belong, like the Ballymacarrett men, to dense, multiplex networks. While unemployment in the Hammer has led to a breakdown of networks and a corresponding blurring of gender differences, male unemployment in the Clonard has led to the younger women seeking work, finding work together, and developing a pattern of social interaction similar to the traditional pattern for working-class *men*. This change in social pattern has resulted in a changing *linguistic* pattern for the Clonard community, with the young women acting as innovators. As we can see, changes in network structure can be an important social mechanism of linguistic change.

I have described two variables in the process of change in inner-city Belfast. Prestigious raised variants of (ɛ) are being introduced into Belfast speech by younger *women*, while backing of (a) has been introduced by Ballymacarrett *men* and this new vernacular norm is now being adopted by the young Clonard women.

8.3.4 *Oberwart, Austria*

Susan Gal (1978; 1979) investigated language shift in the bilingual town of Oberwart, in eastern Austria, which until 1921 was part of Hungary. In this community a shift is occurring from German-Hungarian bilingualism to the exclusive use of German. Since the Second World War, there has been a change in the connotations of the two languages. Hungarian, the national language until 1921, used to have great prestige as the language of intellectuals and the upper classes, while German used to be a language of outsiders, associated with merchants, bureaucrats, and people from other villages. Now, Hungarian is increasingly associated with peasant status, while knowledge of German is an economic necessity for anyone wanting employment of any kind apart from working on the land. (Since the war, the proportion of adult males working in full-time agriculture has dropped from 100 per cent to 19 per cent.)

Gal carried out a survey to establish patterns of linguistic usage. For example, she asked people which language they would use at the doctor's, in the post office, at work, with their friends, with their

Figure 8.6 Percentage of G and GH language choices of informants with peasant and non-peasant social networks in three age groups (Gal 1978: 10)

brothers and sisters, with their grandparents. She established that the shift from Hungarian to German is being led by the young *women*. Figure 8.6 gives the results of her survey (answers were coded G for German, H for Hungarian, and GH for where people said they could use either language). This figure shows that for men there is a regular pattern: use of G increases as the sample gets younger, but in all three age groups, speakers with peasant networks use more H than speakers with non-peasant networks. For women, the pattern is different. In the older group, there are no women with non-peasant networks, a reflection of women's limited lives before 1945. The middle group of women gives responses which match those of the men; those with peasant networks prefer Hungarian, while those with non-peasant networks increasingly choose German. The youngest group of women is unlike all other groups: first, they use more G and less H than any other group; second, their language choice is not influenced by whether or not they belong to peasant networks.

How do we explain this pattern? Gal argues that the young women's rejection of Hungarian represents a rejection of peasant life. They have observed the lives of their mothers and grandmothers: they have seen that the life of a peasant wife is hard. So they are consciously choosing *not* to marry peasant men (see Table 8.1), and this choice is reflected in their choice of language.

Table 8.1: Endogamous* marriages of all bilingual Oberwarters and bilingual male peasant Oberwarters (Gal 1978: 13)

	Endogamous* marriages of all marriages (%)	Endogamous* marriages of male peasants (%)
1911–40	71	87
1941–60	65	54
1961–72	32	0

Source: Marriage Register, City of Oberwart.

Endogamy means marriage within the tribe.

Ironically, this means that young peasant men have been forced to marry women from other towns and villages, and these women are frequently monolingual German speakers. So the Oberwart women's rejection of peasant life has both a direct *and* an indirect impact on the shift from Hungarian to German.

8.3.5 South Carolina

In her work on the changing speech of South Carolina, Patricia Nichols (1982; 1983) draws attention to the importance of another factor in linguistic change: the differing economic opportunities open to women and men in specific speech communities. She carried out fieldwork in two black communities in South Carolina, one on the mainland and one on a nearby island, in order to investigate the shift from an English creole known as Gullah to a more standard variety of English. The variables she investigated were:

1. the *for-to* complementiser
    e.g. *I come for get my coat*
2. the static-locative preposition *to*
    e.g. *Can we stay to the table?*
3. third person singular pronouns *ee* and *um*
    e.g. *and ee was foggy and they couldn't see but I ain't see she fuh tell um nothing*

Nichols found that the women in her sample did not behave uniformly. As Figure 8.7 shows, older mainland women were the

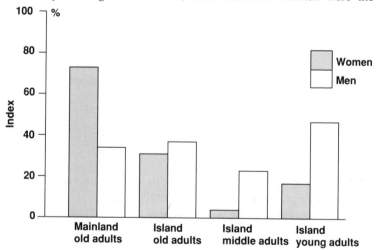

Figure 8.7 The distribution of creole and non-standard grammatical variants by age, gender and area in South Carolina (based on Nichols 1983: 60)

heaviest users of Gullah variants, scoring higher on these than their male contemporaries, but young and middle-aged island women, in complete contrast, were the most advanced in the shift to standard English. Nichols explains this finding in terms of local job opportunities. Men of all ages in the area she studied work in the construction industry, while older women work in the domestic and agricultural jobs to which black women have until recently been confined. None of these groups has much incentive to speak Standard English, and the older women have little opportunity even to encounter Standard English speakers. Given the circumstances of their lives, these women have no reason not to maintain their vernacular. The younger island women, on the other hand, have different work opportunities in white-collar and service jobs. These jobs require Standard English and bring the younger women into contact with Standard English speakers. Thus the younger black women have both the incentive and the opportunity to acquire the standard variety.

8.4 Gender Differentiation and Linguistic Change

The dialectological evidence given in section 8.2 shows women as innovators; the sociolinguistic evidence given in section 8.3 shows both women and men initiating linguistic change. In order to make sense of these two patterns, one involving women as innovators, the other involving men as innovators, we need to distinguish between **conscious** and **unconscious** change, or 'change from above' and 'change from below' as Labov calls them (Labov 1972a). There are some linguistic changes which speakers are conscious of and which are actively encouraged: these tend to be associated with the middle class. There are other changes which go on *below* the level of public consciousness: these tend to be associated with the working class. Women seem to initiate changes above the level of social awareness: such changes tend to be in the direction of the prestige norms. Men, on the other hand, seem to initiate changes below the level of social awareness: such changes tend to be *away from* the accepted norms.

The shift to centralised diphthongs on Martha's Vineyard is a good example of change taking place *below* the level of social awareness. According to Labov, the native Vineyarders are not aware of this feature in their language. As a result, he found no style-shifting associated with the diphthongs; speakers have no control over this feature in their speech and their pronunciation is therefore the same whatever the context. As we have seen, it is *men* who are (unconsciously) initiating and furthering this change in the local language.

Labov's work in New York City revealed several variables where change was taking place *above* the level of consciousness. Figure 8.1 – postvocalic (r) – is a very good example of this. Note the steep slope for all groups: (r) is clearly subject to a great deal of style-shifting, with the lower middle class in particular shifting from low usage of (r) in casual speech to very high usage of (r) in Word List Style. The variable (a) – see section 8.3.1 – is another typical example of change taking place from above the level of consciousness. Here it is women who are revealed as being particularly conscious of the variant, as is shown by the extent of their style-shifting.

In Belfast, female speakers are innovating towards a *prestige* norm with raised variants of (ɛ), while male speakers are responsible for the introduction of a new *vernacular* norm, backing of (a), to the inner city. In Norwich change is taking place in two directions at once, with female speakers innovating towards a prestige norm and male speakers innovating away from the prestige norm. The rural Suffolk vernacular norm which working-class men are taking as their model happens to coincide with the RP norm which female speakers are imitating. This fortuitous coincidence of change from below with change from above means that the shift to the rounded vowel (that is, [ɒ] in place of traditional Norwich [ɑ]] has a good chance of success. In the bilingual community of Oberwart in Austria, where Hungarian has come to symbolise peasant life, it is young women who are leading the switch from Hungarian to the high-prestige language, German. Similarly, in the South Carolina communities studied by Nichols, it is the younger women who are shifting their linguistic usage in the direction of Standard English, away from the local (creole) norms.

Many sociolinguists have argued that linguistic change is associated with women, particularly women of the lower middle class. But as the data presented in this chapter reveal, women are sometimes linguistically innovative, sometimes linguistically conservative. Women, like men, respond to local circumstances: they make linguistic choices in the context of particular speech communities.

It does seem, however, as though women are more sensitive to status-giving prestige norms (whether the prestige norms are those of Standard English or those of a higher-ranked group, as in the case of the Clonard young women imitating the prestigious Ballymacarrett community), while men are more sensitive to vernacular norms, which represent solidarity and values traditionally associated with masculinity. Two factors frequently put forward in the past to 'explain' women's linguistic behaviour were sensitivity and conservatism. (Note that men's language was taken as given and so did not need explaining.) As we have seen, both women and men are linguistically sensitive, but to different models. Women's conservatism is merely the converse of male innovation: when male speakers initiate change, then women speakers can be described as conservative – they conserve older forms. Conversely, when female speakers initiate change, then male speakers can be described as conservative (though conservatism is not often ascribed to men, except in the work of traditional dialectologists). Conservatism and sensitivity are two sides of the same coin, and neither sex has the monopoly of either of them.[6]

The idea that only middle-class women are innovative seems no longer tenable when we observe the Clonard young women in Belfast who are leading the change to a more backed (a) in their community, or the young peasant women in Oberwart who are leading the switch to German, or the young Black women in South Carolina who are shifting towards Standard English.

This may be because of changing structures in society, and the new roles being taken on by women. In Belfast, for example, where male unemployment is now very high in some parts of the city, young women are going out to work and are participating in dense, multiplex social networks similar to those which used to be typical of *men* in the community. In the communities studied by Nichols in South Carolina, younger women have opportunities which older women did not have: they work in service industries or white-collar jobs, and have escaped the domestic and agricultural labour of their mothers' generation. These choices, these changes in life-style, have significant linguistic reflexes.

As I have said, linguistic change can take place only in the context of linguistic variation, and linguistic variation reflects and maintains social variation. Societies vary in all kinds of ways, but male and female roles are distinguished in some way in all known societies. It is not surprising, then, that the linguistic variation arising from socially constructed differences between women and men turns out to have a significant role in facilitating linguistic evolution.

In conclusion, it is not true to say that either women or men are linguistically the innovative sex. As we have seen, some linguistic change is initiated by female speakers and some by male speakers. However, it is true to say that male/female differences in language seem to be intimately involved in the mechanism of linguistic change. This being the case, the study of linguistic change can only benefit from the growing interest in the sociolinguistic analysis of gender differentiation in speech.

Notes

1   'Autrefois la chambre où nous sommes, on la nommait le *pailé*, maintenant nous l'appelons la *tsābra*, et ma femme, qui veut être plus fine que nous, la nomme *kabiné*' (Gilliéron 1880: iv, as quoted in Pop 1950: 180).
2   'les femmes accueillaient . . . avec empressement toute nouveauté linguistique'.
3   'Une fois que la femme a accepté l'innovation, c'est de son langage que celle-ci passera dans le langage de la jeunesse, parce que les enfants suivent plutot l'exemple des femmes' (Gauchat 1905: 218, quoted in Pop 1950: 194).
4   Labov labels this variable (eh).
5   Trudgill actually scores these variables the other way round, with the highest score representing consistent *non*-standard pronunciation, and 0 representing the prestige form. For consistency in this book (see Chapter 4), all figures showing social stratification have been presented in the same way.
6   Eckert (1989) is critical of accounts of gender-based variation which treat gender as a simple binary opposition. In her work on the Northern Cities Chain Shift in the Detroit area (a pattern of vowel shifting involving the fronting of low vowels, and the backing and lowering of mid vowels), she shows how significant for adolescents are the two categories 'Jock' (roughly: middle class, school-focused) and 'Burnout' (working class, focused on the adult community outside the school). Gender is implicated in the linguistic change in progress in Detroit, but Eckert argues strongly for the importance of *intra*-gender variation (female Jocks and female Burnouts, for example, emerge as very different). She urges sociolinguists to bear in mind that gender and other social categories don't necessarily operate as independent variables.

CHAPTER 9

The social consequences of gender differences in language

9.1 Introduction

This chapter will examine the social, as opposed to linguistic, consequences of linguistic differentiation based on gender. First, the problem of miscommunication between women and men will be assessed in the light of current knowledge of interaction patterns. Second, the question of disadvantage will be raised in the context of the differing linguistic behaviour of girls and boys in the classroom. Work on miscommunication in adult conversation tends to take gender differences in language as a given, and concentrates on the specific aspects of conversational interaction where communication between women and men can break down. Studies of classroom interaction, by contrast, tend to be critical of the social pressures which bring about gender differences in language. Many researchers feel that girls are failing to fulfil their potential in school, and that language is one of the contributing factors – they are therefore not content to adopt a different-but-equal stance.

9.2 Miscommunication between Women and Men

There is considerable evidence that the patterns of interaction typical of all-female groups differ from those typical of all-male groups (see sections 6.5 and 7.3.3).[1] It has been argued that these different patterns of interaction lead to miscommunication between the sexes. Some commentators (Maltz and Borker 1982; Tannen 1991) have even gone so far as to describe conversation between women and men as 'cross-cultural' communication. I shall begin by summarising the main characteristics of all-female and all-male talk before identifying and discussing areas of potential miscommunication.

In all-female groups, women adopt paralinguistic strategies which signal involvement: they lean forward, they turn their heads towards each other, they look at each other directly. Men, by contrast, lean back, and often avoid looking at each other. In all-women groups, women often discuss one topic for half an hour or more; they share a great deal of information about themselves and talk about their feelings and their relationships. Men on the other hand jump from one topic to another, vying to tell anecdotes which centre around themes of superiority and aggression. They rarely talk about themselves, but compete to prove themselves better informed about current affairs, travel, sport, etc. The *management* of conversation also differs significantly between women's and men's groups. Women are careful to respect each other's turns and tend to apologise for talking too much. Members of all-women groups are concerned that everyone should participate and dislike any one person dominating conversation. Men in all-men groups, by contrast, compete for dominance and over time establish a reasonably stable hierarchy, with some men dominating conversation and others talking very little. Individual men frequently address the whole group (33 per cent of the time on average, in Aries's (1976) experimental groups), while individual women rarely do (6.5 per cent of the time on average), preferring an interpersonal style involving one-to-one interaction.

Turn-taking patterns in all-male conversation seem to correspond to those predicted by the model developed by Sacks et al (1974) (see Figure 6.1) in that talk is structured by two main rules: (1) one speaker speaks at a time; (2) speaker change recurs. Turn-taking patterns in all-female conversation are far more complex: more than one speaker may speak at a time, with speakers working collaboratively to produce talk.[2]

Maltz and Borker (1982) have analysed some of the ways in which these differences could cause miscommunication in mixed conversations. They argue very strongly that women and men develop different rules for engaging in, and interpreting, friendly conversation, and that these rules are learned in same-sex peer groups during childhood and adolescence (see section 7.3.3 for extended discussion of these ideas). Here I shall look at eight problem areas, elaborating on them in the light of earlier discussion.[3]

9.2.1 Minimal Responses

Women use frequent and well-placed minimal responses in conversation. For women, the use of forms like *yeah* and *mhm* means 'I'm listening and I support your right to hold the floor'. Men use minimal responses less frequently than women. For men, these forms seem to mean something more like 'I agree with you'. The different use and interpretation of minimal responses can lead to serious miscommunication. First, men think women are agreeing with them, and are irritated when this turns out not to be the case. Second, women are disconcerted by men's infrequent use of minimal responses and accuse them of not listening.

9.2.2 The Meaning of Questions

Questions seem to have a different meaning for women and men. As we saw in sections 6.2.2 and 6.5, women use questions more than men: they use them as part of a general strategy for conversational maintenance. Questions are speech acts which require a subsequent speech act (an answer), so using questions is a way of ensuring that conversation continues. Moreover, women use questions rhetorically: if a woman says *what on earth am I going to do about David?*, she isn't asking for a lecture on what to do, she's inviting the addressee(s) to join her in her exasperation about her current (problematic) relationship. But this is not how questions are used by men. Men interpret questions as simple requests for information, and respond by giving information, sometimes at length. We have here a clash between direct and indirect modes: men interpret questions at face value while women see them as facilitating the flow of conversation. This is clearly an area which has the potential for miscommunication.

9.2.3 Links Between Speaker Turns

When a speaker takes a turn in conversation, s/he can begin by explicitly acknowledging the contribution of the previous speaker(s) and can then continue the current topic, or talk on a topic directly connected with what has gone before. It seems that this is a pattern typically adopted by women. Men on the other hand do not feel they have to make a link with the previous speaker's contribution; on the contrary, men are more likely to ignore what has been said before and to concentrate on making their own point. In mixed conversation, this means that women become resentful at having their comments ignored, while men will miss the cut and thrust of conversations played according to their rules.

9.2.4 Topic Shifts

Shifts between topics tend to be abrupt in all-male conversations, whereas women typically build on each others' contributions, so topics are developed progressively in conversation and topic shift occurs gradually. An extreme example comes from Dorval's (1990) research on the talk of same-sex friends. Two 12-year-old boys recorded by Dorval cover fifty-five topics in the twenty minutes allowed for talk. No topic is pursued for more than a few turns; the boys jump from topic to topic and topics are often unconnected with each other. By contrast, two 12-year-old girls recorded in the same setting spend most of the twenty minutes discussing one topic (their reactions to one of them falling out with another friend). Elaboration and continuity are key notions in the analysis of women's talk, but may not be relevant to an understanding of men's talk.

9.2.5 Self-Disclosure

Women tend to see conversation as an opportunity to discuss problems, share experience and offer reassurance and support. In this respect, all-female conversations are therapeutic. The following extract is taken from a conversation between four girls aged 14 who have been friends for many years. They are talking in D's bedroom; the topic is period pains.

(1) A: I get really bad back a– back ache down there

    B: so do I, back aches, I can't go like that, and I can't

$\left\{\begin{array}{l}\text{A:}\\\text{B:}\\\text{C:}\end{array}\right.$
A: but . ho– hot water
B: go like that and I just (...........)
C: yeah

$\left\{\begin{array}{l}\text{A:}\\\text{C:}\\\text{D:}\end{array}\right.$
A: bottles help =
C: ⌐help so much
D: = hot water bottles help me⌐as well

For men, the discussion of personal problems is not a normal component of conversation. Men may therefore respond to another speaker's self-disclosure as if it were a request for advice. They do not respond with a matching self-disclosure, but take on the role of expert, offering advice, often lecturing the other speaker(s). The following example (from Tannen 1991: 49) describes the breakdown of communication between husband and wife when a husband responds to a wife's self-disclosure by giving advice. The wife has had a lump removed from her breast, and is upset when she looks at the stitches because they have left a seam which has changed the contour of her breast. When she tells a woman friend, the friend's response is: *I know. It's like your body has been violated.* When she tells her husband, he responds: *You can have plastic surgery to cover up the scar tissue and restore the shape of your breast.* The wife felt comforted by her friend's response, but was upset by her husband's. The statement of a problem, then, has quite different meaning for women and men, and their linguistic responses differ accordingly.

9.2.6 Verbal Aggressiveness

Loud and aggressive argument is a common feature of speech in all-male groups: such arguments often focus on trivial issues and are enjoyed for their own sake. Shouting, name-calling, threats and insults are all part of male verbal aggressiveness (some of these are well documented: see for example Labov (1972b) on ritual insults among Black adolescents). Women, however, try to avoid displays of verbal aggressiveness – they find such displays unpleasant and interpret them as meant personally. They tend to express conflict indirectly rather than directly. As a result, verbal conflict is problematic in mixed talk since most women will see displays of verbal aggression as disrupting conversation, while for men such displays are part of the conventional structure of conversation.[4] Even among female speakers who demonstrate some skill in verbal insulting (such as the Black and working-class women described in Goodwin 1982, 1990; Eder 1990), it is clear that they use insults to establish norms of behaviour, rather than to maintain status hierarchies. In other words, ritual insults, when used, serve a different social function for female speakers.

9.2.7 Listening

In conversation, participants have two main roles, as speakers and as listeners. The evidence from all-female groups is that women value highly the role of listening. They use many minimal responses, they do not interrupt in the sense of preventing a speaker from finishing a turn (see section 9.2.8), and they actively encourage others to speak. Men, on the other hand, seem to construe conversation as a competition where the aim is to be speaker. This means that their chief conversational strategy is to seize a turn whenever possible, and then to try to hold on to it. This results in the typical pattern in all-men groups of a few men dominating conversation while the rest say little. Listening is not highly valued by men. These two approaches to conversation inevitably lead to clashes in mixed interaction. Women's behaviour is perceived by men as a failure to assert their right to speak rather than as active listening; men's behaviour is perceived by women as insensitive to their right to speak as well as to listen (women often complain that they feel men ignore their contributions to conversation and take advantage of their listening skills). Not surprisingly, the evidence is that in mixed interaction women tend to speak less, initiating only about one-third of all conversations.

9.2.8 Simultaneous Speech

Simultaneous speech, which occurs when more than one speaker speaks at the same time, has different meaning for male and female speakers, and is a potent source of miscommunication. Male speakers value speakership and therefore try to grab the floor (see section 9.2.7). One way of doing this is to start to speak before the current speaker has finished their turn. Example (2) illustrates this strategy:

(2) *Female*: I guess I'll do a paper on the economy business he
        laid out last week if ⌈I can . . .
     Male: ⌊you're kidding! that'd be a
        terrible topic

        (from West and Zimmerman 1977)

Simultaneous speech of this kind is known as **interruption** and is a violation of the current speaker's right to complete their turn (see section 6.2.1). Men respond to interruptions by carrying on speaking: keeping the floor is one of the skills boys learn in the same-sex peer-groups of childhood and adolescence.

Women's talk, on the other hand, contains frequent instances of simultaneous speech, but these can rarely be described as interruptions (see section 6.5). Women interpolate remarks, offer enthusiastic comments, as well as nodding and making minimal responses (*mhm, yeah*) during another speaker's turn. In the context of all-woman interaction, such behaviour is not seen as an attempt to deny the current speaker the right to complete her turn, but as evidence of active listenership and of co-participation. In example (1) above, for example, C's utterance *help so much* overlaps D's statement *hot water bottles help me as well*. C is clearly supporting D's statement; she is not attempting to grab the floor.

Simultaneous speech in all-female talk arises from a wide range of conversational strategies. Women will complete each other's turns, and may even say the same thing at the same time where they have shared knowledge of the topic under discussion, as example (3) illustrates:

(3) [topic = local political crisis]
  {J: and apparently ⌈Jane Bull ((xx))
  {R: ⌊well in fact it . felt very

  {J: ⌈she had this
  {R: threatened because [didʒə] did you hear ⌊she had this

  {J: grammar school meeting =
  {R: grammar school   = that's right

At other times, speakers may make contributions to a common topic, voicing different themes. The following is a brief extract from a long discussion of parents and funerals:

(4) {A: I've [bf] for many years ((have wondered)) about my
  {E: cos that's what funerals are for

  {A: *own* mother's funeral
  {E: . they're for the relatives

Such contrapuntal talk is not unknown in other cultures (see Reisman 1974), but has been largely overlooked in the analysis of English conversation (see Coates 1991, forthcoming a, for a detailed account).

The crucial difference between these two kinds of simultaneous speech is that in the first type (illustrated in example 2), the second speaker ignores or contradicts what the first speaker is saying, while in the second (examples 3 and 4), the two speakers are *both* making a contribution to a mutually agreed topic of conversation. The first kind of simultaneous speech often causes conversational breakdown; the second never does. These different kinds of simultaneous speech come into conflict in cross-gender talk. Women will tend to fall silent when interrupted by a man (see section 6.2.1): their experience of all-female conversation provides them with no strategies to resist interruption.

Male speakers, conversely, will interpret any overlapping speech as interruption, and will therefore protest when a woman talks contrapuntally.[5]

These areas of potential miscommunication arise directly from the different overall styles of women's and men's conversations. Women tend to organise their talk **co-operatively,** while men tend to organise their talk **competitively.** These different modes of organisation entail different conversational rules. In particular, women and men differ in their expectations of what constitutes a normal component of conversation, of how conversations should progress, of how important it is to respect the current speaker's right to finish a turn, and of how important it is to actively support the current speaker. In mixed-sex groups, it seems that women put far more effort than men into maintaining and facilitating conversation.

Some may view the miscommunication that arises in conversations between the sexes as an interesting clash of styles (Maltz and Borker 1982; Tannen 1991). But it can be argued that their competence in a different style disadvantages women in interaction with men. In mixed conversations, women do more of the interactive work, supporting others' topics, respecting others' turns, facilitating conversational flow through the use of questions. The end-product of all this is that male speakers dominate talk. Nor is this fortuitous. Power relations are reproduced through talk, and it would be naïve to deny that there must be some relationship between these gender-differentiated conversational styles and existing power structures.[6]

But is it adequate to respond that women need to change their style of talking? Many would argue that some features of women's talk are desirable for everyone. So perhaps it is male speakers who need to broaden their repertoire of speech styles. In discussions of this topic, male students have expressed to me their unhappiness at their inability to express their feelings or to discuss them with other men. Teachers at Hackney Downs Boys School in London started a Skills For Living course, one of whose aims was to help boys to talk about themselves. The teachers found that 'boys' ways of communicating with each other within the classroom tended to be rigid, stylised, and competitive, often making it impossible to discuss issues in a personal or meaningful way' (*Guardian* Women, 12 March 1985). The growing body of research in this area suggests that male inexpressivity is now seen as problematic (see Pleck 1975; Fitzpatrick and Indvik 1982; Franks 1984; Noller and Fitzpatrick 1988; Seidler 1989).

Both women and men, then, seem to be disadvantaged by the

existence of these two different modes of conversational interaction: women's collaborative, supportive style leads to their being dominated in mixed groups and unfavourably evaluated in public domains such as law and politics where a more masculine, adversarial style is valued. Men's competitive style, on the other hand, may make it difficult for them to express their feelings or establish close friendships. 'Language comes to be used as a weapon for the defence of masculine identity, rather than as a mode of expressing connectedness with others, or honesty about emotional life' (Seidler 1989: 7).

9.3   Language and Disadvantage

Chapter 6 analysed in detail certain aspects of communicative competence where male and female speakers differ. In this section I shall focus on the school – on the classroom in particular – to look at the differentiated competence of girls and boys and the way this affects their education. By analysing what goes on in the microcosm of the school setting, I shall test the claim that girls are a disadvantaged group and that the *language* used by girls and boys is in some way tied up with this disadvantage.

Disadvantage is a term widely used by those writing on education.

> Disadvantage . . . signifies a relatively enduring condition descriptive of the lifestyles of certain social groups – the working class, immigrant populations and ethnic minorities among them – which contributes to poor academic achievement for children at school, and generally lowered chances of success in the larger society.
> (Edwards 1979b: 1)

Notice that this (relatively recent) definition of disadvantage does not mention women in its examples of disadvantaged social groups. It is only recently, as we saw in sections 1.2.1 and 1.3, that researchers have seriously considered the possibility that women are a social group in their own right, and that they are moreover a disadvantaged social group.

Educationalists tend to demonstrate a link between disadvantaged social groups and their language by looking at *dialect* differences. For example, the under-achievement of children of West Indian origin in British schools has been associated with their use of varieties of English related to creoles such as Jamaican Creole; similarly, the under-achievement of children from working-class backgrounds in

British schools is often said to be linked to their use of non-standard (regional) varieties of English.

No such simple link between non-standard language and disadvantage can be made for girls. First, girls are members of the whole spectrum of social class and ethnic groups in society, as are boys. Female speakers are not a homogeneous group using a single dialect. Second, the clearest finding to emerge from the sociolinguistic studies reviewed in Chapters 4 and 5 was that female speakers tend to use more standard speech than comparable male speakers. In school, as Jenny Cheshire's (1982a) research showed, girls are more adept than boys at switching to a more standard dialect, even if their speech outside school is relatively non-standard. As far as dialect differences go, then, girls should be at an advantage rather than a disadvantage in the school setting.

When we examine the relationship between gender, educational disadvantage and language, it is *communicative competence* we need to focus on, not grammar or pronunciation. As we saw in Chapter 7, young children acquire gender-appropriate language, and this includes differentiated communicative competence. In the school setting, this differing understanding of when to speak, when to remain silent, how to mark speech for politeness, when it is permissible to interrupt, etc. helps to contribute to different outcomes for girls and boys.

Their differentiated communicative competence enables boys to dominate in the classroom. The classroom, in other words, mirrors the outside world: male dominance is acted out in the classroom, and this limits girls' opportunities to learn. How is this achieved, and what part does language play? The linguistic strategies of teachers and pupils are both implicated. I shall look in turn at the linguistic behaviour of girls and boys in the classroom, at the way teachers organise classroom activity, at the choice of subject-matter in class, and at examinations and assessment.

Boys' talk in the classroom differs from girls' both in style and in quantity. Boys tend to brag; after a school test they will say it was 'easy', 'simple', while the girls tend to express anxiety about their performance (their comments are of course unrelated to their results). Boys' confidence is also apparent in the way they respond to questions: they participate actively, call out answers, make lots of guesses, while girls listen more passively (Stanworth 1981; Spender 1982; Kelly et al. 1984; Whyte 1986; Kelly 1987). Pupils themselves are aware of this discrepancy: 'they all make a lot of noise, all those boys. That's why I think they're more intelligent than us' (female pupil reported in Stanworth 1981: 48). Girls' silence in class is despised by boys, but tends to be supported by the girls who are hostile towards girls who adopt a more assertive role. Girls are explicitly taught that loudness is 'unfeminine' (Payne 1980) and it seems that girls' sense of their own identity as female makes them feel that the speech acts of arguing, challenging and shouting are inappropriate behaviour for them.

Quietness is an ideal held up to schoolchildren throughout their school life. Many schools equate *quiet* behaviour with *nice* behaviour. The English infant school defines the quiet child as well-behaved and the noisy child as badly behaved (King 1978: 61). King asked infant teachers to rate pupils according to their conduct: the results showed that good children (in the teachers' eyes) are girls, particularly girls from the middle class. As King comments: 'Girls seem to be closer to the definition of how children should be, than boys from the same social background' (1978: 126). Girls achieve this goal by conforming to the school's demand for quietness. Whether quietness *is* a desirable quality is a debatable point: recent innovations in educational practice have stressed the importance of *active* learning – for children to learn, they need to be actively involved in the learning process. Being actively involved means *talking*, among other things: asking questions, making suggestions, offering comments. The quiet child, if quiet means passive and unassertive, is a child who is unable to participate fully in learning.

One consequence of boys' more noisy, undisciplined behaviour in the classroom is that they get more attention. Recent research carried out in the United States, Britain and Sweden, analysing teacher–pupil interaction patterns, has arrived at the same result: boys get more of the teacher's attention than girls (Sears and Feldman 1974; Spender 1982; Wernersson 1982; Sadker and Sadker 1985). Spender (1982) estimates that teachers normally give two-thirds of their attention to boys. This is confirmed by Joan Swann's (1989) research on classroom interaction. Swann and her colleagues made video-recordings of two twenty-minute sequences of small group teaching in two English primary schools. On average, boys contributed more to the sessions, both in terms of the number of turns taken and the number of words uttered, though in both schools there were examples of quieter boys and more talkative girls. Table 9.1 gives a detailed breakdown of results.

In the first group, where spontaneous contributions were welcomed, boys took advantage of this mode to chip in forty-one times to the girls' thirteen. The boys' behaviour seems to have been directly related to the teacher's *gaze* behaviour: analysis of the tape where the teacher's gaze can be seen reveals that she

Table 9.1: Contribution to classroom talk from girl and boy pupils in two classes (based on Swann 1989: 132)

Pupils	Amount spoken		
	Total words spoken	Total spoken turns	Average words per turn
Class One			
Sarah	79	17	4.6
Laura	20	5	4.0
Donna	37	5	7.4
Unidentified girls	18	9	2.0
Total girls	154	36	4.3
Matthew	133	23	5.8
Trevor	83	20	4.1
Peter	55	10	5.5
Unidentified boys	48	20	2.5
Total boys	319	73	4.4
Class Two			
Kate	127	9	14.1
Lorraine	13	7	1.8
Anne	23	8	2.9
Emma	8	4	2.0
Unidentified girls	—	—	—
Total girls	171	28	6.1
Mark	47	9	5.2
Ian	80	23	3.5
John	35	5	7.0
Darren	101	15	6.7
Unidentified boys	3	2	1.5
Total boys	266	54	4.9

looked towards the boys for 61.3 per cent of the time. Moreover, the teacher looks at the boys *at critical points* – when a question requires an answer.

In the second group, calling out was not encouraged, yet the boys still dominated. The teacher selected the child whose hand went up first. This favoured more confident pupils (usually boys), as did the teacher's gaze behaviour (she looked towards the boys 65 per cent of the time and maintained her gaze towards them when she began a question). Girl pupils, on the other hand, themselves contributed to their low level of participation by raising their hands *after* the teacher had directed her gaze to the pupil she intended to select.

Swann (1989) argues that these findings confirm that differences between girls and boys are not categorical, since some boys are quieter and some girls are more talkative. However, the boys do succeed in dominating classroom talk, though by different means in the two classrooms surveyed. In other words, to be dominant, a speaker has to use the resources available *in a given context*. Swann also makes the point that boys' domination of classroom talk is achieved in part at least through the behaviour of the girls and of the teacher: in other words, she sees girls and teachers as *colluding* in boys' dominance.

The claim that teachers pay boys more attention and encourage them to talk more has led to calls for intervention in the process. While some commentators are pessimistic (e.g. Spender 1982), others point to the example of the Girls Into Science and Technology (GIST) project (Kelly et al 1984; Whyte 1986). In this project, a cohort of 2,000 children in ten co-educational comprehensives in Greater Manchester were followed through from the time they entered secondary school (11 years old) until they made their option choices at the end of Year Nine (13–14 year olds). The project aimed simultaneously to explore *why* girls do not opt for science (specifically physics and chemistry) or craft subjects, *and* to initiate strategies to combat this tendency. The GIST team believed that teachers *can* change the balance of teacher–pupil interaction towards greater equality. They observed thirty-four lessons: all the teachers involved had been briefed on the aims of the project and all knew that girls tend to receive less attention in class. In twenty of the lessons, the teachers involved managed to give the girls as much attention as the boys or more. It should be noted that this measure was crude since it ignored the amount of talk involved (every interaction scored 1 regardless of length) and also ignored the context in which teachers addressed girls or boys. However, the GIST project does at least suggest that Spender (1982) is over-pessimistic in her view that teachers cannot achieve equality in their interaction with girls and boys. On the other hand, it emerged

199

that women teachers were far more successful than men at giving girls a fair share of their attention: 75 per cent of the female teachers observed achieved an interaction ratio which was equal for girls and boys or which favoured girls, while only 50 per cent of male teachers achieved this.

Like Spender, the GIST team found that teachers' perceptions of how they interacted with pupils were at odds with quantitative observations. Most were surprised to find how much attention they gave to boys. A male head of science who successfully achieved a balance in his class remarked afterwards that 'he had *felt* as if ninety per cent of his attention was being devoted to the girls' (Whyte 1986).

The language that pupils use to each other reflects and reinforces their unequal status. Boys in secondary school often ridicule girls: they groan when girls ask questions and make rude comments. The GIST observers give examples of this, and comment that they observed *no* examples of girls ridiculing or putting down boys. The unequal roles assigned to girls and boys are well illustrated in a Dutch experiment (described in Millman 1983: 7) which set out to investigate male/female interaction. Dutch children were divided into same-sex and mixed-sex pairs for a science experiment. The analysis of the resulting videos revealed that same-sex pairs worked cooperatively, but in the mixed-sex pairs the boys adopted a dominant role which the girls accepted: the boys set up the experiment and reported the results to the teacher while the girls helped and then cleared up afterwards.

Teachers' awareness of the different communicative competence of girls and boys also affects the choice of topics to be discussed in school. Lessons are organised to reflect boys' interests, because teachers have learned that boys will object – loudly – to topics they see as effeminate, while girls will accept 'boys' topics' (Clarricoates 1978). Teachers have varying success in their efforts to include girls. Elizabeth Sarah (1980) involved girls in a discussion of Space Travel by using passages with the pronoun *he* changed to *she*. The boys in her class hotly disputed the idea of spacewomen, and all wrote about space*men* in the follow-up work; the girls, however, wrote about spacewomen. Sarah claims that they obviously felt actively involved in the class project. Elliot, on the other hand, tried to facilitate girls' participation in his lesson on the topic of War, only to find that the boys ridiculed the girls' contributions, and the girls felt very uncomfortable at being forced to assert themselves in a mixed class (Elliot, cited in Spender 1980b: 150). Both these teachers have grasped the nettle of girls' non-participation in classroom discussions, but even so they have chosen as class topics subjects which are conventionally associated more with boys' interests.

Even in a situation where girls should have the advantage, it seems that various forces conspire to minimise or overturn this 'abnormal' pattern. British public examinations in English now involve a compulsory oral communication component. This means that students are tested on both individual and group talk. One aspect of group talk which is assessed is **interpersonal skill**. Since interpersonal sensitivity is at the heart of girls' communicative competence, we would expect girls to do well in this aspect of the new examination. A recent study (Jenkins and Cheshire 1990; Cheshire and Jenkins 1991) analyses three groups of 14-year-old girls and boys taking part in group discussion as part of the GCSE oral test, as well as examining teachers' assessment of these discussions. This study confirms that girls achieve scores as good as or better than their male counterparts.

However, Cheshire and Jenkins make some worrying observations. First, the conversational work done by the girls helped the entire group; boys were enabled to play a constructive role in discussion through the girls' contributions, but the girls did *not* receive support from the boys in return. In other words, on the evidence of this study, girls are carrying out their traditional role in conversation – doing the 'interactional shitwork' (Fishman 1980b) – and boys are benefiting from it. Second, the researchers discovered that teachers used different criteria to assess girls' and boys' contributions: they were very generous in their comments on boys' efforts to be cooperative, but judged the girls more harshly. Third, there was evidence that male and female assessors perceive and evaluate boys' and girls' conversational skills differently.

This last finding also emerges from research done by Shan Wareing (1993) on the oral communication component of the Scottish equivalent of GCSE English. Her analysis of the responses of teachers in six different schools to video-tapes of girls and boys engaged in group discussion revealed that male teachers generally gave higher marks to students displaying *competitive* skills (challenging, refuting, holding the floor for extended turns), while female teachers generally gave higher marks to students displaying *cooperative* skills (supporting other speakers, linking contributions carefully to the previous speaker's, asking questions to draw other participants into the conversation).

In conclusion, we can say that the relationship between girls or women as a group, the language they use, and disadvantage is a complex one. First, the relationship between women and disadvantage is not always straightforward. In school, for example, girls do relatively well: this was one of the reasons why recognition of women as a disadvantaged group was slow to emerge. Girls do better than boys throughout primary school, particularly in English, and in public examinations at 16. However, this success rests almost entirely on girls' ability in subjects at the Humanities end of the spectrum: English, modern languages, history, etc: 70 to 80 per cent of all examination entries in physics are from males, as are 60 per cent of entries in chemistry (Kelly 1987). In terms of technology, 82 per cent of GCSE exam entries in 1990 were for boys, and 88 per cent of those 18 year olds gaining a pass in A level Technology were boys (DES 1991). This means that, despite their good results, girls are at a disadvantage in a society which values technology and science.

If we look at education outcomes in terms of what happens to pupils *after* school, it is quite clear that girls are at a disadvantage. As employees, women are concentrated in poorly paid, low prestige jobs; they constitute less than 10 per cent of those employed in the majority of top professions (architects, barristers, accountants, university professors, top civil servants, and so on.) The 1991 statistical survey, *Social Trends*, shows that the proportion of female students in higher education (universities, polytechnics and colleges of higher education) has increased from 41 per cent to 47 per cent between 1981 and 1991, but this is still less than half.

Overall, research into classroom life has discovered many ways, both linguistic and non-linguistic, in which girls and boys are treated differently. The differential usage of interactional resources by teachers, girls and boys inside the classroom is a key element in sustaining male dominance. All participants in the classroom collude in this: teachers by paying more attention to boys, boys by talking more and at greater length than girls, girls by talking less. Moreover, the cooperative conversational skills which girls bring to the classroom are not valued. Schools tend to view favourably the adversarial style of debate more typical of male peer groups. On the other hand, in situations where students are expected to work collaboratively, boys benefit from girls' interactive skills. Some schools are making brave efforts to combat these social pressures, by, for example, encouraging teachers to make sure they talk to and listen to girls as much as boys, but such efforts can do little to alter the fact that society constructs male and female roles as different and *unequal*.

9.4 Women, Men and Language: Conclusions

This book has set out to demonstrate that in our society, and others like it, there are clear male/female differences in language. In a society where gender is a highly significant category, language has a key role to play in the contribution of that category. Linguists have the task of describing and explaining the role language plays. The emergence of sociolinguistics as a discipline reflects the increase in studies of linguistic variation of all kinds, but while descriptions become more refined, explanations are still tentative and unsophisticated.

In this chapter I have looked at two areas where gender differences in language have socially undesirable consequences. In section 9.2 I described ways in which women's and men's differing understanding of how conversational interaction works can lead to miscommunication. In section 9.3 I looked at work in schools which suggests that talk in the classroom directly reinforces male dominance and female subordination. These two areas illustrate nicely the two different approaches to language and gender differences outlined in section 1.4. Discussion of miscommunication between adult speakers in mixed conversations assumes that women and men talk differently and have different rules for conversation because they belong to different subcultures. Discussion of girls' under-achievement in the education system and its linguistic correlates, on the other hand, assumes that differences in girls' and boys' language are directly related to girls' oppression and boys' dominance. The first approach emphasises the **difference** in the gender roles and identities of women and men, the second emphasises the hierarchical nature of gender relations and the **dominance** of men.

The two topics covered in this chapter illustrate the need for both approaches. An analysis of classroom interaction which ignored the dimension of dominance and subordination would have little explanatory power. On the other hand, to insist that the conversational patterns typical of all-female groups can be explained by calling women an oppressed group is to do them less than justice. Women are an oppressed group, but the use of the dominance model alone leaves unexplored women's different linguistic strategies. As we saw in section 6.5, women's conversational style is based on solidarity, while men's is based on power, a difference arising directly from women's and men's membership of a patriarchal society. But women's solidarity-oriented talk is as deserving of sociolinguistic description in its own right as men's power-oriented talk.

There is a great deal still to be done in the area of gender differences and language.[7] There is a need for more detailed sociolinguistic studies at both individual and group levels. We must remember that gender differentiation in language does not exist in a vacuum: it interacts in a complex way with other kinds of social differentiation. Moreover, we are beginning to understand that theories which talk about 'language' and 'gender' as if they were free-floating, separate entities are misleading. As children, we become language users and, through using language, become gendered members of the community: both language and gender are developed through our participation in everyday social practice. In other words, language and gender are inextricably linked. But the fact that gender is accomplished through talk is only now being addressed seriously by sociolinguists.

Notes

1   Many of the generalisations in this section refer more accurately to white middle-class women and to white middle-class men; however, Goodwin's work on the language of Black children in Philadelphia (Goodwin 1980, 1990) and Wodak's work on the language of working-class adults in Vienna (Wodak 1981) confirm the general pattern (Goodwin's work is discussed in section 6.2.2; Wodak's work is discussed in section 6.5). Research by Bent Preisler in the north of England (Preisler 1986), which looked at women and men in three occupational groups (managerial, clerical, and manual) in both mixed- and single-sex groups, shows that many linguistic features are typical of women's speech regardless of age or social class.

2   This summary draws on the work of Kalcik 1975; Aries 1976; Jones 1980; Wodak 1981; Coates 1989a; 1989b; 1991; Tannen 1991; Sheldon 1992.

3   All the examples in this section are taken from my data, except where stated.

4   In her study of computer-mediated discussion, Susan Herring (1992) established that women not only produce less adversarial discourse, but tend to avoid participating in discussion which is adversarial.

5   Male irritation at – and incomprehension of – women's all-in-together style is nicely illustrated by this quotation from Kingsley Amis's novel *Stanley and the Women* (1984: 234): 'From the start she paid close attention to everything I said . . . She . . . made some faces and a few noises at high or low points but *she came out with*

none of those dispensable prompts I had known females to hand out so as to stay in shot while someone else tried to talk' (my italics).

6 For a powerful statement in support of interpreting cross-gender miscommunication in terms of power politics, see Troemel-Ploetz 1991.

7 For discussion of theoretical incoherence in language and gender studies, and for suggestions as to the way forward, see Cameron (in press), Eckert and McConnell-Ginet (in press); Uchida 1992.

Bibliography

Ardener, Shirley (ed.) (1975) *Perceiving Women*, Mallaby Press, London.

Ardener, Shirley (1978) The nature of women in society, pp. 9–48 in Ardener, Shirley (ed.) *Defining Females*, Croom Helm, London.

Argyle, Michael, Lalljee, Mansur and **Cook, Mark** (1968) The effects of visibility on interaction in a dyad, *Human Relations* **21**: 3–17.

Aries, Elizabeth (1976) Interaction patterns and themes of male, female and mixed groups, *Small Group Behaviour* **7** (1): 7–18.

Aries, Elizabeth, and **Johnson, Fern** (1983) Close friendship in adulthood: conversational conduct between same-sex friends, *Sex Roles* **9** (12): 1,183–96.

Baptiste, Tamsin (1990) A contrastive study of male and female complimenting behaviour in British English, unpublished BA dissertation, Roehampton Institute.

Barnes, Douglas (1971) Language and learning in the classroom, *Journal of Curriculum Studies* **3** (1).

Bate, Barbara, and **Taylor, Anita** (eds) (1988) *Women Communicating: Studies of Women's Talk,* Ablex, Norwood, NJ.

Bem, Sandra (1974) The measurement of psychological androgyny, *Journal of Consulting and Clinical Psychology* **42**: 155–62.

Bem, Sandra (1975) Sex role adaptability: one consequence of psychological androgyny, *Journal of Personality and Social Psychology* **31** (4): 634–43.

Bernard, Jessie (1972) *The Sex Game.* Atheneum, New York.

Bevan, J. (1990) Compliments and compliment-responses in British English, unpublished MA project, Birkbeck College, University of London.

Blom, Jan-Petter and **Gumperz, John** (1972) Social meanings in linguistic structures: code switching in Norway, pp. 407–34 in Gumperz, John and Hymes, Dell (eds) *Directions in Sociolinguistics.* Holt Rinehart & Winston, New York.

Bloom, Lois (1970) *Language Development: Form and Function in Emerging Grammars.* MIT Press, Cambridge, Massachusetts.

Bloom, Lois (1975) *One Word At A Time.* Mouton, The Hague.

Bloomfield, Leonard (1933) *Language.* George Allen & Unwin, London.

Bodine, Ann (1975a) Sex differentiation in language, pp. 130–51 in Thorne, Barrie and Henley, Nancy (eds) *Language and Sex: Difference and Dominance*. Newbury House Publishers, Rowley.

Bodine, Ann (1975b) Androcentrism in prescriptive grammar, *Language in Society* **4** (2): 129–56.

Bosmajian, Haig (1974) *The Language of Oppression*, Public Affairs Press, Washington DC.

Bragg, Melvin and **Ellis, Stanley** (1976) Word of Mouth. BBC TV, London.

Breakwell, Glenys (1979) Women: group and identity?, *Women's Studies International Quarterly* **2**: 9–17.

Bridge, Joseph C. (1917) *Cheshire Proverbs and Other Sayings and Rhymes Connected with the City and County Palatine of Chester*. Phillipson and Golder, Chester.

Brouwer, Dede, Gerritsen, Marinel and **de Haan, Dorian** (1979) Speech differences between women and men: on the wrong track?, *Language in Society* **8**: 33–50.

Brown, Penelope (1980) How and why are women more polite: some evidence from a Mayan community, pp. 111–36 in McConnell-Ginet, S. et al. (eds) *Women and Language in Literature and Society*. Praeger, New York.

Brown, Penelope and **Levinson, Stephen** (1978) Universals in language usage: politeness phenomena, pp. 56–289 in Goody, Esther (ed.) *Questions and Politeness*. Cambridge University Press.

Brown, Penelope, and **Levinson, Stephen** (1987) *Politeness*, Cambridge University Press, Cambridge.

Brown, Roger (1976) *A First Language*. Penguin Books, Harmondsworth.

Brown, Roger and **Gilman, A.** (1972) The pronouns of power and solidarity, pp. 252–282 in Giglioli, P. P. (ed.) *Language and Social Context*. Penguin Books, Harmondsworth.

Brun, A. (1946) *Parlers régionaux, France dialectale et unité française*. Didier, Paris.

Bruner, Edward M. and **Kelso, Jane Paige** (1980) Gender differences in graffiti: a semiotic perspective, in Kramarae, Cheris (ed.) *The Voices and Words of Women and Men*. Pergamon Press, Oxford.

Cameron, Deborah (1985) *Feminism and Linguistic Theory*. Macmillan, London.

Cameron, Deborah (1990) Introduction: why is language a feminist issue?, pp. 1–28 in Cameron, Deborah (ed.) *The Feminist Critique of Language: A Reader*, Routledge, London.

Cameron, Deborah (in press) The future of feminist linguistics, in Mills, Sara (ed.) *Language and Gender*, Longman, London.

Cameron, Deborah, and **Coates, Jennifer** (1989) Some problems in the sociolinguistic explanation of sex differences, pp. 13–26 in Coates, Jennifer, and Cameron, Deborah (eds) *Women in their Speech Communities*, Longman, London.

Cameron, Deborah, McAlinden, Fiona, and **O'Leary, Kathy** (1989) Lakoff in context: the social and linguistic functions of tag questions, pp. 74–93 in Coates, Jennifer, and Cameron, Deborah (eds) *Women in their Speech Communities*, Longman, London.

Chambers, J. K., and **Trudgill, Peter** (1980) *Dialectology*, Cambridge University Press, Cambridge.

Chaney, J. (1981) *Social Networks and Job Information – the Situation of Women who Return to Work*. EOC/SSRC, Manchester.

Cheshire, Jenny (1978) Present tense verbs in Reading English, pp. 52–68 in Trudgill, Peter (ed.) *Sociolinguistic Patterns in British English*. Edward Arnold, London.

Cheshire, Jenny (1982a) *Variation in an English Dialect*. Cambridge University Press.

Cheshire, Jenny (1982b) Linguistic variation and social function, pp 153–66 in Romaine, Suzanne (ed.) *Sociolinguistic Variation in Speech Communities*. Edward Arnold, London.

Cheshire, Jenny (1984) Language and sexism, in Trudgill, Peter (ed.) *Applications of Sociolinguistics*. Academic Press, London.

Cheshire, Jenny, and **Jenkins, Nancy** (1991) Gender issues in the GCSE oral English examination: Part 2, *Language and Education* **5** (1): 19–40.

Clarke-Stewart, Alison (1973) Interactions between mothers and their young children: characteristics and consequences, *Monographs of the Society for Research in Child Development* **153,** 38 (6–7).

Clarricoates, Katherine (1978) 'Dinosaurs in the classroom': A re-examination of some aspects of the 'hidden' curriculum in primary schools, *Women's Studies International Quarterly* **1** (4): 353–64.

Coates, Jennifer (1984) Syntactic variation on Merseyside, Paper presented to the SSRC workshop on varieties of British English syntax. University of Salford, 8–10 January.

Coates, Jennifer (1987a) *Language and Sexism*, L.A.U.D. Paper No. 173, University of Duisburg.

Coates, Jennifer (1987b) Epistemic modality and spoken discourse, *Transactions of the Philological Society*, 110–31.

Coates, Jennifer (1989a) Gossip revisited: language in all-female groups, pp. 94–121 in Coates, Jennifer, and Cameron, Deborah (eds) *Women in their Speech Communities*, Longman, London.

Coates, Jennifer (1989b) Women's speech, women's strength?, *York Papers in Linguistics* **13:** 65–76.

Coates, Jennifer (1991) Women's cooperative talk: a new kind of conversational duet?, pp. 296–311 in Uhlig, Claus, and Zimmerman, Rudiger (eds) *Proceedings of the Anglistentag 1990 Marburg*, Max Niemeyer Verlag, Tubingen.

Coates, Jennifer (forthcoming a) No gap, lots of overlap: turn-taking patterns in the talk of women friends. *Text*.

Coates, Jennifer (forthcoming b) *Women Talking to Women*, Basil Blackwell, Oxford.

Coates, Jennifer, and **Cameron, Deborah** (1989) *Women in their Speech Communities,* Longman, London.

Corsaro, William, and **Rizzo, Thomas** (1990) Disputes in the peer culture of American and Italian nursery-school children, pp. 21–66 in Grimshaw, Allen (ed.) *Conflict Talk,* Cambridge University Press.

Crystal, David and **Davy, Derek** (1975) *Advanced Conversational English.* Longman, London.

Dale, Philip (1976) *Language Development.* Holt Rinehart & Winston, New York (2nd edn).

Daly, Mary (1988) *Webster's First New Intergalactic Wickedary of the English Language,* Women's Press, London.

Davies, Reginald T. (ed.) (1963) *Medieval English Lyrics.* Faber & Faber, London.

DeFrancisco, Victoria L. (1991) The sounds of silence: how men silence women in marital relations, *Discourse & Society* **2** (4): 413–24.

Delphy, Christine (1981) Women in stratification studies, in Roberts, H. (ed.) *Doing Feminist Research,* Routledge, London.

Delphy, Christine (1984) *Close to Home: A Materialist Analysis of Women's Oppression,* Hutchinson, London.

De Klerk, Vivian (1992) 'How taboo are taboo words for girls?', *Language in Society* **21,** 277–289.

De Lyon, Hilary (1981) A sociolinguistic study of aspects of the Liverpool accent. Unpublished M. Phil. thesis, University of Liverpool.

Department of Education and Science (DES) (1991) *Statistical Bulletin,* December 1991. HMSO, London.

Deuchar, Margaret (1987) Sociolinguistics, in Lyons, John, Richard Coates, Margaret Deuchar, Gerald Gazdar (eds.) *New Horizons in Linguistics 2.* Penguin Books, Harmondsworth.

Deuchar, Margaret (1989) A pragmatic account of women's use of standard speech, pp. 27–32 in Coates, Jennifer, and Cameron, Deborah (eds) *Women in their Speech Communities,* Longman, London.

Deuchar, Margaret and **Martin-Jones, Marilyn** (1982) Linguistic research in minority and majority communities: goals and methods. Paper given at the Sociolinguistics Symposium, Sheffield, 29–31 March 1982.

Dobson, Eric J. (1969) Early modern standard English, in Lass, Roger (ed.) *Approaches to English Historical Linguistics,* Holt Rinehart & Winston, New York.

Donovan, Josephine (1980) The silence is broken, pp. 205–18 in McConnell-Ginet, Sally, et al. (eds) *Women and Language in Culture and Society,* Praeger, New York.

Dorval, Bruce (1990) *Conversational Organisation and its Development,* Ablex, Norwood, NJ.

Dubois, Betty Lou and **Crouch, Isabel** (1975) The question of tag questions in women's speech: they don't really use more of them, do they?, *Language in Society* **4:** 289–94.

Eakins, Barbara W. and **Eakins, R. Gene** (1978) *Sex Differences in Human Communication*. Houghton Mifflin Company, Boston.

Eckert, Penelope (1989) The whole women: sex and gender differences in variation, *Language Variation and Change* **1**: 245–67.

Eckert, Penelope and **McConnell-Ginet, Sally** (in press) Think practically and look locally: language and gender as community based practice, *Annual Review of Anthropology*.

Edelsky, Carole (1976) The acquisition of communicative competence: recognition of linguistic correlates of sex roles, *Merril-Palmer Quarterly* **22**: 47–59.

Edelsky, Carole (1977) Acquisition of an aspect of communicative competence: learning what it means to talk like a lady, in Ervin-Tripp, Susan and Mitchell-Kernan, Claudia (eds) *Child Discourse*. Academic Press, New York.

Eder, Donna (1990) Serious and playful disputes: variation in conflict talk among female adolescents, pp. 67–84 in Grimshaw, Allan (ed.) *Conflict Talk*, Cambridge University Press.

Edwards, John R. (1979a) Social class differences and the identification of sex in children's speech, *Journal of Child Language* **6**: 121–7.

Edwards, John R. (1979b) *Language and Disadvantage*. Edward Arnold, London.

Eisikovits, Edna (1987) Sex differences in inter-group and intra-group interaction among adolescents, pp. 45–58 and Pauwels, Anne (ed.) *Women and Language in Australian and New Zealand Society*, Australian Professional Publications, Sydney.

Eisikovits, Edna (1988) Girl-talk/boy-talk: sex differences in adolescent speech, pp. 35–54 in Collins, Peter, and Blair, David (eds) *Australian English*, University of Queensland Press.

Ellis, Havelock (1894) *Man and Woman*, Walter Scott Publishing Co.

Elyan, Olwen, Smith, Philip, Giles, Howard and **Bourhis, Richard** (1978) RP-accented female speech: the voice of perceived androgyny?, pp. 122–31 in Trudgill, Peter (ed.) *Sociolinguistic Patterns in British English*. Edward Arnold, London.

Elyot, Thomas (1531) *The Governour*. Scolar Press, Menston, Yorks, 1970.

Emler, Nicholas (forthcoming) *Secrets, Scandals, Rumours and Reputations: The Gossip Process in Everyday Life*, Harvester Wheatsheaf.

Engle, Marianne (1980a) Family influences on the language development of young children, pp. 259–66 in Kramarae, C. (ed.) *The Voices and Words of Women and Men*. Pergamon Press, Oxford.

Engle, Marianne (1980b) Language and play: a comparative analysis of parental initiatives, in Giles, Howard, Robinson, W. Peter, and Smith, Philip M. (eds) *Language: Social Psychological Perspectives*. Pergamon Press, Oxford.

Erickson, Frederick (1990) The social construction of discourse coherence in a family dinner table conversation, pp. 207–38 in Dorval, Bruce (ed.) *Conversational Organisation and its Development*, Ablex, Norwood, NJ.

Ervin-Tripp, Susan (1972) An analysis of the interaction of language, topic and listener, in Fishman, Joshua (ed.) *Readings in the Sociology of Language*. Mouton, The Hague.

Fichtelius, Anna, Johansson, Irene and **Nordin, Kerstin** (1980) Three investigations of sex-associated speech variation in day school, pp. 219–25 in Kramarae, Cheris (ed.) *The Voices and Words of Women and Men*. Pergamon Press, Oxford.

Fischer, John L. (1964) Social influences on the choice of a linguistic variant, in Hymes, Dell (ed.) *Language in Culture and Society*. Harper International, New York.

Fishman, Pamela (1978) Interaction: the work women do, *Social Problems* **24**: 397–406.

Fishman, Pamela (1980a) Conversational insecurity, pp. 127–32 in Giles, Howard, Robinson, W. Peter, and Smith, Philip M. (eds) *Language: Social Psychological Perspectives*. Pergamon Press, Oxford.

Fishman, Pamela (1980b) Interactional shitwork, *Heresies* **2**: 99–101.

Fitzpatrick, Mary Anne, and **Indvik, J.** (1982) The instrumental and expressive domains of marital communication, *Human Communication Research* **8** (3): 195–213.

Flannery, Regina (1946) Men's and women's speech in Gros Ventre, *International Journal of American Linguistics* **12**: 133–5.

Fletcher, Paul, and **Garman, Michael** (1986) *Language Acquisition*. Cambridge University Press (second edition).

Flexner, Stuart B. (1960) Preface to *Dictionary of American Slang*. Thomas Y. Crowell, New York.

Foster, Susan (1990) *The Communicative Competence of Young Children*, Longman, London.

Francis, W. Nelson (1983) *Dialectology: An Introduction*. Longman, London.

Franks, Helen (1984) *Goodbye Tarzan – Men After Feminism*, George Allen & Unwin, London.

Frazer, J. G. (1900) A suggestion as to the origin of gender in language, *Fortnightly Review* **73**: 79–90.

Gal, Susan (1978) Peasant men can't get wives: language change and sex roles in a bilingual community, *Language in Society* **7**: 1–16.

Gal, Susan (1979) *Language Shift*, Academic Press, New York.

Gardette, P. (1968) *Atlas linguistique et ethnographique du Lyonnais*, volume IV: Exposé méthodologique et tables. Centre Nationale de la Recherche Scientifique, Paris.

Gauchat, L. (1905) *L'unité phonetique dans le patois d'une commune*. D. S. Niemeyer, Halle.

Giles, Howard, Robinson, W. Peter and **Smith, Philip M.** (eds) *Language: Social Psychological Perspectives*. Pergamon Press, Oxford.

Gleason, Jean Berko (1980) The acquisition of social speech routines and politeness formulas, in Giles, Howard, Robinson, W. Peter, and Smith, Philip M. (eds) *Language: Social Psychological Perspectives*. Pergamon Press, Oxford.

Gomm, Isabel (1981) A study of the inferior image of the female use of the English language as compared to that of the male. Unpublished BA dissertation, Edge Hill College, Ormskirk.

Goodwin, Marjorie Harness (1980) Directive-response speech sequences in girls' and boys' task activities, pp. 157–73 in McConnell-Ginet et al (eds) *Women and Language in Literature and Society*. Praeger, New York.

Goodwin, Marjorie Harness (1982) Processes of dispute management among urban black children, *American Ethnologist* **9**: 799–819.

Goodwin, Marjorie Harness (1988) Cooperation and competition across girls' play activities, pp. 55–94 in Todd, Alexandra Dundas, and Fisher, Sue (eds) *Gender and Discourse: The Power of Talk*, Ablex, Norwood, NJ.

Goodwin, Marjorie Harness, (1990) *He-said-she-said. Talk as Social Organisation among Black Children*. Indiana University Press, Bloomington.

Goodwin, Marjorie Harness, and **Goodwin, Charles** (1987) Children's arguing, pp. 200–48 in Philips, Susan, Steele, Susan, and Tanz, Christine (eds) *Language, Gender and Sex in Comparative Perspective*, Cambridge University Press.

Goody, Esther (ed.) (1978) *Questions and Politeness*. Cambridge University Press.

Graddol, David, and **Swann, Joan** (1989) *Gender Voices*, Basil Blackwell, Oxford.

Grant, W. (1914) *The Pronunciation of English in Scotland*. Cambridge University Press.

Greif, Esther Blank (1980) Sex differences in parent–child conversations, pp. 253–8 in Kramarae, Cheris (ed.) *The Voices and Words of Women and Men*. Pergamon Press, Oxford.

Grimshaw, Allen (ed.) (1990) *Conflict Talk*, Cambridge University Press.

Gumperz, John (ed.) (1982) *Language and Social Identity*. Cambridge University Press.

Haas, Adelaide (1978) Sex-associated features of spoken language by four-, eight-, and twelve-year-old boys and girls. Paper given at the 9th World Congress of Sociology, Uppsala, Sweden, 14–19 August.

Haas, Adelaide (1979) Male and female spoken language differences: stereotypes and evidence, *Psychological Bulletin* **86**: 616–26.

Haas, Mary (1944) Men's and women's speech in Koasati, *Language* **20**: 147–9.

Harris, Sandra (1984) Questions as a mode of control in magistrates' courts, *International Journal of the Sociology of Language* **49**.

Hasan, Ruqaiya, and **Cloran, Carmel** (1990) A sociolinguistic interpretation of everyday talk between mothers and children, in Halliday, M. A. K., Gibbons, J, and Nicholas, H. (eds) *Learning, Keeping and Using Language: Selected Papers from the 8th World Congress of Applied Linguistics*, Benjamins, Amsterdam.

Herring, Susan (1992) Gender and participation in computer-mediated linguistic discourse, paper presented at LSA annual meeting, Philadelphia, Jan 9–12 1992.

Herring, Susan, Johnson, Deborah and **DiBenedetto, Tamra** (in press) Participation in electronic discourse in a "feminist" field, in *Locating Power: Proceedings of the 1992 Berkeley Women and Language Conference*.

Hirschmann, Lynette (1974) Analysis of supportive and assertive behaviour in conversations. Paper presented at Linguistic Society of America meeting, July 1974.

Holland, Janet (1980) *Work and Women*, Bedford Way Papers 6. University of London Institute of Education.

Holmes, Janet (1984) Hedging your bets and sitting on the fence: some evidence for hedges as support structures, *Te Reo* **27**: 47–62.

Holmes, Janet (1987) Hedging, fencing and other conversational gambits: an analysis of gender differences in New Zealand speech, pp. 59–79 in Pauwels, Anne (ed.) *Women and Language in Australian and New Zealand Society*, Australian Professional Publications, Sydney.

Holmes, Janet (1988) Paying compliments: a sex-preferential politeness strategy, *Journal of Pragmatics* **12**: 445–65.

Hudson, Emmet (1992) 'Swearing: a linguistic analysis', unpublished MA dissertation, Birkbeck College, London.

Hughes, Susan (1992) 'Expletives of lower working-class women', *Language in Society* **21**, 291–303.

Humm, Maggie (1989) *The Dictionary of Feminist Theory*, Harvester Wheatsheaf, London.

Humphrey, Caroline (1978) Women, taboo and the suppression of attention, pp. 89–108 in Arderner, Shirley (ed.) *Defining Females: the Nature of Women in Society*. Croom Helm, London.

Hymes, Dell (ed.) (1964) *Language in Culture and Society*. Harper International, New York.

Hymes, Dell (1972) On communicative competence, pp. 269–93 in Pride, J. B. and Holmes, Janet (eds.) *Sociolinguistics*. Penguin Books, Harmondsworth.

Ide, Sachiko (1991) How and why do women speak more politely in Japanese?, pp. 63–79 in Ide, Sachiko, and McGloin, Naomi H. (eds) *Aspects of Japanese Women's Language*, Kurosio Publishers, Tokyo.

Ingram, David (1989) *First Language Acquisition*, Cambridge University Press.

Irigaray, Luce (1990) Women's exile, Interview with Luce Irigaray, translated by Couze Venn, pp. 80–96 in Cameron, Deborah (ed) *The Feminist Critique of Language*, Routledge, London.

Jenkins, Nancy, and **Cheshire, Jenny** (1990) Gender issues in the GCSE oral English examination: part 1, *Language and Education* **4**: 261–92.

Jespersen, Otto (1922) *Language: Its Nature, Development and Origin*. George Allen & Unwin, London.

Jones, Deborah (1980) Gossip: notes on women's oral culture, pp. 193–8 in

Kramarae, Cheris (ed.) *The Voices and Words of Women and Men*. Pergamon Press, Oxford.

Kalcik, Susan (1975) '. . . like Ann's gynaecologist or the time I was almost raped' – personal narratives in women's rap groups, *Journal of American Folklore* **88**: 3–11.

Kamuf, Peggy (1980) Writing like a woman, pp. 284–99 in McConnell-Ginet et al. (eds) *Women and Language in Literature and Society*. Praeger, New York.

Kelly, Alison (1987) The construction of masculine science, pp. 127–39 in Arnot, Madeleine, and Weiner, Gaby (eds) *Gender and the Politics of Schooling*, Hutchinson, London.

Kelly, Alison, Whyte, Judith and Smail, Barbara (1984) *Girls Into Science and Technology: Final Report*. Equal Opportunities Commission, Manchester.

Kessler, Suzanne and McKenna, Wendy (1978) *Gender: An Ethno methodological Approach*. John Wiley & Sons, New York.

Key, Mary Ritchie (1975) *Male/female Language*. Scarecrow Press, Metuchen, New Jersey.

King, Ronald (1978) *All Things Bright and Beautiful?* John Wiley & Sons, New York.

Kirby, J. (1746) *A New English Grammar*, Scolar Press, Menston, Yorks, 1971.

Knowles, Gerald (1974) Scouse: the urban dialect of Liverpool. Unpublished PhD thesis, University of Leeds.

Kramarae, Cheris (ed.) (1980a) *The Voices and Words of Women and Men*. Pergamon Press, Oxford.

Kramarae, Cheris (1980b) Perceptions and politics in language and sex research, in Giles, Howard, Robinson, W. Peter, and Smith, Philip M. (eds) *Language: Social Psychological Perspectives*. Pergamon Press, Oxford.

Kramarae, Cheris (1981) *Women and Men Speaking*. Newbury House, Rowley, Massachusetts.

Kramarae, Cheris (1982) Gender: How she speaks, in Ryan, Ellen Bouchard, and Giles, Howard, (eds) *Attitudes Towards Language Variation*. Edward Arnold, London.

Kramarae, Cheris, and Treichler, Paula (1983) *A Feminist Dictionary*, Pandora Press, London.

Kramer, Cheris (1974) Folklinguistics, *Psychology Today* **8**: 82–5.

Kramer, Cheris (1975) Stereotypes of women's speech: the word from cartoons, *Journal of Popular Culture* **8** (3): 624–38.

Kurath, Hans (1972) *Studies in Area Linguistics*. Indiana University Press.

Labov, William (1969) The logic of non-standard English, *Georgetown Monographs on Language and Linguistics* **22**: 1–31.

Labov, William (1971) Variation in language, in Reed, C. E. (ed.) *The Learning of Language*. National Council of Teachers of English, New York.

Labov, William (1972a) *Sociolinguistic Patterns*. University of Pennsylvania Press, Philadelphia.

Labov, William (1972b) *Language in the Inner City*. University of Pennsylvania Press, Philadelphia.

Lakoff, Robin (1975) *Language and Woman's Place*. Harper & Row, New York.

Leet-Pellegrini, Helena M. (1980) Conversational dominance as a function of gender and expertise, pp. 97–104 in Giles, Howard, Robinson, W. Peters, and Smith, Philip M. (eds) *Language: Social Psychological Perspectives*. Pergamon Press, Oxford.

Liebermann, Philip (1967) *Intonation, Perception and Language*. M.I.T. Press, Cambridge.

Local, John (1982) Modelling intonational variability in children's speech, pp. 85–103 in Romaine, Suzanne (ed.) *Sociolinguistic Variation in Speech Communities*. Edward Arnold, London.

Luhman, Reid (1990) Appalachian English stereotypes: language attitudes in Kentucky, *Language in Society* **19**: 331–48.

Macaulay, R. K. S. (1977) *Language, Social Class and Education*. Edinburgh University Press.

Macaulay, R. K. S. (1978) Variation and consistency in Glaswegian English, pp. 132–43 in Trudgill, Peter (ed.) *Sociolinguistic Patterns in British English*. Edward Arnold, London.

Maccoby, Eleanor E. and **Jacklin, Carol Nagy** (1974) *The Psychology of Sex Differences*. Stanford University Press, Stanford.

McConnell-Ginet, Sally (1988) Language and gender, pp. 75–99 in Newmeyer, Frederick (ed) *Linguistics: The Cambridge Survey*, vol. IV, Cambridge University Press, Cambridge.

McConnell-Ginet, Sally, Borker, Ruth and **Furman, Nelly** (eds) (1980) *Women and Language in Literature and Society*. Praeger, New York.

MacDonald, M. (1980) Schooling and the reproduction of class and gender relations, in Barton L., Meighan R. and Walkers S. (eds) *Schooling, Ideology and the Curriculum*. Falmer Press.

McIntosh, Angus (1952) *An Introduction to a Survey of Scottish Dialects*. Nelson.

MacLean, Ian (1980) *The Renaissance Notion of Woman*. Cambridge University Press.

McTear, Michael (1985) *Children's Conversation*, Basil Blackwell, Oxford.

Maltz, Daniel N. and **Borker, R. A.** (1982) A cultural approach to male–female miscommunication, pp. 195–216 in Gumperz, John (ed.) *Language and Social Identity*. Cambridge University Press.

Maynard, Douglas (1986) Offering and soliciting collaboration in multi-party disputes among children (and other humans), *Human Studies* **9**: 261–85.

Meditch, Andrea (1975) The development of sex-specific patterns in young children, *Anthropological Linguistics* **17** (9): 421–33.

Miller, P., Danaher, D. and **Forbes, D.** (1986) Sex-related strategies for coping with interpersonal conflict in children aged five and seven, *Developmental Psychology* **22**: 543–8.

Millman, Valerie (1983) *Sex Stereotyping in Schools: the Role and Responsibilities of the Teacher*. Equal Opportunities Commission, Manchester.

Mills, Jane (1989) *Womanwords: A Vocabulary of Culture and Patriarchal Society*, Longman, London.

Milroy, James and Milroy, Lesley (1978) Belfast: change and variation in an urban vernacular, pp. 19–36 in Trudgill, Peter (ed.) *Sociolinguistic Patterns in British English*. Edward Arnold, London.

Milroy, James and Milroy, Lesley (1985) Linguistic change, social network and speaker innovation, *Journal of Linguistics* 21: 339–84.

Milroy, Lesley (1980) *Language and Social Networks*. Basil Blackwell, Oxford.

Milroy, Lesley (1982) Social network and linguistic focusing, pp. 141–52 in Romaine, Suzanne (ed.) *Sociolinguistic Variation in Speech Communities*. Edward Arnold, London.

Milroy, Lesley (1987) *Observing and Analysing Natural Language*, Basil Blackwell, Oxford.

Moi, Toril (1985) *Sexual/Textual Politics*, Methuen, London.

Montaiglon, A. and Raynaud, G. (eds) (1872–90) *Recuil general et complet des fabliaux des XIIIe et XIVe siecles* (6 vols). Librairie des Bibliophiles, Paris.

Muscatine, Charles (1981) Courtly literature and vulgar language, in Burgess, G. S. (ed.) *Court and Poet, Selected Proceedings of the 3rd Congress of the ICLS (Liverpool 1980)*, Liverpool.

Nelson, Katherine (1973) Structure and strategy in learning to talk, *Monographs of the Society for Research in Child Development*, 149, 38 (1–2).

Nelson, Marie Wilson (1988) Women's ways: interactive patterns in predominantly female research teams, pp. 199–232 in Bate, Barbara, and Taylor, Anita (eds) *Women Communicating: Studies of Women's Talk*, Ablex, Norwood, NJ.

Newbrook, Mark (1982) Sociolinguistic reflexes of dialect interference in West Wirral. Unpublished PhD thesis, Reading University.

Nichols, Patricia (1982) Black women in the rural south: conservative and innovative, pp. 45–54 in Dubois, Betty Lou, and Crouch, Isabel (eds) *American Minority Women in Sociolinguistic Perspective*, Mouton, The Hague.

Nichols, Patricia (1983) Linguistic options and choices for Black women in the rural South, pp. 54–68 in Thorne, Barrie, Kramarae, Cheris, and Henley, Nancy (eds) *Language, Gender and Society*, Newbury House Publishers, Rowley Mass.

Noller, Patricia, and Fitzpatrick, Mary Anne (1988) *Perspectives on Marital Interaction*, Multilingual Matters, Clevedon.

O'Barr, William and Atkins, Bowman K. (1980) 'Women's language' or 'powerless language'?, pp. 93–110 in McConnell-Ginet et al. (eds) *Women and Language in Literature and Society*. Praeger, New York.

Ochs, Elinor, and Schieffelin, Bambi B. (eds) (1979) *Developmental Pragmatics*, Academic Press, New York.

Ochs, Elinor and Schieffelin, Bambi B. (1983) *Acquiring Conversational Competence*. Routledge & Kegan Paul, London.

Ong, Walter J. (1967) *The Presence of the Word*, Yale University Press, New Haven, Connecticut.

Orton, Harold (1962) *Introduction to the Survey of English Dialects*. E. J. Arnold, Leeds.

Patterson, D. (1860) *The Provincialisms of Belfast Pointed Out and Corrected.* Belfast.

Payne, Irene (1980) A working-class girl in a grammar school, pp. 12–19 in Spender, Dale and Sarah, Elizabeth (eds) *Learning to Lose.* Women's Press, London.

Pée, W. (1946) *Dialect-Atlas van West-Vlaanderen en Fransch-Vlaanderen.* De Sikkel, Antwerp.

Perkins, Michael (1983) *Modal Expressions in English.* Frances Pinter, London.

Philips, Susan, Steele, Susan, and **Tanz, Christine** (eds) (1987) *Language, Gender and Sex in Comparative Perspective,* Cambridge University Press.

Pizzini, Franca (1991) Communication hierarchies in humour: gender differences in the obstetrical/gynaecological setting, *Discourse & Society* **2** (4): 477–88.

Pleck, Joseph (1975) Man to man; is brotherhood possible?, in Glazer-Malbin, N. (ed) *Old Family, New Family,* Van Nostrand.

Poole, J. (1646) *The English Accidence.* Scolar Press, Menston, Yorks, 1967.

Pop, Sever (1950) *La Dialectologie: Apercu historique et methodes d'enquêtes linguistiques.* Université de Louvain.

Preisler, Bent (1986) *Linguistic Sex Roles in Conversation,* Mouton de Gruyter, Berlin.

Pringle, Janis (1991) Is cooperative talk possible among men?, unpublished MA dissertation, University of London.

Reid, Euan (1976) Social and stylistic variation in the speech of some Edinburgh schoolchildren. Unpublished MLitt thesis, University of Edinburgh.

Reid, Euan (1978) Social and stylistic variation in the speech of children: some evidence from Edinburgh, pp. 158–71 in Trudgill, Peter (ed.) *Sociolinguistic Patterns in British English.* Arnold, London.

Reisman, K. (1974) Contrapuntal conversation in an Antiguan village, in Bauman R., and Sherzer, J. (eds) *Explorations in the Ethnography of Speaking,* Cambridge University Press.

Romaine, Suzanne (1978) Postvocalic /r/ in Scottish English: sound change in progress?, pp. 144–57 in Trudgill, Peter (ed.) *Sociolinguistic Patterns in British English.* Edward Arnold, London.

Romaine, Suzanne (ed.) (1982) *Sociolinguistic Variation in Speech Communities.* Edward Arnold, London.

Romaine, Suzanne (1984) *The Language of Children and Adolescents: The Acquisition of Communicative Competence.* Basil Blackwell, Oxford.

Rosaldo, Michelle Z. and **Lamphere, Louise** (eds) (1974) *Woman, Culture and Society.* Stanford University Press, California.

Ryan, Ellen Bouchard and **Giles, Howard** (eds) (1982) *Attitudes Towards Language Variation.* Edward Arnold, London.

Sachs, Jacqueline (1987) Preschool boys' and girls' language use in pretend play, pp. 178–188 in Phillips, Susan, Steele, Susan, and Tanz, Christine (eds) *Language, Gender and Sex in Comparative Perspective*, Cambridge University Press.

Sachs, Jacqueline, Lieberman, Philip and **Erickson, Donna** (1973) Anatomical and cultural determinants of male and female speech, pp. 74–84 in Shuy, Roger and Fasold, Ralph (eds) *Language Attitudes: Current Trends and Prospects*. Georgetown University Press, Washington, DC.

Sacks, Harvey, Schegloff, Emanuel, A. and **Jefferson, Gail** (1974) A simplest systematics for the organisation of turn-taking for conversation, *Language* **50**: 696–735.

Sadker, Myra, and **Sadker, David** (1985) Sexism in the schoolroom of the '80s, *Psychology Today* March: 54–7.

Sapir, Edward (1961) Male and female forms of speech in Yana, in Mandelbaum, David (ed.) *Selected Writings of Edward Sapir on Language, Culture and Personality*. University of California Press, Berkeley.

Sarah, Elizabeth (1980) Teachers and students in the classroom: an examination of classroom interaction, pp. 155–64 in Spender, Dale and Sarah, Elizabeth (eds) *Learning to Lose*. Women's Press, London.

Sattel, Jack (1983) Men, inexpressiveness and power, pp. 118–24 in Thorne, Barrie, Kramarae, Cheris, and Henley, Nancy (eds) *Language, Gender and Society*, Newbury House Publishers, Rowley, Mass.

Schieffelin, Bambi (1990) *The Give and Take of Everyday Life: Language Socialisation of Kaluli Children*, Cambridge University Press.

Sears, P. and **Feldman, D.** (1974) Teacher interactions with boys and with girls, in Stacey, J., Bereaud, S. and Daniels, J. (eds) *And Jill Came Tumbling After: Sexism in American Education*. Dell Publishing, New York.

Sebba, Mark (1983) *Language Change among Afro-Caribbeans in London*, mimeo, Dept of Language, University of York.

Sebba, Mark (in press) *London Jamaican*, Longman, London.

Seidler, Victor (1989) *Rediscovering Masculinity – Reason, Language and Sexuality*, Routledge, London.

Sheldon, Amy (1990) Pickle fights: gendered talk in preschool disputes, *Discourse Processes* **13** (1): 5–31.

Sheldon, Amy (1992) Conflict talk: sociolinguistic challenges to self-assertion and how young girls meet them, *Merrill-Palmer Quarterly* **38** (1): 95–117.

Shipman, V. C. (1971) Disadvantaged children and their first school experiences, Educational Testing Service Head Start Longitudinal Study.

Siegler, David and **Siegler, Robert** (1976) Stereotypes of males' and females' speech, *Psychological Reports* **39**: 167–70.

Smith, Philip M. (1979) Sex markers in speech, pp. 109–46 in Scherer, Klaus R. and Giles, Howard (eds) *Social Markers in Speech*. Cambridge University Press.

Smith, R. K. and **Connolly, K.** (1972) Patterns of play and social interaction in pre-school children, in Jones, N. B. (ed.) *Ethological Studies of Child Behaviour*. Cambridge University Press.

Smith, W. G. and **Heseltine, J. E.** (eds) (1935) *The Oxford Dictionary of English Proverbs*. Oxford University Press.

Soskin, William and **John, Vera** (1963) The study of spontaneous talk, in Barker, R. (ed.) *The Stream of Behaviour*. Appleton-Century-Crofts, New York.

Spender, Dale (1980a) *Man Made Language*. Routledge & Kegan Paul, London.

Spender, Dale (1980b) Talking in class, pp. 148–54 in Spender, Dale and Sarah, Elizabeth (eds) *Learning to Lose*. Women's Press, London.

Spender, Dale (1982) *Invisible Women – The Schooling Scandal*. Writers and Readers Publishing Cooperative, London.

Spender, Dale and **Sarah, Elizabeth** (eds) (1980) *Learning to Lose*. Women's Press, London.

Stanford Research Institute (1972) Follow-through pupil tests, parent interviews, and teacher questionnaires, Appendix C.

Stanworth, Michelle (1981) *Gender and Schooling*. WRRC Publications Collective.

Stone, M. (1983) Learning to say it in cup of tea language, *The Guardian* (Women's Page), 19 April 1983.

Strodtbeck, Fred and **Mann, Richard** (1956) Sex role differentiation in jury deliberations, *Sociometry* **19**: 3–11.

Streeck, Jurgen (1986) Towards reciprocity: politics, rank and gender in the interaction of a group of schoolchildren, pp. 295–326 in Cook-Gumperz, Jenny, Corsaro, William, and Streeck, Jurgen (eds) *Children's Worlds and Children's Language*, Mouton de Gruyter, Berlin.

Stubbs, Michael (1983) *Discourse Analysis*, Basil Blackwell, Oxford.

Swacker, Marjorie (1975) The sex of the speaker as a sociolinguistic variable, pp. 76–83 in Thorne, Barrie and Henley, Nancy (eds) *Language and Sex*. Newbury House, Rowley, Massachusetts.

Swann, Joan (1989) Talk control: an illustration from the classroom of problems in analysing male dominance in education, pp. 122–40 in Coates, Jennifer, and Cameron, Deborah (eds) *Women in their Speech Communities*, Longman, London.

Swift, Jonathan (1735) *Works*. Faulkner, Dublin.

Tajfel, Henri (1974) Social identity and intergroup behaviour, *Social Science Information* **13** (2): 65–93.

Tajfel, Henri (ed.) (1978) *Differentiation between Social Groups: Studies in the Social Psychology of Intergroup Relations*. Academic Press, London.

Tajfel, Henri (1981) *Human Groups and Social Categories*. Cambridge University Press.

Tannen, Deborah (1990a) Gender differences in conversational coherence: physical alignment and topical cohesion, pp. 167–206 in Dorval, Bruce, (ed) *Conversational Organisation and its Development*, Ablex, Norwood, NJ.

Tannen, Deborah (1990b) Gender differences in topical coherence: creating involvement in best friends' talk, *Discourse Processes* **13** (1): 73–90.

Tannen, Deborah (1991) *You Just Don't Understand: Women and Men in Conversation*, Virago, London.

Thomas, Beth (1989) Differences of sex and sects: linguistic variation and social networks in a Welsh mining village, pp. 51–60 in Coates, Jennifer, and Cameron, Deborah (eds) *Women in their Speech Communities*, Longman, London.

Thorne, Barrie and **Henley, Nancy** (eds) *Language and Sex: Difference and Dominance*. Newbury House, Rowley, Massachusetts.

Thorne, Barrie, Kramarae, Cheris, and **Henley, Nancy** (eds) (1983) *Language, Gender and Society*, Newbury House Publishers, Rowley, Mass.

Todd, Alexandra Dundas (1983) A diagnosis of doctor–patient discourse in the prescription of contraception, pp. 159–87 in Fisher, Sue, and Todd, Alexandra D. (eds) *The Social Organisation of Doctor–Patient Communication*, Center for Applied Linguistics, Washington, DC.

Todd, Alexandra Dundas, and **Fisher, Sue** (1988) *Gender and Discourse: The Power of Talk*, Ablex, Norwood, NJ.

Troemel-Ploetz, Senta (1991) Review essay: selling the apolitical, *Discourse and Society* 2 (4): 489–502.

Trudgill, Peter (1972) Sex, covert prestige and linguistic change in the urban British English of Norwich, *Language in Society* 1: 179–95.

Trudgill, Peter (1974a) *The Social Differentiation of English in Norwich*. Cambridge University Press.

Trudgill, Peter (1974b) *Sociolinguistics*. Penguin Books, Harmondsworth.

Trudgill, Peter (ed.) (1978) *Sociolinguistic Patterns in British English*. Edward Arnold, London.

Trudgill, Peter (1983) *On Dialect*. Basil Blackwell, Oxford.

Trudgill, Peter (1984) *Applications of Sociolinguistics*. Academic Press, London.

Tucker, Susie (1961) *English Examined*. Cambridge University Press.

Uchida, Aki (1992) 'When "difference" is "dominance"; A critique of the "anti-power-based" cultural approach to sex differences', *Language in Society* 21 (4), 547–68.

Walters, J. (1981) Variation in the requesting behaviour of bilingual children, *International Journal of the Sociology of Language* 27: 77–92.

Wareing, Shan (1993) *Cooperative and Competitive Talk: The Assessment of Discussion at Standard Grade*, unpublished PhD thesis, University of Strathclyde.

Weitz, Shirley (1977) *Sex Roles: Biological, Psychological and Social Foundations*. Oxford University Press.

Wells, Gordon (1979) Variation in child language, in Lee, V. (ed.) *Language Development*. Croom Helm, London.

Wernersson, I. (1982) Sex differentiation and teacher–pupil interaction in Swedish compulsory schools, in Secretariat of the Council of Europe (ed.) *Sex Stereotyping in Schools*. Swets & Zeitlinger.

West, Candace (1984a) When the doctor is a 'lady': power, status and gender in physician–patient encounters, *Symbolic Interaction* 7: 87–106.

West, Candace (1984b) *Routine Complications: Troubles with Talk between Doctors and Patients*, Indiana University Press, Bloomington, Indiana.

West, Candace (1990) Not just 'doctors' orders': directive-response sequences in patients' visits to women and men physicians, *Discourse & Society* **1** (1): 85–112.

West, Candace, and **Zimmerman, Don** (1977) Women's place in everyday talk: reflections on parent–child interaction, *Social Problems* **24**: 521–9.

West, Candace, and **Zimmerman, Don** (1983) Small insults: a study of interruptions in cross-sex conversations between unacquainted persons, in Thorne, Barrie, Kramarae, Cheris, and Henley, Nancy (eds) *Language, Gender and Society*, Newbury House Publishers, Rowley, Mass.

Whyte, Judith (1986) *Getting the GIST*, Routledge & Kegan Paul, London.

Williams, I. F. (1912) *Phonetics for Scottish Students: The Sounds of Polite Scottish Described and Compared with those of Polite English* (2nd edn). James Maclehose & Sons, Glasgow.

Williams, J. and **Giles, Howard** (1978) The changing status of women in society: an intergroup perspective, pp. 431–46 in Tajfel, Henri (ed.) *Differentiation between Social Groups*. Academic Press, London.

Wilson, T. (1560) *The Arte of Rhetorique*. Clarendon Press, London (1909).

Wilson, T. (1724) *The Many Advantages of a Good Language to any Nation*. Scolar Press, Menston, Yorks, 1969.

Wodak, Ruth (1981) Women relate, men report: sex differences in language behaviour in a therapeutic group, *Journal of Pragmatics* **5**: 261–85.

Wolfson, Nessa (1983) An empirically-based analysis of complimenting in American English, pp. 82–95 in Wolfson, Nessa, and Judd, E. (eds) *Sociolinguistics and Language Acquisition*, Newbury House, Rowley, Mass.

Woods, Nicola (1989) Talking shop: sex and status as determinants of floor apportionment in a work setting, pp. 141–57 in Coates, Jennifer, and Cameron, Deborah (eds) *Women in their Speech Communities*, Longman, London.

Woolf, Virginia (1979) *Women and Writing*. Women's Press, London.

Yaguello, Marina (1978) *Les Mots et les femmes*. Petite Bibliothèque Payot, Paris.

Zimin, Susan (1981) Sex and politeness: factors in first- and second-language use, *International Journal of the Sociology of Language* **27**: 35–58.

Zimmerman, Don and **West, Candace** (1975) Sex roles, interruptions and silences in conversation, pp. 105–29 in Thorne, Barrie and Henley, Nancy (eds) *Language and Sex: Difference and Dominance*. Newbury House, Rowley, Massachusetts.

Index

acquisition 14, 143–167
adolescents 5, 6, 7, 76–7, 94–100,
    186
adversarial style, *see* competitive
    style
affective meaning 120–1
age 4, 5, 56, 62, 67, 84
aggravated forms 124–6
all-female groups 187–195, 203
all-male groups 187–195, 203
androcentric 19, 24, 30, 51, 116
    rule 16, 18, 29
androgyny 83, 139
anthropology 3, 13, 38–45
appropriateness 106–7
    gender-appropriate
        behaviour 143–167 passim,
        197.
argument 159–60
assimilation 8, 9, 12
asymmetrical discourse 123–4
Atkins, Bowman K. 132–5, 139–40

Belfast 87, 88, 89–93, 101, 102, 103,
    104, 172, 177–9, 184, 185
    (th) 90–1
    (a) 91–3, 178–9
    (ε) 177–8
Borker, Ruth 157–8, 187–8, 194
Brown, Penelope 85, 103, 129–132
Brun, Auguste 169–170

Cameron, Deborah 6, 120, 121, 123
change (linguistic) 14, 17, 22, 33,
    38, 65–7, 166, 168–186
    conscious 183–4
    in apparent time 174, 179, 183
    in real time 174, 179
    linguistic variable involved in
        change 65–7, 68
    unconscious, *see* conscious
Cheshire, Jenny 89, 94–100, 101,
    102, 103, 127, 196, 201
child language 143–167
classroom *see* school
Clonard young women 92–3, 104,
    179, 184–5
Coates, Jennifer 117–18, 138–9, 140
    n3, 193, 204 n2 & n3
code-switching *see* style-shifting
codification 17, 25
collaborative talk *see* cooperative talk
commands *see* directives
communicative competence 13,
    106–40, 144, 152–7, 166, 196–202
competitive style 10–11, 137, 139,
    158, 194–5
compliments 115, 128–9
conflict 158, 160
conservatism 40, 46, 47, 48, 170–1,
    185
contact with speakers of other
    languages 43–4
control of topic *see* topic control

conversational dominance   107–114, 115, 139, 153–4, 158, 194–5, 196–200, 202, 203
cooperative talk   10, 137, 138, 158, 194–5
correctness   23, 61, 67
correct usage   17
    see also Standard English
Corsaro, William   158–9
covert norms see norms
covert prestige   80–82

Deuchar, Margaret   6, 84–5
diachronic   171, 174
dialectology   3, 6, 13, 38, 45–56, 169–171
difference approach   13, 202–3
directives   124–6, 160–1
disadvantage   195–202
doctor-patient talk   11, 125–6, 134–5
dominance
    approach   12, 202–3
    in classroom   195–200
    in conversation see conversational dominance
dominant group   7, 35–6
Dorval, Bruce   162–5

Eckert, Penelope   186 n6, 205 n7
Edinburgh   74–6, 149–151
    (au) 150
    (r) 75–6
Eisikovits, Edna   76–7, 80, 101, 151–2
elaborated code   27, 37 n2
ethnic group   4, 6, 56, 62, 67, 84
explanations   42–4, 48, 77–85, 100–102

face   84–5, 129–132
face-threatening talk   118
'female style' see 'women's language'
femininity   83, 197
feminist dictionary   30
fieldworker   50, 53–5
Fishman, Pamela   112–3, 116, 122

folklinguistics   16–36, 129
    folklinguistic beliefs   16, 22, 46, 155, 156

Gal, Susan   179–182
Gauchat L.   170–171
gender   3, 4, 5, 56, 67–77, 81, 83, 85–6, 203–4
    gender-appropriate see appropriate
    gender-exclusive differences   44, 157
    gender-preferential differences   44, 157, 166
    gender role   44, 166, 185, 203
GIST (Girls Into Science and Technology)   199–200
Glasgow   70–72, 77, 78, 149–50
    (i)   70–2, 77
    (glottal stop)   78
Goodwin, Marjorie   124–6, 137, 159–60, 165, 204 n1
gossip   11, 107, 135–6
grammar   23–8, 53, 106, 143, 196
grammarians, early   16

Harris, Sandra   123
hedges   115, 116–119, 138
Herring, Susan   115, 116
he-said-she-said   159–60
Holmes, Janet   117–8, 120–121, 130
homogeneous
    community   7
    group   196
    speech   90
    speech community see speech community
Hymes, Dell   106–7
hypercorrection   66–7, 68, 78, 86 n6, 172
    hypercorrect pattern   78
hypotaxis   26–8

identity   7–12 passim,   84, 197
imperative see directive
inexpressiveness   114, 194

informants 5, 6, 45–50, 51, 64–5, 66, 74–5, 79
  women as 45–50
innovation (speaker) 168–186
insecurity 66, 78
interruption 109–111, 114, 134–5, 139, 153–4, 192–4
interview 5, 64, 70

Jespersen, Otto 18, 19, 20, 25–8, 31–3, 34, 126
Jones, Deborah 135–6

Labov, William 6, 61, 66–7, 86 n5, 94, 101, 102, 127, 140, 171–4
Lakoff, Robin 19, 20, 22–3, 25, 116–8, 119, 122, 127, 132–3, 134, 135
lame 102
  women as lames 102–3
Levinson, Stephen 85, 129
lexicon see vocabulary
linguistic change see change
linguistic variable 62
  stable 65, 90, 92
  undergoing change 65–7, 171–9, 182–3, 184
linguistic variation see variation
listening 192
literacy 28–30
Local, John 147–8
long-term participant observation see participant observation
lower middle class 65–7, 71, 78, 172, 184
  LMC women 70, 78

Macaulay R. K. S. 70–2, 78
majority
  approach 6
  group 6, 7
  language 6
  view 5
male-as-norm see androcentric
Maltz, Daniel 157–8, 187–8, 194
man-made language 30

marker 74, 76, 77, 99–100, 149
Martha's Vineyard 172, 173–4, 183–4
masculinity 83, 156, 185
'men's language' 38, 42, 44, 139, 156–7
Merseyside see West Wirral
middle class 63, 78, 145, 174, 183
  children 153
  group 65, 78
  speakers 81, 84, 85, 137
Milroy, James 87, 105 n1, 168, 177–9, 184–6
Milroy, Lesley 87, 88–93, 101–4, 105 n1, 168, 172, 177–9, 184–6
minimal response 109, 111–2, 114, 115, 116, 138, 139, 189
  delayed minimal response 111–2, 114
minority 6
  approach 6
  group 6, 8, 12, 13, 144
  language 6
miscommunication 14, 187–195, 203
mitigated forms 124–6, 158
modal meaning 120–1
morphology 106
  differences 39–40
  features 94–5
muted group 35–6

negative face see face
Network Strength Scale 90, 92
Network Strength Score 89, 92, 102, 104
Newbrook, Mark 72–4, 78, 86 n6
New York City 66–7, 171–4, 184
  (r) 66–7, 171–2, 184
  (a) 172, 173–4, 184
Nichols, Patricia 173, 182–3, 185
non-standard
  forms 62, 65, 70, 73, 77, 79, 80, 83, 86, 95, 101, 103, 149–150, 152, 173–9 passim
  language 80, 104, 195
  varieties 6, 62, 81, 86 n2

norm   10, 19, 81, 90, 92, 97, 100–102, 103, 140
   adult   156
   linguistic   7, 78, 82, 88, 102
   prestige   68, 101, 102, 176, 183, 184
   standard   54, 74, 81, 83, 90, 95, 102
   vernacular   81, 83, 90, 92, 97, 100, 102, 103, 176, 179, 184
   written   26, 31
   see also male-as-norm
norm-enforcement mechanism   88, 93, 104
Norwich   64–5, 68–70, 78, 79–80, 172, 174–7, 184
   (ng)   64–5, 68–70, 78
   (er)   79
   (a)   79
   (e)   174–5
   (o)   175–7, 184

O'Barr, William   132–5, 139–40
Oberwart, Austria   179–182, 184
obliges   160–1 see also directives
occupational status see status
oppression   12, 203–4
over-report   79–80

parataxis   26–8
participant observation   5, 89, 94
peer group   13, 94, 95, 96, 100, 101, 102, 157
phonological
   differences   39, 67–76 passim, 171–9
   variation see variation, phonological
phonology   53, 106, 143, 174
politeness   41, 85, 129–132, 139, 152, 154–5, 156, 166
positive face see face
power   84–5, 113, 136, 194, 203
powerful language   132–5
powerful speakers   123
powerless language   132–5, 139–40
Preisler, Bent   116–7, 120

prestige   61–2, 81, 83
   form/variant   62–77 passim, 79, 81
   see also norm, prestige
pronunciation   30–33, 38–9, 48, 106, 169, 173, 174
psychological androgyny see androgyny

quantitative sociolinguistic
   studies   13, 31, 56, 61–86 passim, 171–183 passim
questionnaire   50–53
questions   122–4, 138, 189
   meaning of   189
   see also tag questions
quiet behaviour   35, 197–9

Reading   94–100 passim, 103
Rizzo, Thomas   158–9
role see gender role
Romaine, Suzanne   74–6, 149–151
R.P. (Received Pronunciation)   30, 74, 83, 176, 184
   speakers   83–4

Sachs, Jacqueline   160–2
sampling (techniques)   5, 48
school   14, 35, 100–101, 187, 195–202
Scouse   67–8, 72, 78
self-disclosure   118, 190–191
self-evaluation tests   79–80
sensitivity
   of lower middle class   66–7
   of women   47, 78–9, 80, 132, 185
sexism   3
   sexist   27, 49, 144
Sheldon, Amy   158
silence   34–6, 111, 113–4, see also quiet behaviour
simultaneous speech   138–9, 192–4
single-sex discourse   118–9, 139
social class   4, 5, 8, 37 n2, 56, 61, 62, 73, 81, 85, 145, 196, 204 n1
social group   4, 12, 84, 144, 169, 195, 201
   women as   7–12

social network   13, 87–105 *passim*,
    179, 185
social psychology   3, 8, 83–4
social status *see* status
social stratification   7, 61, 62–5, 174,
    175, 176
social variation *see* variation
socialisation   13, 166
sociolinguistics   3, 4–7, 45, 54, 56,
    105, 171
    see also quantitative sociolinguistic
        studies
solidarity   82–4, 101, 136, 140, 173,
    185
South Carolina   182–3, 184
speaker innovation *see* innovation
speech community   4–5, 12, 45, 55,
    82, 100, 140
    homogeneous   4–5, 45
Spender, Dale   35, 115, 196, 197,
    199, 200
stable linguistic variable *see* linguistic
    variable
Standard English   5, 17, 23, 30, 44,
    80, 81, 86 n1, 100, 101, 147, 148,
    182–3, 184
standard norm *see* norm
status   8, 12, 40, 82–4, 123, 135, 184,
    200
    status-based model   101
    status consciousness   47
stigma   61–2
    stigmatised accent   30
    stigmatised form   69, 70, 78, 79,
        80, 150
stratification *see* social stratification
Streeck, Jurgen   154, 157
style-shifting   70, 100–101, 151, 173,
    183–4
stylistic variation *see* variation
subculture   7, 13, 157–165, 166, 203
subordination *see* oppression
support   113, 136, 138, 140
Survey of English Dialects   46, 47,
    48, 50
Swann, Joan   153, 197–9

swearing   20–23, 126–8, 139, 152,
    155–6, 157
Sydney, Australia   76–7, 151–2

taboo   20–23, 43
    language   20–23, 126–8, 166
tag questions   115, 119–122, 123,
    132, 156
Tajfel, Henri   8–12
Tanner, Deborah   162–5, 187, 191
talkativeness *see* verbosity
Thomas, Beth   104
topic   112, 115–6, 118, 136, 138,
    161–2, 188, 189, 190
    topic-control   113, 139
    topic development   138
    topic shift   190
Trudgill, Peter   61, 64–5, 68–70,
    79–80, 86 n4, 172, 174–7
turn-taking
    in conversation   107–114, 138,
        189–190, 192–4
    violations   114
Tyneside   147–8

under-report   79–80

variable *see* linguistic variable
variation   3, 23
    linguistic   4, 12, 13, 23, 44, 45, 56,
        62, 67, 136, 169, 185, 203
    phonological   148–151, 171–9
    social   4, 12, 56, 169, 185
    stylistic   4, 56, 169, 173
verbal aggressiveness   191–2
verbosity   33–6, 115–6, 152–3, 166
vernacular   5, 21, 28, 46, 55, 62,
    63, 70, 71, 80, 81, 86 n2, 90–93
    passim, 101, 102, 103, 176, 178–9
    Culture Index   97, 99, 127
    loyalty   97, 99, 100, 103
    norms *see* norms, vernacular
    speech   100, 103–5
vocabulary   17–20, 51, 53, 143, 169

West, Candace   11, 13, 108–112, 125–6, 134–5

West Wirral   72–4, 78
  (ing)   72–3
  (h)   72–3
  (k)   72–3
  (a)   73–4
  (o)   78, 86 n6

woman-to-woman interaction   135–9
  see also all-women groups

'women's language'   38, 43, 44, 114–129 passim, 136, 138–9

Woods, Nicola   134–5

working class   63, 75, 76, 145, 174, 183
  communities   88, 89, 90, 93, 101
  group   6, 65, 78, 94–100, 174, 179
  men   73, 81, 94, 176
  speakers   70, 77, 80, 83–4, 86, 137, 174, 204 n1
  women   81, 104, 128, 176

young Clonard women see Clonard young women

Zimmerman, Don   13, 108–112